Resolving Conflicts at Work

Kenneth Cloke

Joan Goldsmith

Foreword by Warren Bennis

Resolving Conflicts at Work

Eight Strategies for Everyone on the Job

Revised Edition

JOSSEY-BASS
A Wiley Imprint
www.josseybass.com

Published by Jossey-Bass
A Wiley Imprint
989 Market Street, San Francisco, CA 94103-1741   www.josseybass.com

Jossey-Bass books and products are available through most bookstores. To contact Jossey-Bass directly call our Customer Care Department within the U.S. at 800-956-7739, outside the U.S. at 317-572-3986, or fax 317-572-4002.

Jossey-Bass also publishes its books in a variety of electronic formats. Some content that appears in print may not be available in electronic books.

Credits appear on page 341.

Library of Congress Cataloging-in-Publication Data

Cloke, Ken, date.
  Resolving conflicts at work : eight strategies for everyone on the job /
Kenneth Cloke, Joan Goldsmith ; foreword by Warren Bennis.— Rev. ed.
        p. cm.
  Includes index.
  ISBN-13 978-0-7879-8024-5 (alk. paper)
  ISBN-10 0-7879-8024-2 (alk. paper)
  1. Conflict management. 2. Interpersonal relations. 3. Personnel management—Psychological aspects. 4. Psychology, Industrial. I. Goldsmith, Joan. II. Title.
  HD42.C56 2005
  650.1'3—dc22

                                                        2005007391

Printed in the United States of America
REVISED EDITION
PB Printing   10 9 8 7 6 5 4 3 2 1

Contents

Foreword:
Conflict: A Leader's Challenge

"I curse you! May you live in an important time," goes that famous Chinese imprecation. No one would argue that we live and work in difficult and conflicted times. Especially leaders of complex, global organizations. Leaders today must be far more adept in resolving conflicts than ever before. We increasingly look to leaders for guidance in navigating through a succession of crises and conflicts, each seemingly more intractable than the last.

As change is now a constant, the conflicts that inevitably accompany it can be seen everywhere. These conflicts create a crisis of leadership that is reflected in the spate of recent corporate scandals that have undermined our faith in business leaders and created a revolving door at the top. As a result, CEOs appointed after 1990 are three times more likely to be fired than CEOs appointed before that date, and seventy-seven of the two hundred largest companies have ousted their leaders and hired new bosses in recent years.

These discouraging facts reflect the failure of leaders to listen and learn from the conflicts in their organizations, as well as the unforgiving personal blame we attach to them as soon as anything important goes wrong.

This growing mistrust of business and government, together with the emerging possibility of a serious global recession, the aftermath of the attacks of September 11, 2001, the war in Iraq, the acrimony seen in the last election, and increasingly fierce corporate competition, are some of the signs that our leaders are no longer able to guide us toward a resolution of our conflicts and, as a result, that we are heading for trouble.

Resistance to addressing conflict in organizations is similar to the resistance that divides nations and communities. As organizations become more complex, they fragment and become more insular, creating tribal patterns and symbolic codes (secrets and jargon, for example) that exclude outsiders and exploit differences for inward gain, thereby sacrificing a fragile harmony for individual and group gain.

Recently, we saw in the case of Enron a complex and startlingly negative example of these destructive patterns, including an organizational culture based on secrecy, dishonesty, and aversion to resolving the conflicts that always arise whenever the truth is told. The courageous whistleblower Sharon Watkins, in her letter to CEO Ken Lay, warned, "Enron could explode in a wave of accounting scandals." She took the risk all leaders with integrity must face—that of breaking with the regressive cultural norms of her environment. Yet, who in Enron took her warning seriously? Who was listening?

At Enron, simply talking about what was actually going on was off-limits. As one executive later told me, "You simply didn't want to discuss . . . anything important in front of the water cooler." Employees were afraid to express their opinions or question unethical or illegal business practices.

Enron is only one example, albeit a dramatic one. Yet, the most difficult thing to do in any organization is to speak truth to power and to create the social architecture that permits, gives license to, and supports openness in communications. Without it, our organizations are doomed to failure.

Ken Lay's real crime was not his infectious greed or whatever malfeasance he may or may not have committed. It was his failure to create a culture and social architecture that were open to reality and willing to engage the conflicts that inevitably accompany truth telling. His primary failure was in not instituting reforms in Enron's organizational culture that would have encouraged employees to get at the truth whatever the cost. That is his greater failure.

The *Challenger* disaster during President Reagan's term of office reflected a similar problem. Those who built the space shuttle knew there was something wrong with the O-rings. The man who reported the problem was fired and later went around the country in a feckless chase trying to convince people that we have to create more open and honest organizational systems.

In 1991, Jack Welch faced a serious disaster at a General Electric plant in Louisville, Kentucky, that cost the company $600 million because the equipment used to make refrigerators was faulty, and the people who were making them knew it. But the truth never came out, at least to the company's headquarters in Fairfield, Connecticut. To Welch's credit, he soon after created a "workout" program to make sure that such episodes will not reoccur. In conflict-adverse environments, the truth is suppressed, and the personal and organizational price paid for doing so, even in these few examples, is enormous.

Research has shown that effective leadership accounts for at least 15 percent of the success of any organization. In these organizations, good leaders make people feel that they are at the heart of things, that they make a difference to its success, and that their conflicts and differences can be overcome by communicating openly and working together to realize their common vision and goals.

Successful leaders engage their employees through compelling, tangible visions. Most important, they commit to these visions by generating and sustaining cultures that build trust, promote self-improvement, make work feel exciting, foster a sense of community, encourage open communications, confront and resolve conflicts, and support people in learning from their mistakes.

I believe subtle yet profound and perceptible changes are now taking place in our philosophy of leadership that are moving us toward the creation of organizational cultures that encourage the honest expression of conflict and promote candid discussion of differences. These changes include:

- A new concept of humanity, based on increased understanding of our complex and shifting needs, that is replacing an oversimplified, innocent, mechanical idea of who we are
- A new concept of power, based on collaboration, reason, and synergy, that is replacing a model of power based on violence, coercion, and threats

- A new concept of values, based on humanistic-democratic ideals, that is replacing a depersonalized, bureaucratic value system that regards property and rules as more important than people and relationships

To this list I can add a fourth change reflected in the central argument Cloke and Goldsmith make in the pages that follow:

- A new concept of conflict, based on personal and organizational learning, creative problem solving, collaborative negotiation, and satisfaction of interests, that is replacing an approach to conflict that seeks to avoid, suppress, or settle it rather than resolve the underlying reasons that gave rise to it and use it to promote personal and organizational improvement

Traditional power-based and bureaucratic approaches to conflict, as Cloke and Goldsmith point out, merely suppress useful information and discourage those who can make a difference from learning how they can use their disputes to expose what is not working and promote change.

The future we face will not necessarily be a "happy" one. Coping with rapid, uncertain change, operating in temporary work systems, grappling with global interdependence, and searching for meaningful relations all augur social strains, psychological tensions, and chronic conflicts, which can be either suppressed or used to reveal the challenges we need to address. Successful leaders value honest communications over power and bureaucracy that is fundamental to creating cultures of collaboration, open communication, and conflict resolution.

No organization can be honest with the public if it is not honest with itself. Creating cultures of honesty, like creating healthy balance sheets, is an ongoing effort that requires attention and diligence from the top.

Successful leaders support *reflective back talk*. They create environments in which people freely offer their honest reactions so that leaders are not taken by surprise. They value differences in perceptions, habits, languages, and styles and plumb them for their unique contributions. They generate trust so that employees feel comfortable communicating openly, honestly, and empathetically. In doing so, as Cloke and Goldsmith observe, they reduce the fear of conflicts and are able to turn them into opportunities for improvement.

It will not be easy to create organizational cultures in which conflicts are openly addressed and candor is routine. The problem of getting leaders to build organizational systems that encourage their colleagues to embrace and learn from conflicts is exacerbated by an increasingly turbulent global economic environment in which greed and unethical competition are creating compound crises and a race for the bottom.

These troubled times call for the theories, strategies, and techniques identified by Cloke and Goldsmith. The core leadership competencies, organizational systems ideas, day-to-day prescriptions, and high-level skills that are presented in the strategies that follow can support each of us in transforming our workplace conflicts into learning opportunities.

The authors of this book offer wisdom, food for thought, and tools to those of us who want to continue improving our abilities to address the conflicts that come our way. We can all become better at learning to live with ambiguity, communicating more openly, participating in conflict with integrity, making a virtue of contingency, and finding unity in the issues that divide us.

Cloke and Goldsmith provide us all with multiple ways of addressing, resolving, transforming, and learning from conflicts. In doing so, they make a significant contribution to organizational health by providing us with methods for resolving the destructive conflicts that plague our era and those that, if we do not heed their message, will be sure to follow.

Warren Bennis
Distinguished Professor of Business Administration
University of Southern California

*This book is dedicated to our families,
from whom we have learned both the pain of conflict
and the joy of resolution: to Dick, Shirley, Bill, Angie, Elka, Nick,
Erin, Orrin, Kristen, and Glen; and Leonard, Miriam, Steve,
Pravina, Sam, Shetu, and Tinku.*

Preface

Philosophers have written that a universe can be found in a single grain of sand. This book is our effort to describe the universe we have found in the sands of conflict, which we have studied, sifted, and reshaped professionally over the past twenty-five years. In the process, we have helped thousands of people in workplaces around the United States and the world resolve their disputes.

We have observed firsthand the pain, loss, and irretrievable damage that have been suffered by individuals, organizations, and relationships as a result of conflict. We have also seen miracles of transformation, people moved to forgiveness and reconciliation, creative solutions revealed, and hundreds of lives, relationships, and organizations reclaimed. These are the two faces of conflict, the destructive and the creative, the impasse and the transformation. Between them is a set of strategies, techniques, and approaches for turning one into the other.

Everyone is capable of seeing both faces of conflict, although most of us focus more on the first than the second. We have all learned how to fight and how to collaborate, how to run away and how to stand up for what we believe in, how to hide what we think and how to say what we really mean, how to resist change and how to embrace it, how to live as though no one else matters and how to challenge ourselves and improve our lives and relationships.

In short, each of us has learned destructive and creative ways of responding to conflict. To shift from the destructive to the creative, from impasse to transformation, we need to search within ourselves for the true meaning of our conflict, become more aware of what we are contributing to it, and decide to listen and learn from our opponents. We need to improve our skills and resist our tendency to slip into negative or destructive responses.

Few of us have received training in how to work collaboratively to resolve conflicts. Few schools teach it. Few corporations, nonprofits, and government agencies have created conflict-prevention programs or orient their employees to constructive approaches to conflict resolution, despite the fact that nearly all organizations and their employees will confront a number of serious conflicts during the course of their working lives.

While some organizations train their leaders or managers in conflict resolution, classes are usually brief and oriented to suppressing conflicts or trying to make them go away. Yet most of these leaders and managers face conflicts on a *daily* basis, spending from 20 to as much as 80 percent of their time trying to resolve or contain them.

When we merely suppress conflicts or try to make them go away, we miss their underlying meaning. As a result, we cheat ourselves, others, and the organization as a whole out of learning from them, correcting what led to them in the first place, preventing future conflicts, and discovering how to improve our ability to resolve and transcend them.

About This Book

We wrote this book to assist everyone who works: employees, leaders, managers, teachers, principals, union representatives, and workers of all kinds in corporations, nonprofits, schools, and government agencies. *Everyone* can increase their skills, not just in making conflicts disappear but in discovering their deeper underlying truths, resolving the reasons that gave rise to them, and using them to drive personal and organizational improvement.

To assist you in discovering these truths for yourself, we present you with eight strategies for resolution, each leading to the center of the conflict. We offer you a diverse set of tools to resolve your conflicts—not just hammers and wrenches, but mirrors and scalpels. The mirrors are to help you reflect on what *you* are doing to encourage the conflict and see how you can use that information to trigger a personal or organizational transformation. The scalpels are to assist you in eliminating unproductive, destructive, and unwanted behavior patterns and free you to approach your conflicts in a more constructive and strategic manner. Our object is not to tell you what to do but to provide you with tools that will lead you to your own truth, as we have been led to ours.

No single tool or technique will work for everyone in every situation at all times. If there is any set principle in conflict resolution, it is that there are no set principles. Success proceeds from a synergistic combination of intellect and emotion, honesty and empathy, reason and intuition, head and heart, and a willingness to integrate and let each guide the other. Everyone can improve their objective and subjective conflict resolution skills and learn better ways of expressing their needs, feelings, and ideas.

We hope you will follow the strategies we describe and work to create an organizational environment in which conflict resolution is creative and strategic, integrated and accepted, celebrated and continually reinvented—an environment in which settlement is not settled for and resolution opens opportunities for organizational transformation and personal mastery.

The strategies we describe invite the magic that comes from listening, collaboration, and forgiveness. Our basic message is to strengthen and follow your intuition, be guided by your heart, deepen and expand your empathy, and be willing to risk being deeply and compassionately honest about what you have seen and experienced. While there are times and places where being open and honest can get you into trouble, for the most part we overcensor ourselves and, in the process, cheat ourselves and others out of learning and growth.

If you are willing to take the risk of being deeply empathetic and honest, we can promise you that your conflict and the strategies for resolving it will open up to you—and to the organization in which you work—extraordinary opportunities for improvement that include personal growth, reduced costs, improved morale, and deeper and more satisfying relationships.

Because everywhere we get stuck and find ourselves at impasse, both personally and organizationally, expresses itself as a conflict, it should be obvious that to obtain the release, resolution, and transformation we desire, we need to learn to move toward, into, and through our disputes. In conflict resolution, the way *out* is *through*.

Finally, while everyone can improve their skills and become more effective at resolving their conflicts, we each need to discover the approach that works best for us. In this book, we have identified eight distinct strategies to help you define your approach to conflict and to assemble a "resolution toolbox" from the dozens of techniques we cite. Your challenge will be to design your own strategy, which begins by looking inside yourself and recognizing that you can choose the direction your conflict will take you.

We encourage you to learn from your opponents and all the people with whom you have been in conflict, without whom it will be impossible to understand fully what your conflict is trying to teach you. We know we cannot teach you anything you do not want to learn, and it is difficult to decide to learn from your opponents. Nonetheless, we invite you to open yourself, your colleagues, and your organizations to conflict and to be willing to learn a new approach to resolution. We are pleased you have chosen to learn with us.

Acknowledgments

Everyone faces their conflicts alone, but no one resolves them alone. The process requires collaboration, support, safe havens, honest feedback, and understanding from those who are willing to reach out and promote peace and reconciliation. The two of us are deeply grateful to all our friends and mediation associates who have traveled this road with us.

We want to thank our friends and family for having taught us many lessons about conflict and resolution and for having been deeply committed to transforming their own lives and the lives of others as well. We also want to thank the many courageous organizational leaders on all levels with whom we have worked who have allowed us to try out many of the ideas we present here.

A special thanks goes to Warren Bennis for believing in us and in our book. Finally, we want to thank our editors, Alan Rinzler and Seth Schwartz, our indexer and friend, Carolyn Thibault, and our assistant, Solange Raro.

Kenneth Cloke
Joan Goldsmith
Center for Dispute Resolution
Santa Monica, California

We have thought of peace as passive
and war as the active way of living.
The opposite is true.
War is not the most strenuous life.
It is a kind of rest cure compared
to the task of reconciling our differences.
From War to Peace is not from the strenuous
to the easy existence.
It is from the futile to the effective,
from the stagnant to the active,
from the destructive to the creative way of life.
The world will be regenerated by the people
who rise above these passive ways
and heroically seek by whatever hardship,
by whatever toil
the methods by which people can agree.

—*Mary Parker Follett*

Introduction:
Eight Strategies to Move from
Impasse to Transformation

> The rules of the game: learn everything, read
> everything, inquire into everything. . . . When two
> texts, or two assertions, or perhaps two ideas, are in
> contradiction, be ready to reconcile them rather
> than cancel one by the other; regard them as two
> different facets, or two successive stages of the same
> reality, a reality convincingly human just because it
> is complex.
>
> —*Marguerite Yourcenar*

Each of us experiences innumerable conflicts and miscommunications in the course of our lives, many of which affect us deeply and profoundly. It is nearly impossible today to grow up in a family, live in a neighborhood, attend a school, work at a job, have an intimate relationship, raise children, or actively participate as a citizen without experiencing multiple conflicts.

Much of our childhood is spent in conflict with our parents, siblings, and playmates, who teach us the first and most difficult lessons of life, including how to respond to intense emotions and difficult behaviors. Our schools teach us hard lessons about rejection and compromise; about how to succeed and fail in disputes with teachers and peers; and about shame, rage, and fear. Our spouses, partners, neighbors, and children force us to face fresh conflicts over false expectations and assumptions, roles and responsibilities, change and loss.

Thus, our most intimate family relationships are immersed and influenced by conflict and either deepen or dissolve with it. Our society and cultures are saturated with conflicts that scream at us from headlines, ads, and movies that subtly shape our psyches. Our neighborhoods and ethnic communities are deeply divided by racial prejudice, hatred of people who are different, and conflicts over how resources will be used to satisfy needs and expectations.

Yet, for many of us, the principal sources of conflict are the people with whom we work. Our workplaces and organizations are profoundly shaped by conflicts between workers and supervisors, unions and management, competing departments, and difficult behavior by coworkers. Our competitive economy, status-conscious society, and politicized governmental agencies generate chronic disputes between haves and have-nots, ins and outs, us and them, powerful and powerless—all battling over the distribution of scarce resources.

We pay a heavy price for these conflicts—not only individually and relationally but organizationally and socially—in litigation, strikes, reduced productivity, poor morale, wasted time and resources, lost customers, dysfunctional relationships with colleagues, destructive battles with competing departments, stifling rules and regulations, gossip and rumors, and reduced opportunities for teamwork, synergy, learning, and change.

Yet, most of these conflicts are completely avoidable, unnecessary, and quickly resolvable. Many arise from simple miscommunications, misunderstandings, seemingly irrelevant differences, poor choices of language, ineffective management styles, unclear roles and responsibilities, false expectations, and poor leadership. These conflicts can be corrected easily by listening, informal problem solving, dialogue, and collaborative negotiation.

But there are also deeper sources of conflict, which consist of *chronic* disputes that repeat themselves in various forms between different people and personalities, diverse issues, and dissimilar times and locations, yet never completely disappear. The causes of these conflicts have little or nothing to do with the petty, superficial issues people are fighting over but go much deeper into the nature of conflict, the cultures of organizations, and the way work is structured.

How, then, do we resolve these conflicts? We have to begin by recognizing that every chronic conflict we experience contains at least two fundamental truths: the truth of impasse, that we are stuck with a problem from which we would like to escape and cannot, and the truth of resolution, that it is possible for us to become unstuck and move to a higher order of relationship. We can do this by understanding at a deep level what got us stuck in the first place and transforming the way we think, feel, and act about it.

Every organization and workplace generates chronic conflicts—every corporation, school, nonprofit, and government agency. Each of these conflicts reflects in some way a challenge the organization is beginning to face, or has not faced as well as it could. Each reveals a paradigm that has begun to shift, a problem that has yet to be solved, and an opportunity for improvement that has not been understood or seized upon and implemented.

For this reason, every conflict you experience at work will present you with an opportunity to significantly improve your personal life, expand the effectiveness of your organization, increase the satisfaction of your friends, coworkers, and customers, and release you from impasse. To do so, it is necessary to understand how and why you got stuck and develop the strategies and skills that make resolution and transformation possible.

The Dark Side of Conflict

When we are in conflict, we all say things we do not mean and mean things we do not say. Only rarely do we communicate at a deep level what we really, honestly think and feel. We seldom speak from our hearts or expose our most vulnerable parts, or do so in ways the other person can hear. Why do we fall into these traps? Why is it so difficult to do what we know is right?

Our conflicts have the capacity to confuse and hypnotize us, and make us genuinely believe that there is no way out other than through battle. Conflict possesses dark, hypnotic, destructive powers: the power of attachment when it is time to leave, the power of demonization when it is time to forgive, the power of articulate speech when it is time to be silent and listen. Conflict alternately strokes and crushes our egos, fuels and exhausts our will, energizes us and freezes us in fear. It speaks to a deep, ancient part of our soul that thirsts for power and delights in revenge.

When we are engaged in conflict, our emotions become enormously powerful and overwhelming. When we are in the grip of strong emotions, they feel limitless and unstoppable, irresistible and all-defining. Part of the seduction of strong emotions is that they encourage us to define ourselves and what we want in absolute terms, to identify with the seemingly infinite power of our feelings, and to surrender control to something larger than ourselves.

We have all experienced times in our lives when we lacked the skills we needed to communicate honestly and empathetically with others. We have all been aggressive, judgmental, and hypercritical, or passive, apathetic, and defensive. Our efforts at honesty have been misinterpreted as aggression and our empathy as weakness. We have not known how to temper our anger with compassion, how to listen to our opponent's pain when we were being criticized, how to discover what caused our opponents to act as they did, and how to take responsibility for our own miscommunications and conflicts. We have failed to find ways of working collaboratively with our opponents to find solutions to our problems. As a result, we have felt trapped in our conflicts, sensing or believing that there was no exit, no way out.

At the same time, we have resisted apologizing for our behaviors, acknowledging our miscommunications, or recognizing that our emotions originate inside us and often have nothing to do with our opponents. We have become lost in self-aggrandizement and self-denial, sometimes simply by focusing exclusively on what our opponents did or said. We have engaged in conflict because we were unhappy with our lives; because we needed attention, felt rejected, or did not have the courage to stand up for ourselves; because we felt insecure or upset by criticism, were ashamed of our own cowardice or grief, or did not have the skill to respond effectively to someone's behavior. So have our opponents.

Instead of facing up to these internal reasons for being upset, we have become angry with others and claimed our cause was noble, just, true, and right. We have described our opponents in terms of evil, injustice, unfairness, harassment, aggression, dishonesty, betrayal, and insanity, as opposed to describing our relationship with them in terms of misunderstandings, false expectations, miscommunications, and petty incidents that have been blown out of proportion by both sides.

In these ways, we have been seduced by the apparent importance of our conflicts, by principles of "Truth," "Justice," and "Fairness" that we have somehow incorporated into our own actions and isolated or stripped from our opponent's actions. We have become hypnotized by the adversarial process and drawn into battles over issues that, at the time, seemed all-important but in retrospect felt petty and exaggerated. Yet we have all felt powerful and cleansed when we were able to transmute these narrow, petty concerns into feelings of self-importance, unfair treatment, and self-righteousness.

In the process, we have missed the truth: that these petty concerns can be transcended only by expanding our awareness of the deeper reasons that gave rise to them. We can escape them only by being honest with ourselves and others about what is really bothering us, by genuinely listening to those with whom we disagree, and by discovering that we have much to learn from them. We can let go of our emotional investment in the continuation of our conflicts only by collaborating in the discovery and implementation of creative solutions.

The Secret Transformative Power of Conflict

When we become willing to face the dark side of our own participation in conflict, we begin to recognize its extraordinary capacity to transform our lives by shifting the way we understand ourselves, experience others, conduct our relationships, work in organizations, and learn and grow. This secret, transformative power of every conflict lies in the fact that its resolution and the discovery of a better way of being, working, and living happen simultaneously.

If this proposition seems shocking to you, think about a time when your life shifted dramatically and your relationship to the world around you was transformed. Was your transformation connected to a conflict? Did you achieve a flash of realization while in the midst of a dispute? Were you changed as a result of loss, confrontation, criticism, divorce, or the death of someone you loved? Did it occur as a result of negative feedback, discipline, or termination? Before you achieved clarity, did you feel torn between conflicting alternatives? If so, you are not alone.

The ancient Chinese Buddhist philosopher Hui-Wu wrote, "The whole world is a door of liberation, but people are unwilling to enter it." Conflict is one of those doors. We invite you to begin your own transformation by consciously and skillfully engaging in your conflicts, experiencing them completely, turning them into learning experiences and opportunities to practice new skills, and working to reach genuine closure.

By transformation, we mean dramatic, all-encompassing, and lasting change. Transformation is not minor, incremental, small scale, linear, or transitory. It leaves us different from the way we were before. It alters our sense of reality. Transformation means allowing what is stuck in the past to die in order that our present and future might live.

By using the processes we describe in this book, you can create a new sense of yourself and your organization, a new direction in your life, a new understanding of your opponent, and a new approach to resolving future miscommunications, misunderstandings, and conflicts. The energy, focus, and time that form part of your personal *investment* in conflict can also drive your personal and organizational growth, learning, and transformation. These opportunities are open to each of us in every conflict.

Surprisingly, large-scale transformations can require only simple actions. We ask you to make two commitments. First, to change the way you *are* when you are in conflict, to listen and learn—internally to your own voice and sense of truth and externally to the voice of your adversary or opponent. Second, to change the way you *act*, to explore options without biases, to separate problems from people and interests from positions, to explore the reasons for resistance, to act as a leader in your own life, and to do so with courage and commitment.

Within these twin spheres of being and acting, there are innumerable techniques, methods, approaches, questions, and processes that can give birth to transformation, which will be different for each person, organization, and situation. Not every method will work for everyone, every conflict, or at all times. What matters is that you search for what works for you, right now, with one opponent, one conflict at a time. We offer you a toolbox, not a magic wand. Magic is your ability to select the right tool at the right time with the right person.

Eight Strategies to Shift from Impasse to Resolution and Transformation

In each of the eight chapters ahead, we identify strategies that can lead you from impasse to resolution and to personal and organizational transformation. Each will improve your ability to take a do-it-yourself approach and allow you to confront, embrace, struggle with, and resolve your conflicts in your own way. We investigate each strategy; offer detailed directions on how to follow, practice, and redesign it to meet your needs; and suggest ways of transforming yourself and your organization's culture as you go.

While you may prefer a step-by-step guide guaranteed to help you navigate life's difficulties, we have found the recipe approach to conflict resolution hopelessly inadequate. It cannot anticipate the unexpected or account for individual or organizational uniqueness. It cannot appreciate the wholeness of conflict, which is not resolvable by slicing it into smaller pieces. Instead, we offer you a series of somewhat circular, iterative, intersecting strategies that can lead you to the center of your conflict.

By calling them strategies, we want to differ from the usual approach to conflict resolution, which consists of a series of linear steps leading closer and closer to resolution. In our experience, transformation does not take place in steps, and resolution is rarely a linear process. Rather, it is a state of mind, an *intention* that you cannot locate on any map but must find for yourself. There is no guaranteed technique that will lead you there, yet every conflict resolution technique has the potential to open your eyes to the truth, which is that you already know the value of every strategy we are going to suggest but that implementing it requires you to first look inward.

The word *strategy* implies planning, but it also suggests a journey to a place that is unimaginable and indescribable before you arrive. For this reason, we ask you to adopt an attitude of openness, possibility, and curiosity and bring a commitment and desire for resolution to the process. We know from experience that if you pursue any of these strategies, opportunities for transformation will automatically begin to open for you. We invite you to take this journey with us.

Here are the strategies we explore in each chapter:

1. *Change the culture and context of conflict.* Discovering the meaning of the conflict, both for yourself and your opponent, leads not merely to settlement but to increased awareness, acceptance, and resolution of the underlying reasons for your dispute and a need to change the organizational culture in which it occurred.

2. *Listen actively, empathetically, and responsively.* Listening actively, empathetically, responsively, and with an open heart to your opponents will encourage them to do the same for you and lead you to the center of the conflict, where all strategies for resolution and transformation converge.

3. *Acknowledge and integrate emotions to solve problems.* When intense emotions are brought to the surface and communicated openly and directly to your opponents in a way they can hear, invisible barriers are lifted to integration, problem solving, resolution, and transformation.

4. *Search beneath the surface for hidden meaning.* Beneath the surface issues in your conflict lie subterranean fears, desires, interests, emotions, histories, and intentions that can tell you what is really wrong. These can become a powerful source of resolution and transformation.

5. *Separate what matters from what gets in the way.* The road to resolution and transformation lies not in blaming people but in solving problems, not in understanding positions but in satisfying interests, not in debating who was right but in engaging in dialogue over meaning, and not in resurrecting the past but in redesigning the future.

6. *Stop rewarding and learn from difficult behaviors.* In every conflict, you will confront people who are being rewarded for engaging in difficult behaviors. These behaviors paradoxically provide you with excellent opportunities to improve your skills; increase your capacity for empathy, patience, and perseverance; and discover what makes them difficult for you.

7. *Solve problems creatively, plan strategically, and negotiate collaboratively.* Transformation requires the energy, uncertainty, and duality of enigma, paradox, and contradiction, which are part of every conflict. Yet these can lead you to problem-solving, strategic-planning, and collaborative-negotiation techniques that can help you at least to agree to disagree.

8. *Explore resistance, mediate, and design systems for prevention and resolution.* All resistance reflects an unmet need and is a request for authenticity, participation, and communication. Exploring resistance can help unlock your conflict. If you are still in impasse, mediation can address issues you cannot resolve yourself. Designing conflict resolution systems allows organizations to prevent or eliminate the sources of chronic conflict and reduce their cost.

Finally, as we have indicated, because everyone is different and each person is different from moment to moment, there can be no single tried-and-true strategy for conflict resolution that will work for everyone, always, and everywhere. There are no simple step-by-step formulas or methods for shifting a paradigm, opening your opponent's heart, or becoming a different person than you were before. All you can do is to find your own way of combining honesty and empathy, analysis and intuition, reflection and curiosity, precision and kindness, and awareness and equanimity and applying them to the conflict and the opponent you are facing, then seeing what works and what does not and being courageous enough to change as you go.

Strategies for Transforming Organizational Conflicts

Conflicts can be destructive not only interpersonally but organizationally as well. Yet these same conflicts focus our attention on what is not working effectively for someone, thereby allowing us to improve it. For this reason, every organization, from corporations to nonprofits and schools to government agencies, can be revitalized, improved, and profoundly transformed by learning to embrace their conflicts and using them to develop innovative strategies for organizational transformation.

Breaking the downward spiral of unresolved organizational conflicts, whether they result in paralyzing impasses, petty personal disputes, or large-scale systemic dysfunctions, requires courage, leadership, and a strategic focus. The true organizational warriors, as Mary Parker Follett recognized in the quotation that opens this book, are those who refuse to succumb to these petty, personal conflicts or visit harm on others. Rather, they continuously encourage open, honest, and empathetic communications and develop the organizational strategies that allow us to learn from our conflicts.

Moments of insight and transformation in organizations are admittedly rare and frequently frightening. The idea that conflicts can be enriching or transforming may seem illogical or confusing because most of our experience has taught us the opposite. Although we frequently behave badly in conflict and rarely reach moments of resolution or transformation, it is nonetheless clear that the *possibility* of profound personal and organizational transformation is *always* present in every conflict we encounter.

To reveal this possibility, we need to dramatically shift the way we approach our conflicts and the way we behave when we are in them. We need to change how we think about ourselves, our organizations, and the people with whom we are in conflict. Most important, we need to redesign our organizational systems and cultures in ways that encourage constructive engagement and honest dialogue. To develop the organizational will to do so, it is important to focus not merely on what it will cost to resolve these organizational conflicts but what it will cost to *not* resolve them.

The Costs of Unresolved Conflicts

We all know that it takes time to resolve organizational disputes, yet it also takes time to not resolve them. If we count up the time and money we routinely spend on unresolved conflicts, it is nearly always far in excess of the time and money it would take to sit down and work out solutions. This is particularly true for organizational conflicts, as the two of us have observed in the thousands of conflicts we have resolved over the past twenty-five years. Here are a few real-life examples based on direct quotes:

• "I'm so furious! Why can't he understand what I'm trying to tell him!" We heard this from a supervisor trying to comprehend why a manager reporting to him did not reorganize the department as he suggested. We discovered that the supervisor had not actually told his manager what he wanted because he liked the man, assumed he understood what was needed, and did not want to cause him trouble or seem like he was micromanaging. Instead, he communicated poorly, became angry when he had been misunderstood, nearly fired the manager, and cost the organization considerable time and money to fix the problem.

- "I made it very clear to him that I didn't want him to touch me or flirt with me, but I couldn't say so directly because I didn't want to be rude." A woman who filed a sexual harassment lawsuit against her boss told us in mediation that this was why she had been unable to say "no" or ask him to stop. When we spoke with her boss, he said he thought she enjoyed his shoulder massages and flirtatious comments and added, "If she had just told me, I would have stopped immediately." The price they and the organization paid for her lack of communication skills and his failure to read her non-verbal signals ran well over a million dollars, without counting emotional costs and damaged careers.

- "I'm leaving because there are too many people in this organization who won't carry their weight or do their fair share of the work, and no one will call them on it." This statement was made by the director of a company leading a yearlong effort to introduce self-managing teams. She was frustrated to the point of resigning because she could not surface the group's unspoken agreement: "I won't call you on your shortcomings if you don't call me on mine." If we had not helped her find a constructive way to surface and discuss the problem, she would have left, costing the company a highly valued director and the expense of finding and training a qualified replacement.

In each of these cases, people became involved in serious, life-altering conflicts because they were unable to communicate what they really wanted or were afraid of the conflict that would result if they did! Yet each of these individuals, their colleagues, and organizations paid an enormous price for their fear of conflict, unwillingness to tell each other the truth, and lack of skill in listening. In retrospect, nothing they could have said would have been as powerful or destructive as what they thought and did not say.

If we could calculate the total amount of time, energy, money, and resources that are routinely wasted on unresolved organizational conflicts—the intimacies lost; the relationships destroyed; the decreased productivity due to gossip, rumors, absenteeism, stress-

related illnesses, and poor morale; the disruptions, turnover, grievances, and lawsuits; the accidents and workers' compensation cases—
the total would be staggering. On top of these, we have squandered a
potential for growth and learning and missed possibilities for improved relationships and personal and organizational transformations.
These are the true reasons for organizational conflict resolution.

Settlement Versus Resolution

In most organizations, managers and employees have learned to
sweep conflicts under the rug in hopes that they will go away. As a
result, they have developed cultures that encourage people to *not*
fully communicate what they really want and settle for partial solutions or no solutions at all. In doing so, they cheat themselves and
others out of learning from their conflicts and discovering more
skillful ways of handling them.

Denying the existence of our conflicts does not make them disappear but simply gives them greater covert power. Organizations
that encourage people to suppress their disagreements, or reward
them as "good soldiers" for doing so, create cultures that sacrifice
honesty, integrity, creativity, and peace of mind for superficial, fragile, temporary civility.

In most workplaces, employees learn to accept a level of humiliation, abuse, superficiality, and unresolved conflict simply in order
to keep their jobs. Consider, for example, how much humiliation,
abuse, and conflict you have accepted. Do people in the organization embrace and try to learn from conflicts, or do they avoid them
and try to sweep them under a rug? What price have you paid as a
result? What price have others at work paid for being unable to resolve their conflicts or having to dissemble and pretend or carry the
conflict with them for years? What price has the organization paid?

There is an enormous difference between communicating superficially to settle your conflicts and communicating deeply to resolve or learn from them. We settle our conflicts when we are
uncomfortable with them, feel frightened by them, wish to avoid or

suppress them, or think we need to pacify our opponents. We try to make them go away because we experience them as stressful, uncontrollable, violent, frightening, and irrational; because we lack the skill to handle our own intense emotions; or because we do not know how to respond safely to the intense emotions of others. Often we see our conflicts as failures or as expressions of irresponsibility or do not think them important or useful. Sometimes we are simply afraid of hurting other people's feelings.

Yet when we suppress our conflicts, we make the problem disappear before we have had a chance to reveal its underlying sources, correct it, learn from it, or break through to the other side. If this is our approach, we will tend to seek settlement for settlement's sake and cheat ourselves out of opportunities for resolution, learning, and transformation.

It may come as a shock to discover that we do not advocate peace for its own sake or believe that settlement is always better than battle. As we see it, peace without justice quickly turns oppressive. Superficial settlements often lead to silence, sullen acceptance, distrust, and renewed hostilities. By contrast, resolution leads to learning, change, partnership, community, innovation, increased trust, and forgiveness. All these are lost when we "trade justice for harmony" and commit to "peace at any price." Peace, in this sense, is not the absence of conflict but the ability to engage in it constructively.

Into the Eye of the Storm

When we seek resolution, we are drawn toward the center of our disputes, directly into "the eye of the storm." While this may sound irrational, and even dangerous, by moving *toward* our adversaries rather than away from them, we more quickly discover how to listen empathetically, acknowledge what we have in common, clarify and resolve the issues that are dividing us, devise creative solutions, collaboratively negotiate our differences, identify and resolve the underlying reasons for our dispute, learn from each other, and strengthen and revitalize our relationships.

At the center, heart, or eye in every conflict storm is a calm, peaceful place where conflict is transformed and transcended and where learning, dialogue, and insight take place. Journeying into the eye of the storm is, for this reason, a core or metastrategy for moving from impasse to resolution and transformation.

To move toward the center of our conflicts, we first have to change the way we think about our disputes and how we behave in their presence. We cannot run away from confrontation or decide to stop communicating with our opponents. Instead, we need to recognize that because every conflict contains hidden lessons that fuel our growth, change, learning, awareness, intimacy, effectiveness, and successful relationships, we should not be frightened of moving toward their center. As we do so, we can begin to recognize in every conflict the signs of emergence of a new paradigm, the indication of a desire on both sides for a better working relationship, a detailed guide to what is not working for one or both of us, and a request that we work together to make things better.

Paradoxically, we often engage in conflict because we do not believe it is possible to resolve our disputes, so we become more aggressive to avoid feeling defeated. Sometimes we fight because we need to express strong feelings or beliefs about an issue; or when we are trying to remedy an injustice, the other side has refused to listen or negotiate; or conflict offers an antidote to stagnation and apathy.

Being aggressive is sometimes the only way we can spark communication and honest dialogue, not because it is right but because we feel it is the only way to get the other person or the organization to listen. Yet hidden in the allure of principled opposition is the price we pay for having an enemy. This price is explored more fully in the strategies that follow.

Lasting change occurs when we use higher-level skills to move *through* our conflicts to achieve deeper levels of resolution, shifting from divergence to convergence, antagonism to unity, and impasse to transcendence. In this way, conflict resolution is an expression of the *highest* personal, organizational, social, and political responsibility. It is an ancient antidote to unfairness and injustice, a sometimes effective way of bringing about social change, and frequently the only way of expressing opposition to policies and practices we do not like. In each of these cases, it is not conflict that is the problem but the destructive, adversarial ways we engage in it.

How Far Apart Are People in Conflict?

Our greatest sources of inspiration and personal satisfaction come from love rather than hate, from moments of connection with others rather than moments of aggression and hostility. Yet even while we are searching for insight and transformation and trying to rise above the fray, we find ourselves mired in petty squabbles and disputes that make our efforts to rise above them seem almost laughable.

Every conflict we face in life is rich with positive and negative potential. As we have described, they can be a source of inspiration, enlightenment, learning, transformation, and growth—or of rage, fear, shame, impasse, and resistance. The choice is fundamentally not up to our opponents, but to us, and depends on our willingness to face and work through them.

The German philosopher Nietzsche wrote, "When you look into the abyss, the abyss also looks into you." Looking into your conflict means giving up your illusions, no longer seeing yourself as a victim or other people as your enemies. It means giving up your fear of engaging in honest communication with someone you distrust or dislike.

For example, consider the following: how far apart are people when they are in conflict? There are three correct answers: first, they are an infinite distance apart because they cannot communicate at all; second, they are no distance at all because their conflict makes them inseparable; and third, they are exactly *one step* apart because either of them can reach out and touch the other at any moment.

This leads to a follow-up question: if this is so, where are their conflicts located? Again, there are three correct answers: first, they are located in the mind of each person because each person's attitudes, ideas, emotions, and intentions are indispensable to the continuation of the dispute; second, they are located between them because every conflict is a relationship; and third, they are located around them because all conflicts take place within a system, culture, context, or environment that influences how they are conducted.

The answers to these questions suggest that you can improve your ability to resolve conflicts not only by taking that one step that separates you but also by changing the way you think and act in their presence, by working to improve your relationship with your opponent, and by changing the organizational culture or system in which they occur.

Twelve Ways to Begin

If you would like to follow the approach we have identified, where and how might you begin? The starting place for pursuing any of the eight strategies we have identified is your willingness to learn and your commitment to finding a resolution. To begin, you can position yourself to approach and engage your conflicts constructively by engaging in one or more of the following twelve actions. As you review them, notice shifts in the ways you are thinking about yourself, your opponent, and your conflict.

1. Set the stage for dialogue. Move out of your office and into a neutral environment, even one that is warm and open, such as a garden, restaurant, or park. Consider asking your opponent to join you for a walk or for lunch. Be open and friendly rather than hostile and accusative. Invite openness and honesty, and model it in return.

2. Disengage your fight-or-flight response, clear your mind of everything you think you already know about the conflict, and listen empathetically to your opponent. The best way to learn from your conflicts is by listening to your opponent. Active, empathetic, and responsive listening techniques are based on a recognition that all conflict is fundamentally a *request* for communication. To listen, you need to understand and control

your emotional responses. Realize that angry people sometimes need to vent, and refuse to take what they say or do personally. When your fragility makes you angry and defensive, it is easy to forget that you *always* have a choice about how you respond to others. Remember that the largest part of anger has little to do with the people to whom it is directed and everything to do with their actions and behaviors.

3. State clearly and without anger or fear of rejection your emotional needs and self-interests, and listen carefully to those expressed by others. Giving in to anger and fear only encourages the conflict, cheapens the victory, and makes the other side look good or allows your opponent to dismiss your integrity and willingness to listen. Asking for what you want or need is essential if you are going to give up your anger and fear and negotiate as equals.

4. Look below the surface of what is being said to resolve the underlying reasons for the dispute. Your conflict is probably not really about the issues over which you are busily arguing. There are always issues that lie beneath the surface and need to be brought into the open for the conflict to be resolved. Rather than starting with your opponent, start with yourself and think what you might be able to do to respond more powerfully to what lies beneath his or her statements.

5. Separate the person from the problem, the future from the past, and positions from interests. Most people in conflict begin and end with the idea that the other person is the problem, that they are right about what happened, and that there is only one solution, which is theirs. Conflict becomes an opportunity when you treat the problem as an "it" rather than as a "you." Resolution becomes possible when you stop debating over positions (what you want) and start dialoguing over interests (why you want it). Interests can usually be satisfied in multiple and diverse ways, whereas positions are nearly always opposed and represent only a small range of possible out-

comes. Positions are traps that narrow your thinking, perceptions, and imagination. By contrast, interests are rarely mutually exclusive. They can broaden your choices and help you look to the future, which is the only part of the conflict you can do anything about.

6. Brainstorm all the possible solutions to your conflict, listing as many as you can, and ask your opponent to work with you to develop criteria for how to resolve it. When you are in conflict, you probably spend most of your energy trying to get other people to accept your solution, or poking holes in theirs, rather than searching for alternatives that will benefit both of you. Brainstorming is a useful technique for expanding the range of possible solutions and not assuming that the only alternatives are victory and defeat.

7. Negotiate collaboratively rather than aggressively, and clarify the values, standards, or rules that will help resolve the dispute fairly and result in mutual satisfaction. Using a collaborative-negotiation process, agree on a set of shared values, standards, or mutually acceptable ground rules for integrating emotions into problem solving. It is useful to search for what will satisfy the other party's interests as well as your own. A dissatisfied opponent has a strong interest in continuing the dispute.

8. Use informal problem solving, strategic planning, mediation, and similar conflict resolution techniques to reduce resistance, overcome impasse, clarify areas of agreement, and reach closure. It is possible for you to enormously expand the degree of opportunity you are able to find in your conflicts through informal problem solving. If you are stuck, find an experienced third-party professional to mediate the conflict, rather than litigate it.

9. Let go of your judgments about your opponents, and focus instead on improving your own skills in handling their difficult behaviors. Then let go, forgive yourself and the other person, and move on with your life. Your judgments about people are

only justifications for not listening and admissions that you
are unable to respond skillfully to their behaviors. As you dis-
mantle your judgments and assumptions that you are right and
they are wrong, you will discover how locked-in you are to
fighting and how far you are from forgiveness. It is important
to learn how to let go of your conflicts and release yourself
in the present from what has been done to you in the past
and, at the same time, not lose sight of the lessons you have
learned that can help you avoid future conflicts. Finding ways
to forgive yourself and others does not mean forgetting what
happened. It is not "forgive and forget" but "remember and
let go." This is something you do, not for your opponent but
for yourself, in order to get on with your life.

10. Do not surrender just so the conflict will go away. The point is
    not to avoid conflict but to turn it into a collaboration and an
    opportunity for improvement. Conflict resolution does not
    mean giving in but turning opposition into a fruitful collabora-
    tion. When you surrender, you cheat yourself and your oppo-
    nent out of the opportunities for learning, which you achieve
    only by confronting what the conflict is trying to teach you.

11. Recognize the larger organizational and social issues that ex-
    press themselves through your conflict, and discover how you
    can engage in committed actions and contribute to a more
    peaceful world. You are not an island unto yourself. As organi-
    zations and societies become more complex, problematic, and
    riddled with conflict, examine your small disputes closely to
    see if they reflect these larger problems, yet are experienced by
    you as exclusively interpersonal. Examine your own role in
    contributing to change, organizational collaboration, and so-
    cial justice, and engage in committed actions that will allow
    you to grow and feel connected to others.

12. Search for closure. Your conflicts may go on and on because
    you have not completely communicated at a deep-enough
    level what you think or feel or do not believe you have been

fully or completely heard. Finding ways of expressing what you need to say, asking your opponents to express what they need to say, and encouraging them to make sure nothing is held back are useful strategies in allowing you to end the conversation and walk away feeling complete and that something has changed.

Some of these steps may appear counterintuitive to you. We know that embarking on them will require considerable support and guidance as well as self-knowledge, courage, and internal strength. We also know that a skilled mediator will not always be there to help when you are on the spot and haven't got the foggiest notion of what to do or say.

In that moment, our only advice to you is to speak from your heart; let your spirit, authenticity, and integrity shine forth; reach out to your opponent and invite them in; and trust in your intuition. If you can do these things, the rest will seem easy.

Resolving Conflicts at Work

Change the Culture and Context of Conflict

Only someone who is ready for everything, who
doesn't exclude any experience, even the most
incomprehensible, will live the relationship
with another person as something alive and will
himself sound the depths of his own being. For if
we imagine this being of the individual as a larger
or smaller room, it is obvious that most people
come to know only one corner of their room, one
spot near the window, one narrow strip on which
they keep walking back and forth. In this way they
have a certain security. And yet how much more
human is the dangerous insecurity that drives those
prisoners in Poe's stories to feel out the shapes of
their horrible dungeons and not be strangers to the
unspeakable terror of their cells. We, however, are
not prisoners.

—*Rainer Maria Rilke*

Every society, organization, group, and family creates a culture of
conflict, a complex set of words, ideas, values, behaviors, attitudes,
archetypes, customs, and rules that powerfully influence how its
members think about and respond to conflict. Cultures of conflict are shaped in and by our experiences. They set parameters
for what we believe is possible when we are in conflict and define
what we can reasonably expect, both of ourselves and of others.

They shape our capacity to ask questions, alter how we see our opponents and ourselves, and tell us what is acceptable and what is not.

Every workplace and organization, school and neighborhood, family and relationship generates spoken and unspoken rules about what we should and should not say and do when we are in conflict. Each of these entities produces a separate and distinct culture that exerts enormous pressure on us to respond to conflict in traditionally expected ways.

Many organizational cultures place a premium on conflict avoidance, whereas others reward accommodation or compromise. A number of highly competitive corporate cultures give high marks for aggression. Most possess a subtle set of rules regarding who can behave how, with whom, and over what.

As we scan our current organizational cultures, we search in vain for signs of meaningful support for genuine collaboration with our opponents; open, creative dialogue regarding problems; honest, empathetic, self-critical leadership in addressing and responding to conflicts; and preventative, persistent, systemic approaches to resolution.

Instead, we find dismissive attitudes that regard conflict resolution as pointless or "touchy-feely"; conflict-averse cultures that reward avoidance and accommodation; aggressive, hypercompetitive cultures that permit retribution and reprisal for speaking the truth; bureaucratic rules that encourage passive-aggressive behavior; hypocritical, self-serving leadership; and covert systems that are creating chronic, avoidable conflicts.

Sadly, in most organizational cultures, it is rare that aggression, avoidance, and accommodation require explanation whereas collaboration, honesty, openness, and forgiveness seem vaguely unacceptable. Algerian novelist Albert Camus, observing a similar phenomenon, wrote, "Through a curious transposition peculiar to our times, it is innocence that is called upon to justify itself."

Conflict Messages in Popular Culture

The seductive, hypnotic power of aggression is enhanced by powerful images that are communicated through popular media to which we are continually subjected. Newspapers are sold with it through the injunction, "if it bleeds, it leads." Television programs alternately accentuate or trivialize it. Sporting events bristle with it. Soap operas play with it. Advertising captures its images or creates a phony, superficial world where it cannot be imagined.

Look carefully at the messages that are broadcast every day through movies, television, newspapers, magazines, radio, and advertising, and ask yourself: what ideas are being communicated about conflict? What behaviors are being reinforced or emulated by paying attention to them? What ideas and behaviors are implicitly regarded as unworthy of attention and emulation by others? How often are conflicts mediated, negotiated, or resolved without violence?

As we experience this continual cultural assault, our threshold of acceptance for violence and aggression is lowered, our capacity for peace making is undermined, and we become more and more addicted to the adrenaline rush of combat, less empathetic and collaborative, and more fearful and conflict-avoidant.

Like addicts, our mass culture is alternately numbed and "shot up" with conflict. In common media imagery, pacifism is equated with idealism, saintliness, and passivity, thoughtfulness with stupidity, caution with cowardice, aggression with passion, and cruelty with seriousness of character.

These distorted images are brought to us not only in movies, music, and newspapers but also through a titillating array of commercial products that encourage and support our addiction. We are presented with subtle images that generate tensions and conflicts that can only be resolved through the purchase of tranquilizing, painkilling, disgrace-averting, druglike products.

Many of the effects of this continuous immersion in conflict are immediate, clear, and pervasive. They include a brutalization of the soul, a loss of capacity for empathy with the suffering of others, an overwhelming fear of violence, an anxiety about social acceptance, a numbing capitulation to unacceptable behaviors, a cynicism about human worth, an avoidance of social intimacy, a political paranoia, a retreat into compliant behavior, and a "bread and circuses" atmosphere. These effects divert our attention from solving problems that seem insurmountable because we are incapable of paying attention to them, banding together to bring about change, or overcoming our fear of criticism, controversy, and retaliation.

Many societies, workplaces, and organizations have, as a result, developed entire ecosystems based on miscommunication and conflict avoidance in which people spend an extraordinary amount of time hiding from honest communications, trapped in unresolved disputes with others, confused over unclear messages, and unsuccessfully trying to make their needs and feelings heard and understood.

People in these cultures spend little time learning what their conflicts are actually about—what caused them; what really upset people's feelings; why they have such a hard time saying what they really think and feel; or talking directly, openly, and honestly. As a result, they fail to learn from their conflicts and cannot see how they might respond more skillfully to their own strong emotions, or to those of others.

A dramatic example of this self-reinforcing spiral of conflict occurred in an engineering and maintenance division of a Fortune 100 manufacturing company in which we consulted. The engineers saw themselves as a highly skilled, well-educated elite corps within the organization. Their mission was to respond to requests from the manufacturing divisions to build equipment that would produce quality products and generate profits. While they were not a revenue-generating center, they considered themselves to be central to the company's vision, mission, and goals.

The other part of the division was a maintenance crew that consisted of electricians, carpenters, and building managers who saw themselves as craftspeople. They were responsible for repairing the equipment that was built or purchased by the engineers and maintaining the machinery and buildings that housed it. Each group occupied a different status level within the division and held the other in disdain. Not only did they develop completely different cultures, languages, and attitudes that disregarded the contributions of the other and described them as obstructionist, their mutual hostility began to undermine their ability to successfully complete routine work projects.

The engineers who introduced new equipment neglected or refused to provide directions, instructions, blueprints, or repair charts to the craftspeople who were required to maintain and repair it. The maintenance staff, in turn, neglected or refused to inform the engineers when they modified the equipment, repaired it, or changed the location of machinery the engineers had installed.

When the maintenance staff aggressively challenged the engineers to supply the information they needed, the response was hostile and dismissive. The engineers saw these requests as unnecessary incursions into their protected, elite, professional domain, whereas the maintenance staff considered the engineer's reactions as stonewalling what they saw as logical and necessary requests.

Maintenance, on the other hand, considered engineering's requests to know when and how the equipment had been modified, became defunct, was moved, or broke down as "none of their damn business." Needless to say, the organizational culture that resulted from this escalation was one of "turfism," competition, mutual suspicion, conflict avoidance, and bureaucratic bungling that cost the organization a great deal and took months to fix.

Changing Conflict Cultures

Our challenge is to release ourselves from these pointless, unproductive cultural patterns and create organizational cultures that value openness, honesty, dialogue, collaborative negotiation, conflict resolution, and the ability to learn from our opponents.

Each of us is capable of improving the way we respond to conflict, and as we do, we also gradually begin to change the cultures we have created or tolerated around us—in our homes, families, schools, organizations, and communities. As we achieve a critical mass in favor of conflict resolution, our larger culture and society will begin to change as well.

Each of us can also make an effort to improve the conflict cultures in our workplaces and organizations. We can, for example, reduce the level of conflict avoidance simply by honestly and non-aggressively communicating our differences and openly discussing our issues with others in a spirit of trying to find better solutions.

In addition, we can empathize with our opponents and acknowledge their contributions to our learning or improvement. We can discuss disagreements publicly and not allow them to be swept under the rug. We can be self-critical about the role we have played in our conflicts. We can agree not to engage in caustic insults and vitriolic e-mail attacks on others. We can encourage our colleagues to let go of ancient, unresolved grievances and create common ground with each other. We can encourage consensus regarding vision, mission, goals, and shared values. We can publicly identify covert passive-aggressive behaviors and unethical leadership behaviors and ask people whether they want to engage in them. We can encourage our coworkers to honestly and empathetically communicate their thoughts and feelings about how they are interacting and ask them how they would prefer to interact in the future. We can invite our opponents to engage in dialogue and collaborative negotiation to solve our common problems. And we can reach forgiveness and reconciliation within ourselves and let others know how and why we did so.

By engaging in these activities, we can start to reorient the conflict-averse, -avoidant, and aggressive elements in our organizational cultures. More important, we can increase everyone's awareness of the subtle forms of violence and prejudice we routinely practice against each other and choose to both be committed and behave collaboratively when we are in conflict. The contrast between these opposing cultural attitudes can be found, for example, in the metaphors and language people use when they are in conflict.

The Language of Conflict

The words we use to describe our conflicts reflect the hidden assumptions we have formed about ourselves, our opponents, and the meaning of our conflicts. These words shape our expectations and experiences and limit our interactions, processes, and relationships. The language we use when we are in conflict reveals a great deal about our secret biases, limitations, fears, and even what we are capable of imagining as solutions.

Rather than being static, language evolves dynamically and both affects and is affected by the culture that produces and uses it. This causes national languages to break down into thousands of "sublanguages" that include, as Russian language theorist Mikail Bakhtin wrote,

> . . . social dialects, characteristic group vernacular, professional jargons, generic languages, languages of generations and age groups, tendentious languages, languages of the authorities, of various circles and of passing fashions, languages that serve the specific sociopolitical purposes of the day, even of the hour (each day has its own slogan, its own vocabulary, its own emphases).

Thus, not only does each separate organizational department, hierarchical level, and job title and function create its own language, but each team, group, clique, and relationship does as well. In a similar way, everyone in conflict creates a unique language to describe their experiences and reveals through their choice of words what the conflict means to them, how they see their opponents, and how they intend to interact with them.

In other words, each of us has a choice about how we describe the conflicts in our lives. We can describe them as experiences that imprison us, as battles, as opportunities for learning, or as fascinating journeys. Our choice between these contrasting attitudes will shape the way our conflict unfolds. More important, by changing the language we use to describe conflict, we automatically change what is possible and what we can imagine doing in response to it.

Consider a conflict in which you are presently engaged. Your language choices will reveal as much about yourself as about the person you are describing. Consider the words you are using to describe your opponent. If, for example, you describe him or her as "arrogant," stop for a moment and see if you can think of a positive word you might use in place of the word arrogant. If, for example, you wanted to describe your opponent favorably, you might use words such as "self-confident" or "determined." Yet, by choosing the word arrogant over the word self-confident, you have revealed as much about your own self-confidence as about your opponent's arrogance.

Think of it this way. If you are completely convinced and unambiguous in your self-confidence, why should someone else's arrogance make you angry, as opposed to sad or disappointed? Is it possible that your opponent sees his or her arrogance simply as self-confidence? Could your anger represent an overreaction or overcompensation for your own lack of self-confidence?

Similarly, every insult that is hurled at you by your opponent can be traced like a thread running backwards into the subconscious psyche of the person who chose it. From the insults your opponent uses to describe you, it is possible not only to learn what upsets him or her but to make a reasonable guess as to why and form a better understanding of what you might do to create a different response.

If you listen closely, you will discover that beneath every insult and accusation lies a *confession*, and beneath every confession lies a *request*. For example, if your opponent calls you a "bully," you can hear it as a confession that your opponent feels intimidated by you or becomes frightened when you raise your voice. More deeply, you can hear it as a request that you treat him or her more respectfully or speak softly or less judgmentally in the future.

No matter what insult a person chooses, there is a positive way of saying the same thing. Every decision to use a negative word or phrase in place of a positive or neutral one indicates a sensitivity or weakness on the part of the speaker that can be used by the listener to gain a deeper understanding of what the speaker actually feels. This information can then be used by the listener to turn the insult into a request. In this way, even insults and accusations can be turned upside down and transformed into sources of learning, growth, skill building, resolution, and transformation.

The same point can be made regarding the language we use to describe our conflicts. In conflict resolution workshops, we often ask, "What is one word or phrase that expresses what you do or feel when you are in conflict?" People's initial responses often include words like anger, frustration, silence, shame, fear, stress, avoidance, and repression, nearly all of which are negative. We then ask whether there are any *positive* outcomes from conflict, and people call out words like change, intimacy, learning, growth, opportunity, communication, resolution, forgiveness, listening, trust, and completion.

The positive words represent what we all want, what is possible, and what is at stake in our conflicts, while the negative words represent how we feel, what we are doing to each other, and how we are trying to get it. But if you try to use negative means to achieve positive ends, you will quickly discover that it is nearly impossible to "get there from here," that anger does not translate into trust, any more than shame builds self-confidence.

Try this yourself. Consider a recent conflict or miscommunication you experienced. List the first words that come to mind regarding your opponent, both negative and positive, without censoring yourself, and see what feelings and ideas emerge from your subconscious. Then ask yourself what led you to use the negative words, how you might implement the positive ones, and how it might be possible to resolve your conflicts by turning the negatives into positives. For example, if you feel frightened by your opponent, consider what it might take to overcome your fear, talk calmly about the problem, and let it go.

You may find that the positive words reflect a deeper understanding that working through your conflict could dramatically improve your relationships and communications, while the negative ones reflect a profound frustration at your inability to do so. Yet the negative words are likely to keep you locked in conflict and stuck in cycles of distrust, while the positive ones, to become real, require you to get to the bottom of the reasons why you came up with the negative words in the first place and to honestly and empathetically participate in dialogue with your opponent. Doing so automatically starts to transform the negative words into positive ones at their source inside you.

Metaphors and the Meaning of Conflict

Although the reasons we cite for engaging in conflict are grounded in facts and logic, our experience of conflict is emotional. But rather than participate in direct emotional communication with people we do not trust, we transmit our feelings indirectly through the language we use to describe the facts or reinforce our logic. For this reason, the language of conflict is highly charged and full of allusion, metaphor, and symbolism.

Poets, novelists, and lyricists have invented a rich cultural language that allows us to express in any tongue the complex and convoluted emotional truth of our conflicts. Listen to your words when you are in conflict. What metaphors, symbols, and allusions do you use to make your feelings known? What words do you wrap around your emotions to express or disguise them? How do these words differ when you describe your opponent and when you describe yourself? How do they express how you feel about the conflict?

Consider, for example, three common conflict metaphors and a variety of popular phrases that expose our underlying beliefs about the nature and meaning of our conflicts. These metaphors are drawn from organizational cultures in which we have worked. They employ phrases whose meanings may or may not have been intended. Yet, by scrutinizing the language you use in conflict, you can discover how simple words and phrases are able to shape what you feel and how you respond. Listen to the symbolism and hidden meanings, for example, in the following phrases.

Conflict as War

Common Phrases

"Your position is indefensible."

"We shot down that idea."

"We've got a battle on our hands."

"He dropped a bomb on me."

"Let's line up the troops/man the barricades."

"I won."

Using warlike metaphors to describe our conflict reveals an underlying belief that the other person is out to get us, that we have no choice but to fight back using the same tactics, and that nothing can be done to resolve the dispute short of total victory. Yet the other person may only be acting in self-defense as a result of hearing our aggressive metaphors and combative language; and may respond favorably to a different set of tactics and be willing to negotiate a compromise or interest-based solution.

What is worse, it often happens that victory is turned into defeat and defeat is transformed into victory. For example, crushing the other side generally has the effect of reducing the winner's capacity for compassion, collaboration, forgiveness, and reconciliation and increases other people's sympathy for the loser. And the winner tends to repeat winning behavior while the loser is forced to learn, change, and try something new.

Unfortunately, aggressive, hostile, warlike attitudes and a willingness to do battle against our opponents are richly rewarded in many highly competitive corporate cultures. Yet warlike attitudes toward external opponents can easily be turned inward to generate fiercely competitive attitudes toward colleagues *within* the organizational culture, reducing collaboration and increasing distrust among coworkers.

Reassessing our language, checking the assumptions that lie hidden in combative metaphors, and using more collaborative terminology will encourage us to find and use new metaphors that encourage teamwork. One example of an unlikely corporate leader who found fresh options to this warlike approach to conflict is Jeffrey Katzenberg, now CEO of Dreamworks, Inc. In an interview describing the culture at his new company, Katzenberg, who was well known for his hyperaggressive conflict style as head of Disney Studios, spoke of his realization as follows to a *New York Times* reporter:

> I am aware that for a long period of time I operated like a mercenary soldier. Someone else wrote the music, and I marched to their tune. And if someone poked me in the chest, I would hit them with a baseball bat. And if they hit me with a bat, I would blast them with a bazooka. And I would escalate this until I reached nuclear-bomb time. This was the way I was taught. . . . And it's a very angry place to come from in life. It's a hostile, angry, and predatory way to live life. The truth is, if you asked me to look back and say, because I behaved that way, that's why I was successful, I would now say: No. If I had been more conciliatory, I would have been more successful.

The use of warlike metaphors reveals an underlying assumption that our opponents are evil, allowing us to justify the evil we intend to do to them in return. Demonizing them disarms our compassion and gives us permission to hurt them as we feel they have hurt us. In doing so, we offer an inadequate reason for *why* others hurt us. The reason may be that we unknowingly caused them harm. Or someone else may have hurt them in the past in a similar way. Or they may have decided to pass their pain onto us rather than experience it themselves. Or they may feel that a preemptive strike will protect them from the future harm they think we are going to cause them. Or they may be frightened of being fired and trying to create a diversion by pointing at our responses and minimizing the importance of their own behaviors. While each of these is harmful to us, none can properly be called evil.

By explaining this dynamic, we are not excusing their behavior. Rather, we are questioning the underlying assumption that allows us to think we can demonize them without at the same time victimizing ourselves, or injure them without also injuring ourselves. Demonizing and retaliation only make us more brutal, insensitive, and uncaring and call for similar actions in response. It is not necessary that we make the person who hurt us evil in order to communicate our displeasure and refusal to tolerate what the other person has done.

Metaphors of warfare generate hatred that does not automatically disappear once our opponent leaves. Warlike metaphors harm us by filling us with rage, hostility, fear, stress, and the seeds of physical illness. As a result, we may aggressively express our rage at our opponent simply to let go of it, without appreciating that we have triggered a need on the other's part to respond in kind, continued the conflict, and turned it in a circle.

The good news is that while warfare and hatred can be internalized through metaphors, so can love and forgiveness. To see how, contrast the military approach we have just examined to a different metaphor and set of phrases that view conflict as an opportunity for learning, transformation, improved relationships, better solutions, and personal and organizational change.

Conflict as Opportunity

Common Phrases

"This issue presents us with a real challenge."

"What would you like to see happen instead?"

"We now have a chance to make things better."

"You have a good point. What could we do together to address it?"

"Your feedback has helped me see some ways I could improve, for example, by communicating more respectfully. Is that right?"

"What are all the possibilities for solving this problem?"

This simple shift in language reflects a profound transformation in the way we think about conflict. Metaphors that describe conflicts as opportunities for improvement signal a transition from assuming our opponents are evil to assuming they are allies and can help us solve our problems. They move us from assuming negative outcomes to expecting positive ones. By doing so, they create possibilities for learning, growing, and improving relationships.

Shifting to metaphors of opportunity will allow you to engage in an open-ended exploration of your common problems and pursue a broad range of outcomes that take you beyond victory and defeat. When conflict is viewed as an opportunity, anything becomes possible. More important, you become the shaper of your own conflict experiences, in charge of where and how they end, and responsible for their outcomes.

By adopting metaphors of opportunity, you will be able to see your conflict as containing multiple possibilities, not only for learning and improvement but for deeper personal intimacy, improved appreciation of your opponent, better and more lasting solutions, clearer communications, and more trusting relationships. Viewed in this light, every conflict represents a possibility of personal and organizational improvement. These possibilities cannot be mandated. They occur only when you search for the information your conflict has hidden from you and is waiting for you to discover.

Yet these hidden opportunities do not reveal themselves easily. For example, we were recently asked to assist a small but highly successful corporation in resolving a conflict between its two top officers who were battling for control of the company, although their ostensible fight was over who would get the best office, the plushest furniture, the largest head count, and the biggest expense account.

Our way of helping them shift from metaphors of war to those of opportunity consisted of asking them if they would be willing to transfer their competition to something that really mattered to the company, such as who could create the greatest customer satisfaction, inspire their teams to produce the best results, or reduce costs and streamline operations the most. They laughed, admitted they had been acting like children, and agreed to use their conflict to help drive organizational improvement.

As you confront your problems and conflicts, instead of fighting against them and exhausting yourself and others, consider whether it would not be more interesting and enjoyable to find out why they happened the way they did and what you can do to resolve them better, faster, or move them to a higher level. In these ways, it is possible to locate the opportunities hidden in the conflict.

Shifting your language and thinking to metaphors of opportunity will also force you to take responsibility for what you have contributed to the conflict. The more you acknowledge your own contribution, the greater the opportunity you will create, not only for resolution and innovative outcomes, but for personal growth and organizational improvement. Your willingness to examine the assumptions that underlie your approach to conflict will bring you face to face with your inner nature. The more you do to find your authentic conflict voice, the easier you will find it to recognize and elicit the authentic voices of others.

Metaphors of war focus your attention on the past, your opponent, and the difficulty of resolution. Metaphors of opportunity focus your attention on the future, yourself, and the ways you might learn from the conflict and use it to drive change.

Another example of a conflict metaphor asks you to think of your conflict as a journey. Considering your conflict a journey focuses your attention on the present rather than the past or the future; on the relationship between you and your opponent rather than on what your opponent or you are doing, saying, thinking, or feeling; and on the *process* of discussing, negotiating, and resolving your dispute, rather than on the difficulty or opportunity of achieving a resolution. When we think of conflict as a journey, we become less concerned with the goal or destination and more focused on the process. We decide to relax and enjoy the ride.

Conflict as Journey

Common Phrases

"Your ideas point in the right direction."

"Here is what I really enjoy about working with you."

"We're off to a good start."

"Where do you want to go with that?"

"Is this process/conversation working for you?"

"We're on the road to a solution."

"I think we've arrived at an agreement!"

When you approach your conflict as a journey, process, or voyage that takes you to a new location, you transcend the idea that you are trapped in your conflict. This allows you to move beyond the idea that you can learn from your conflict, to recognize that the journey itself is worthwhile. In doing so, you increase your capacity to move *with* rather than against your opponent, to see what is new and unknown as interesting rather than frightening. You may even learn to anticipate with pleasure your next opportunity to travel the path of conflict in search of growth and discovery.

Seeing your conflict as a journey also encourages you to explore your relationship with your opponents, discover your "hot buttons" and the reasons you allow them to be pushed, and take pleasure in finding better solutions in partnership with your opponent. Journeys create expectations and anticipations of growth, self-improvement, awareness, and forgiveness. They offer release from the stress of feeling trapped and from making enemies of people you have not taken time to know or understand.

At a conflict resolution seminar we conducted for Los Angeles school principals, one of the participants told a story about transforming his school by shifting his attitude toward conflict and viewing it as a journey. His school was run-down and needed a face-lift. Several teachers told him he should paint over a faded, peeling mural that had been at the school for many years. He did so, and several other teachers and staff protested, telling him they had liked the mural, which had respected their ethnic diversity.

Instead of becoming defensive or counterattacking, he implemented an alternative strategy. He met with the entire faculty and asked them to join him in a journey of discovery to see what they could learn from this experience. He invited all sides to express their arguments and defenses and to examine their mutual responsibility for the misunderstanding and conflict. He began by admitting his own errors, something he would not have done if he were describing the conflict as a war. This led to a consensus decision-making process that resulted in an improved educational program for students, an agreement to replace the mural with a new one designed by the entire school community, and a renewed sense of partnership and trust.

Your conflict can become an *external* journey in search of an authentic opponent or an *internal* quest in search of your authentic self. Your ability to hear your inner voice will be reflected externally in your ability to listen to others, just as your ability to accept yourself will be reflected in your capacity to feel compassion for others. Each is a journey toward wisdom and more honest, empathetic, and balanced relationships.

There are many other metaphors you can apply to your conflicts. Try to discover them in the words you and your opponent use during shouting matches and arguments and in the midst of insults and problem-solving conversations. As you investigate these hidden messages, see whether you can use the information expressed through metaphor to move toward better solutions. As you gradually become more skillful, you can begin to intentionally shift and reframe the metaphors your opponent is using and create metaphors of openness, freedom, and optimism to counter metaphors of entrapment, enslavement, or despair.

Creating Opportunities and Journeys: Changing the Context of Conflict

It is difficult in the midst of conflict to deepen your capacity for empathy and intimacy with your opponent. Your anger can quickly transform someone who made an innocent mistake into a stereotypical demon or villain, at the same time leaving you feeling powerless and victimized. Similarly, defensiveness can prevent you from communicating openly and honestly with your opponents or listening deeply and carefully to what they mean *beneath* the words they are saying.

On the other hand, as you engage in dialogue with your opponents, you resurrect the human side of their personalities—and express your own as well. By acting with integrity in conflict, you increase your awareness and stimulate self-improvement in others. Uncontrolled anger, defensiveness, fear, and shame defeat these possibilities and leave you feeling weaker. Everyone feels more powerful when they face their problems, negotiate their differences, and search for resolution, and everyone feels weaker when they succumb to their negative emotions and refuse to talk with each other or even try to resolve their differences.

It is a bitter truth that victories won in anger lead to long-term defeat. Anger causes everyone to feel they lost and encourages opponents to turn away from each other in the future. In conflict, *everyone* suffers, everyone feels betrayed, everyone's heart is broken. If there is no resulting dialogue or resolution, both parties carry these unresolved injuries with them into their next conflict.

If, on the other hand, we are genuinely able to experience our conflicts as opportunities to learn what is not working and how to fix it or as interesting journeys of imagination and discovery, we will not be so frightened by anger. Instead, we will experience it, perhaps, as an indication of frustration and caring, as an opportunity to learn how to be honest without making others mad, or as a chance to experience it and become more aware of how it works.

Clearly, finding a solution to your conflict depends on your ability to understand what caused it. This depends, in turn, on your ability to listen to your opponent as you would to a teacher. Doing so will allow you to halt the cycle of escalation and search for insight and opportunities for improvement. Thus, different—even antagonistic—points of view can help you create a larger, more complex picture of what may otherwise have appeared to be a simple, narrow problem and identify richer, more creative, comprehensive, and effective solutions.

Finally, your conflict can lead you to a deeper understanding, not only of your opponent, yourself, and the conflict, but of the complex relationship, holistic interaction, and large-scale evolution of these elements within your organizational culture. Increased awareness of the deeper causes and subtle nature of conflict in general, the intricacies of interpersonal communication and group process, and why people get angry with each other can help you develop a more profound understanding of the chronic *systemic* sources of your conflict.

As a result, you will become less inclined to respond with fight-or-flight reflexes and more inclined to listen. This is the opportunity of opportunities through which it becomes possible to gain insight, act with greater self-awareness, and prevent your conflicts from escalating to the point where these opportunities become hidden.

When you alter how you see your opponent, you *automatically* alter your definition of yourself, which in turn automatically alters your understanding of the causes, content, and context of your conflict. Thus, by seeing your conflicts as opportunities or journeys, you will automatically increase your capacity to listen and resolve conflicts, strengthen your relationships, and improve the way you approach conflicts in the future.

The Impact of Context: Failing to Notice the Opportunities and Journeys

If it is possible for us to see our conflicts as opportunities or journeys, why do we persist in engaging in them as a form of warfare? What fuels our negative attitudes toward conflicts? How do we get trapped in them? Why do we respond to perceived hostility or aggression in such futile, counterproductive, self-defeating ways?

The answers to these questions can be found in the *context* we create for perceiving and participating in our conflicts. Once we have defined our opponent as evil, resorting to aggression and warfare becomes automatic. The metaphors we use and the language we apply in thinking about the problem, and what we do in response to it, become congruent with our sense of the context in which it occurs.

The principal driving force that largely determines the character of our participation in conflict, the nature of our conflict cultures, and our choice of symbolic language to describe the issues and opponents we are facing is the biological context of our instinctual and habitual responses to aggression, hostility, and opposition.

Let us begin by diagramming our typical responses to any perceived aggression. Assume that the first move in our conflict is made by the other person, whom we will call A, and that A has engaged in some action that we, B, perceive as aggressive, hostile, or directed against us. To make this clear, we will illustrate the opening move in the conflict, as B sees it, as follows:

$$A \longrightarrow B$$

We are not concerned here with what A actually did or intended, with the subject matter of the dispute, or with whether some third party did something to trigger A's actions; we are concerned only with what B *perceives*. From B's perspective, A is behaving hostilely, and in analyzing B's initial response, that is all that counts.

On the basis of this diagram, what can we predict about what B will do next? What options are available to B, based on perceived hostility coming from A? The next chart illustrates the most common responses to perceived aggression. As you scan this chart, think about the responses you use most often. If you recognize any of B's typical responses in what your opponent is directing toward you, you can assume you have become A in your opponent's eyes.

If A attacks B (A $\longrightarrow$ B), B can respond in several ways:

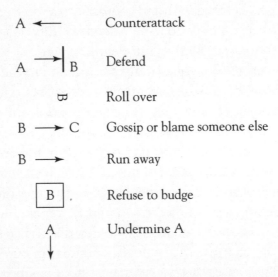

A $\longleftarrow$	Counterattack
A $\longrightarrow\!\big|$ B	Defend
ꓭ	Roll over
B $\longrightarrow$ C	Gossip or blame someone else
B $\longrightarrow$	Run away
B .	Refuse to budge
A $\downarrow$	Undermine A

Notice that for each of B's responses, A appears more dominant and powerful, while B seems weaker and merely responsive to A's cues. Notice also that A "gets something" from every one of B's responses:

- If B counterattacks, A will succeed in getting B's attention and earn support or sympathy from others by no longer appearing to be the one who initiated the dispute.
- If B withdraws, A wins.
- If B becomes defensive, A can say that B is not listening.
- If B gossips, blames C, or refuses to budge, A can criticize B for refusing to accept responsibility for solutions.
- A may even appear the innocent victim of B's unprovoked attack to an outside observer who did not actually see A attack B first!

In each of these responses, B actually does A a *favor* by entering the conflict and paradoxically increases A's power by responding in the ways diagrammed on the previous page. Notice also that to someone who does not know A or is unaware of A's prior aggression, B will not only appear to be the aggressor but will seem "troubled," "crazy," or "a difficult personality" whom it would be wise to avoid.

A and B are both acting out of a context in which anyone who is an opponent is also an enemy. This warlike approach encourages defensive responses based on ancient instinctual reactions and primitive strategies of fight-or-flight that originate in an area of the brain called the amygdala, which regulates our perceptions and responses to aggression. When the amygdala is disabled, for example, through a stroke, fear disappears.

As a result of the evolution of the brain and increased capacity for higher-level thinking, A and B have developed rational prefrontal cortex strategies that are more subtle than simply attacking others, defending ourselves, or running away. These consist, for example, of shifting blame onto others, undermining our opponent's support, and gossiping to C about what A did to us.

Nonetheless, it is extremely rare that A or B regard their conflict as an opportunity or a journey. Neither are they likely in their initial response to a perceived attack to ask their opponent to sit down together; talk openly and honestly about what happened; listen actively, empathetically, and responsively to the other person's point of view; and jointly define, explore, and resolve the problem. This is because they have each already labeled the other's behavior as an attack. If they instead labeled it as a misunderstanding, a natural response to rejection, a request for honest communication, an effort to identify something that is not working as well as it might, or a barrier that could be overcome through joint problem solving, their responses would be quite different.

The difficulty with all the options outlined so far is that none of them have anything to do with listening or support either side in understanding and coming to terms with the underlying issues in the dispute. None assist them in finding solutions to problems or contribute to improving the quality of their relationship. Instead, these options encourage them to think of their conflict as a war and remain trapped in ongoing, chronic hostilities.

Whether we are A or B, we are likely to remain at an impasse until we shift the context or framework we have created for understanding each other, critically examine our assumptions regarding whether our opponent is being *irrationally* aggressive, and halt our instinctual aggressive or defensive responses. Only then can we identify the opportunity in our conflict, see it as a journey, focus on finding solutions to common problems, develop a deeper understanding of the issues, stop reinforcing negative behaviors, and become more skillful in responding to perceived aggression.

How do we reach these positive outcomes? How do we get ourselves to respond positively when we genuinely perceive that aggression is being directed against us by A? What practical, realistic alternatives are available?

The Impact of Context: Creating Opportunities and Journeys

If you want to respond to your conflicts more positively, treat them as opportunities and journeys, and achieve the ends you and your opponent both desire, you will benefit from learning how to disarm your instinctual responses, listen to what your opponent is actually saying, and search together for constructive, collaborative solutions.

But *how* do you overcome your initial fight-or-flight reactions and join someone you fear, dislike, or distrust, who seems to be attacking you? The answers, although simple to suggest, are not at all simple to implement—particularly if you are in the grip of ancient, powerful, and hypnotizing emotions like fear and rage. To make this shift, you need to create a new context for understanding your opponent, yourself, the content of the dispute, your relationship, and the nature of conflict in general.

If, for example, you assume the other person is not attacking *you* but has merely confused you with the problem and probably does not know you well enough to understand or attack who you are, you will begin to hear what he or she is saying differently. You may then be able to respond by focusing your opponent's attention on the problem as an "it" rather than as a "you." Or, if you can hear the other person's attack as a request for assistance, attention, or support, you may be able to say, "How can I help you?" or "How could we work together to solve this problem?" Or, if you can hear the attack as a critique of your communication skills and a request to adopt a more effective way of speaking, you may be able to apologize for not communicating clearly enough and say, "Can you give me some feedback so I can communicate with you better next time?"

None of these responses is likely to be effortless, but each will lead you away from warfare and toward opportunity and encourage you to take the first step on a journey to improved relationships, skills, and self-esteem. As illustrated in the following chart, there are a number of practical, realistic ways you can shift your response from one that is based on a perception of aggression to one that is based on a potential for collaboration:

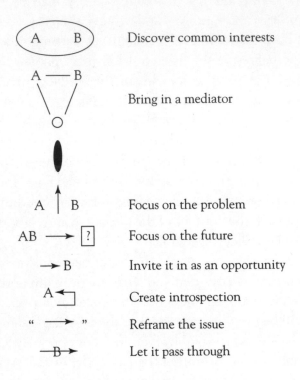

(A B)	Discover common interests
A — B	Bring in a mediator
A ↑ B	Focus on the problem
AB → [?]	Focus on the future
→ B	Invite it in as an opportunity
A ←	Create introspection
" → "	Reframe the issue
—B→	Let it pass through

In each of these collaborative responses, the cycle of aggressive or defensive responses is halted because B is no longer willing to respond as though A were the aggressor, because the focus has shifted from people to problems, because B is engaging in a dialogue about mutual concerns, or because A and B are not arguing about the past but considering together what they want to happen in the future. In other words, B is operating out of an attitude and context that are responsive, empathetic, and collaborative, rather than out of a fight-or-flight instinctual or reflexive reaction.

Notice in this chart that B gains power by engaging in these actions and at the same time eliminates the reasons that prompted A's original and continued aggression. B's collaborative approach rewards A for engaging in dialogue while depriving A of attention and similar rewards for aggressive behavior. This new response by B makes A appear uncooperative if he or she continues to act in an aggressive manner.

Despite the simplicity of these approaches, it is difficult in practice to convert your initial responses to A from negative to positive. In your efforts to do so, it may help you to recognize that A is being aggressive for reasons that have more to do with A's needs than with B's actions. It may also help to recognize that A is using aggression in order to communicate with B and that B's defensive responses are blocking and frustrating that communication. If you can find a way to satisfy A's legitimate needs while not rewarding A's behavior or taking it personally, even by silent acquiescence, in many cases A's aggression will disappear.

As B, you can also halt the escalation of the conflict simply by refusing to accept the role A has created for you. B does not have to be the victim of A's aggression or accept A's definition of the problem or A's version of B's role in their interaction. In other words, it only takes *one* to stop the tango.

Shifting your response from one of counteraggression or defensiveness to listening and collaboration is not easy; yet, it is possible in every conflict. Collaborative responses begin with simple steps that move both parties in the direction they both want to go, form part of a larger strategy to create solutions rather than obstacles, and improve their communication and relationship. In the end, even if all these efforts fail, you will succeed in undermining A's ability to force you into opposition and feel better as a result.

Five Alternative Responses to Conflict

Aggression and collaboration are not the sole responses you can have to conflict. In addition to these, there are several other ways you can respond, each of which reflects a different attitude toward yourself, your opponent, and your conflict. The most common responses are those that follow, each of which focuses your attention either *subjectively* on the people with whom you are in dispute or

objectively on achieving a goal or result. As a result, when you are in
conflict, you are likely to adopt one of the following five responses:

- Avoidance
- Accommodation
- Aggression
- Compromise
- Collaboration

The following chart, drawn from research by Thomas and Kilman,
reveals the relationship between these five alternative approaches, by
differentiating them according to whether your concern for people is
stronger or weaker than your concern for results:

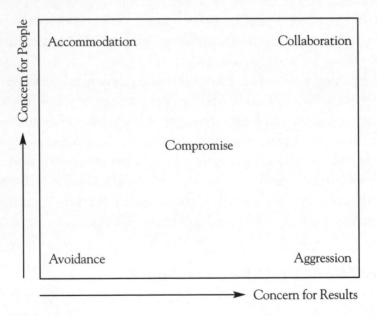

The key to choosing an effective response is deciding what kind of
relationship you would like to have with your opponent and what
results you would like to achieve. If you are primarily concerned
with people as opposed to results, you will be more likely to choose

accommodation. More significantly, whenever you accommodate, you *automatically* communicate that you are more concerned for people than you are for results, just as you communicate the opposite when you act aggressively. When you are collaborative, you communicate both, and your relationships with others and what you want to achieve will appear to be equally important to you.

To understand the differences between these responses, imagine that you have just been asked to work late. If you use avoidance, you will hide in your office or duck out the back door. If you use accommodation, you will do the work but feel resentful and perhaps do it poorly or not complete it. If you use aggression, you will refuse to do it and create an argument. If you use compromise, you will agree to do it today if someone else will do it tomorrow. And if you use collaboration, you will do it together.

None of these responses is wrong. In fact, a skillful person is able to employ each response at the right moment, with the right person, to solve the right problem in the right way. Each is simply a different approach or choice of how to respond to conflict, and there are times when each will be useful and most effective. There is no rule book for employing these responses; there is only your analysis of the situation, your goals, and your real concerns or interests. Here are some of the reasons you might choose one response over another in a given conflict.

Reasons for Avoiding or Dodging Conflict

- You regard the issue as trivial.
- You have no power over the issue or cannot change the results.
- You believe the damage due to conflict outweighs its benefits.
- You need to cool down, reduce tensions, or regain composure.
- You need time to gather information and cannot make an immediate decision.
- You can leave it to others who are in a position to resolve the conflict more effectively.

- You regard the issue as tangential or symptomatic and prefer to wait to address the real problem.

Reasons for Accommodating or Giving in to Conflict

- You realize that you were wrong or want to show you can be reasonable.
- You recognize that the issue is more important to others and want to establish good will.
- You are outmatched or losing, and giving in will prevent additional damage.
- You want harmony to be preserved or disruption avoided.
- You see an opportunity to help a subordinate learn from a mistake.

Reasons for Being Aggressive or Engaging in Conflict

- You want to engage in quick, decisive action.
- You have to deal with an emergency.
- You are responsible for enforcing unpopular rules or discipline.
- You see the issues as vital, and you know you are right.
- You need to protect yourself against people who take advantage of collaborative behavior.

Reasons for Compromising or Negotiating Conflict

- Your goals are moderately important but can be satisfied by less than total agreement.
- Your opponents have equal power, and you are strongly committed to mutually exclusive goals.
- You need to achieve a temporary settlement of complex issues.
- You need a quick solution, and the exact content does not matter as much as the speed with which it is reached.
- Your efforts at either competition or collaboration have failed, and you need a backup.

Reasons for Collaborating or Using Teamwork to Resolve Conflict

- You believe it is possible to reach an integrative solution even though both sides find it hard to compromise.
- Your objective is to learn.
- You believe it is preferable to merge insights that come from different perspectives.
- You need a long-range solution.
- You want to gain commitment and increase motivation and productivity by using consensus decision making.
- You want to empower one or both participants.
- You see it as a way to work through hard feelings and improve morale.
- You want to model cooperative solutions for others.
- You need to help people learn to work closely together.
- You want to end the conflict rather than paper it over.
- Your goals require a team effort.
- You need creative solutions.
- You have tried everything else without success.

   (*Source:* Adapted from Thomas-Kilman Instrument.)

Although each of us should be able to use all of these responses in appropriate circumstances, there will be times when the most effective approach is to walk away or to surrender. There will also be times when there is no alternative other than aggression, which most people assume when their opponents do not agree with them. Nonetheless, it is clear that the best and most satisfying results are produced by responding with collaboration.

Consider, for example, what kind of person you would become if your responses were limited to only one of the five we have described. Thus, if all you ever did was avoid conflict, after a while you would feel numb and disengaged. If all you ever did was accommodate, after a while you would feel used and like a doormat. If all you ever did was respond with aggression, you would be constantly angry, guilty, or incapable of compassion. If all you ever did was compromise, you would end up feeling dissatisfied and compromised. But if all you ever did was collaborate, you would feel successful.

Nonetheless, avoidance, accommodation, compromise, and aggression all feel easier to use when we are in conflict and less time-consuming and more emotionally satisfying than collaboration. In part, this is because we learn avoidance when we are infants and have to accommodate the wishes of our parents as children. We learn aggression and compromise from our siblings and peers at school and at work. But we generally learn collaboration later in life when we work in teams and in our most intimate relationships, where it is often not rewarded and may even be punished. Consider, for example, the word commonly used to describe collaboration in school between students who are taking a test . . .

It is far more difficult to collaborate during conflict because it takes strength to become vulnerable and move toward your opponent when that person is attacking you. In addition, you are unlikely to receive the same sympathy or attention for collaboration as for being a victim, collaboration asks you to become responsible for creating solutions that satisfy mutual interests and not just your own, and popular and organizational cultures do not support collaboration to the extent that they support aggression.

Nonetheless, as we have explained, there remain strong reasons for responding to your opponent with collaboration, the greatest of which is that it is the most effective way of ending your conflict completely and starting on a path to transformation.

The Opportunity of Collaboration

If you are interested in improving your relationship with another person, the best way of doing so is through collaboration. Each of the other responses will leave you and your opponent feeling less than completely successful and create an opening for the conflict to continue. For this reason, we emphasize the collaborative approach, not because it is quicker or easier or always the right response, but because it goes deeper and is more lasting than the others; is more respectful, versatile, and satisfying; builds better relationships; and encourages learning.

For example, a large communications firm in which we worked was attempting to implement a sweeping new structure that had been designed by the CEO without much input from below. As a result, the change process was producing what several managers called "public compliance and private defiance." As we probed the sources of covert resistance, we found that the conflicts and disagreements triggered by the change process were being avoided and swept under the rug by leaders who hoped the problems would simply disappear.

Instead, they were festering and simmering beneath a facade of compliance, being discussed behind closed doors, and fueling a growing resistance to change. We interviewed a cross-section of employees, opened conversations about the real barriers, and drew the underlying conflicts out into the open. As we did so, we were able to see relief and renewed energy bubbling to the surface among staff members who had been frozen in despair.

This renewed energy represented a widespread unspoken desire to participate and collaborate in the change effort from which they had been completely excluded. Opening the process to allow their input on how the CEO's ideas could work even better transformed their defiance into collaborative problem solving. The transformation was so complete that the leadership council, which included several executives who had resisted the change, volunteered to make their annual bonuses contingent on its success.

In our day-to-day lives, we face an unending array of choices about what to say and do and how to behave when we are in conflict. When we step back from the pressures and demands of the moment and develop a collaborative approach that is able to guide our behaviors, we feel more empowered and proactive, open to experience, and better able to locate the transformational potential that is hidden in our conflict.

The shift from feeling victimized, reactive, overwhelmed, destructive, or passive in our conflicts to feeling powerful, proactive, challenged, constructive, or collaborative is already a transformation in the context we are using to approach our conflicts and in our ability to select a strategy that supports our intentions and commitments. Consciously choosing a strategy and sticking to it will make us feel less driven by the choices of others, the emotional whims of the moment, and the dictates of circumstance.

Learning to Collaborate in Conflict

As we have indicated, it is natural for you to seek to avoid, accommodate, behave aggressively, and compromise in your conflicts, but you will not find it nearly so natural to meet with your opponent in a mutual search for collaborative solutions, despite your awareness that collaboration consistently yields the greatest opportunities and the most exciting journeys.

Once you choose to create a context of collaboration for your conflict, the next step is to learn how to respond to your opponents in ways that bring them closer rather than push them farther away. Instead of papering over your conflicts, giving in to them, sweeping them under the rug, escalating them through rage, or compromising them, you will want to improve your skills in being able to engage them in a collaborative way.

The following actions are designed to assist you in reaching out and creating a more collaborative relationship with your opponent. As you review these actions, bring to mind a conflict in which you are presently engaged and try to answer the questions that follow each action. Here are some initial ways to start to collaborate and learn from your conflicts:

• Begin by recognizing and affirming that your conflict can be a positive experience, clarify opportunities for growth and learning, and indicate a need to change a system or shift a paradigm. Can you think of any ways your conflict can be experienced positively? How could it become a learning experience or an opportunity for growth? What does it suggest might need to change?

• Use empathy to place yourself in the other person's shoes. Try to see things from the other person's point of view, while at the same time recognizing that there is a difference between understanding the other people's behavior and condoning it, between forgiving them and what they did. Why do you think they acted as they did? How do they see your actions? What could you learn about their motivation or interests that could help you understand what they want? How could you respond to them more skillfully as a result?

• Shift your focus from holding on to power and supporting your position to sharing responsibility and satisfying both sides' interests. If you let go of the desire to hold on to your power or position, what might you learn as a result? What changes would you be willing to make? What would happen if your opponent did the same? What are your interests? What are your opponent's? What interests do you share? How might both be satisfied?

• Focus your efforts beyond settlement and on fully resolving all the underlying issues in your dispute. What would accommodation, or settlement for settlement's sake, leave out of the equation? What are the deeper underlying issues in your dispute? What would it take to resolve them? How can you bring these issues up so they can be resolved?

• Be deeply honest, both with yourself and your opponent, and give empathetic and timely feedback. What feedback can you give the other person in the conflict that is truthful and at the same time moves the conflict toward resolution? How long has it taken for you to give it? Why has it taken so long? What could you do to shorten it? What feedback might the other person give you? Have you requested that person's feedback? If not, what is stopping you? How could you benefit from your opponent's feedback? What honest feedback can you give yourself?

• Speak and act with impeccable integrity and clarity, without judgment, from your heart and spirit and not just from your head.

Have your actions and communications been crystal clear and of the highest integrity? If not, why not? What can you say to the other person that comes straight from your heart and at the same time is clear and nonjudgmental? Instead of holding on to judgments and answers, can you ask questions that allow the issue of who they are to remain open?

• Search for small-scale collaborative alternatives that increase cooperation, create common ground, and focus on shared interests. Either alone or with your opponent, brainstorm some of the things you might do together to increase your cooperation and partnership. Identify what you could both do to find or create what you both need and want.

In answering these questions, remember that collaboration, resolution, and transformation are real, practical possibilities that become available to us whenever we begin to search collaboratively for opportunities and journey together through our conflicts.

Listen Actively, Empathetically, and Responsively

I want to write about the great and powerful thing
that listening is. And how we forget it. And how
we don't listen to our children, or those we love.
And least of all—which is so important too—
to those we do not love. But we should. Because
listening is a magnetic and strange thing, a creative
force. . . . This is the reason: When we are listened
to, it creates us, makes us unfold and expand.
Ideas actually begin to grow within us and come
to life. . . . Who are the people, for example, to
whom you go for advice? Not to the hard, practical
ones who can tell you exactly what to do, but to the
listeners; that is, the kindest, least censorious, least
bossy people you know. It is because by pouring out
your problem to them you then know what to do
about it yourself. . . . So try listening. Listen to your
wife, your children, your friends; to those who love
you and those who don't; to those who bore you;
to your enemies. It will work a small miracle—and
perhaps a great one.

—Brenda Ueland

We have all observed and participated in countless ineffective,
pointless, and destructive communications. We have all felt misunderstood and experienced the immense costs and destructive
consequences of miscommunications at the hands of others. Yet

despite this wealth of experience, we have still not fully appreciated the price we pay every day for poor communication or focused sufficient attention on improving our communication skills.

Many of the conflicts and miscommunications we experience in life result from the assumption that we communicate successfully merely by speaking clearly and that if we could only make the other person listen, they would automatically understand and agree with us. Yet even when we speak a common language, a listener may hear the words we use from a completely different context or frame of reference and attribute an entirely different meaning to them.

Even minute differences in backgrounds, including gender and cultural assumptions, unacknowledged biases, slight variations in perception, and unstated needs and desires, can lend the words we use the meaning our listeners want and are able to hear. This capacity for distortion of meaning caused playwright George Bernard Shaw to observe that "The greatest problem with communication is the illusion that it has been accomplished."

Each of us filters what we hear through a largely unconscious, unspoken backdrop of personal history, culture, and context that profoundly shapes the way we understand and interpret events and communications. We all lend a personal shape to reality and interpret it according to our own experiences, needs, desires, and expectations.

These personal frameworks have a powerful impact on our interpretation of the communications we receive and the choices we make as a result. Successful communicators are those who listen for, seek out, and endeavor to understand these historical, cultural, and contextual frameworks and, as a result, send messages that stand a better chance of being understood.

For example, women and men often have great difficulty communicating with one another, as Deborah Tannen recognized in her groundbreaking book *You Just Don't Understand*. As an illustration, many women will interpret an expression of sympathy as a sign of support, whereas many men will interpret it as a recognition of weakness. For many women, making joint decisions may be a sign of intimacy whereas for many men it will be a sign of dependency or powerlessness. Many women will interpret a request by their boss for a status report as an invitation to communicate, but many men will see it as an indication that there is something wrong with their work. For many women, it is important to have their most painful feelings recognized and validated while for many men, talking about their pain implies giving in to it.

Thus, effective communication begins with you, as the speaker, taking responsibility for understanding the language, perspectives, and experiences of the listener and framing your message in terms that are likely to make sense inside the listener's framework of experience.

The "language" of the listener may, for example, include a different perspective or point of view, a different set of needs or interests, or a different frame of reference for understanding the issues in dispute. It may be a difference in the style, etiquette, or culture of communication. It may be that the communication raises collateral issues that have nothing to do with the speaker but make listening difficult for the receiver.

If you do not pay attention to the context that shapes understanding in the listener, you may communicate effectively by accident but will not have communicated well, fully, or strategically and may end up in conflict as a result of an unanticipated misunderstanding. How, then, can you learn to be more strategic in your communications and encourage other people to listen to you?

You can start by actively searching for clues on how to communicate more effectively with the specific people you want to reach, tapping into their contexts and frames of reference, attempting to understand their cultural frameworks, learning how to speak their languages, and then saying what you need to say in ways that are more likely to be understood. You can motivate yourself to do so by recognizing the high cost you are likely to pay for poor communication.

The Cost of Poor Communication

We all pay an enormous, uncalculated price for poor communication, not only personally in lost jobs, divorces, unhappiness, and ruptured relationships, but organizationally in gossip and rumors, inefficiencies, lost revenues, poor morale, missed opportunities, grievances, strikes, and litigation.

For example, three members of the executive staff of a large public service agency described in interviews with us the lack of listening in their workplace and the price they and the organization paid for it:

> Executive staff meetings are not a place where we have true dialogue or air problems or where there is an effort to understand what people are saying. We don't have a social contract outlining acceptable codes of behavior, so no one hears anyone else, really—there are too many insensitive remarks, confidences aren't kept, and attendance is spotty. There is more of a sense of power tripping and power alliances versus operating on principle.

> One of our major blocks to success is Harry's role in the organization. When he [the director] does come to meetings, which is rare, he says nothing. He just sits there and doesn't seem to hear what we're saying. You wonder, does he think this is a waste of time, and things will happen according to a grand plan he is controlling? He rarely speaks supportively or in a problem-solving way.

> There is unevenness of commitment here. No one listens to anyone. I am personally offended by people who fall asleep in meetings or say, "OK, it's time to go now, isn't it?" Harry does this. It seems like a favoritism thing. Some people get favored treatment. People are not behaving decently toward each other.

The results of poor communication in this organization included widespread distrust of management (especially Harry); high rates of absenteeism, tardiness, and stress-related workers' compensation claims; and an increase in interpersonal conflicts. These mishaps in communication paralyzed the organization and made its performance mediocre. Everyone we interviewed was unhappy, and personal feuds and miscommunications had escalated as a result.

We facilitated a two-day retreat with Harry and the entire staff who, to their credit, agreed to participate despite their doubts and distrust. The main goal for the session was to engage in open and honest communication. We agreed on three informal ground rules: no-holds-barred honesty, all communications would be confidential within the group, and there would be no retaliation for anything said during the session.

We surfaced the problems with Harry by asking everyone to identify what was not working in their communications. We reached consensus on a set of standards for effective communication that they all agreed to implement, starting immediately. As they did so, we could feel the sense of depression start to lift. As the retreat progressed, everyone gave each other feedback and received it in return. They specified the behaviors they each needed to change and the actions they could take to become better listeners and improve their communication.

We began the process with Harry by asking him to invite everyone present to give him honest feedback. We asked him not to respond defensively, even if he thought the feedback was inaccurate, and instead try to figure out what was true about it. We asked him to thank each person for offering him honest feedback, to think of what he might do to communicate more successfully, and it then became the next person's turn to receive feedback.

We made sure the feedback was constructive and specific and asked the group to practice constructive communication techniques during the exercise. We interrupted occasionally to encourage listening and responsiveness and to assist people in speaking nonjudgmentally and listening nondefensively. At the end, we asked them to evaluate the exercise, and everyone agreed it had been a great relief to communicate openly and honestly and to finally be able to say what they had all been thinking in private.

By the next quarter, productivity had increased significantly, and morale began to return. One year afterwards, nearly everyone indicated they were happier to be working there. Harry had changed his behavior so completely that he was acknowledged by the group and given a hearty, unsolicited round of applause at a meeting in which the organization's success was celebrated. In a client-satisfaction survey conducted eighteen months later, the group received high ratings in client appreciation and quality of client services.

It became clear to Harry over time that his relationship problems were responses to the frustration his staff felt as a result of having issues or concerns they could not communicate. This frustration led them to multiply their problems, perhaps in an unconscious hope that things would get so bad that Harry, or the leadership of the organization, would finally be forced to do something about them.

Conduct a Conflict Audit

We often hear managers argue that conflict resolution and effective communication take too much of their time or that it costs too much to conduct a retreat at which employees work on improving their communication skills and resolving their disputes. But consider how much time and money this organization wasted by *not* addressing its unresolved conflicts and how little time it took to set things right.

We rarely calculate the emotional and financial costs of living with conflict and do not consider the time it takes to *not* communicate effectively or not resolve our conflicts. We rarely include in bottom-line calculations the time people spend getting upset or sick over unresolved conflicts, the time dissipated in gossiping or talking to others about them, and the time wasted by not focusing on work. We do not weigh in the balance the loss of morale, motivation, customer satisfaction, and future business that result from employee unhappiness or the amount of damage inflicted on work relationships by conflicts between friends, colleagues, and coworkers.

We have worked with a number of organizations to assess the costs of miscommunication and unresolved conflict using a device known as a "conflict audit." The audit consists of a collection of objective data, including the number of disciplinary actions, terminations, grievances, customer-service complaints, stress-related illnesses, workers' compensation claims based on stress, employee turnover and training costs, attorney and human resource budgets, and similar data. In addition, the audit includes a set of subjective questions about conflicts within the organization that elicit morale, motivation, and similar costs. The audit is an effort to identify and measure the conflict and communication problems within an organization and put a price tag on them.

You can conduct a rough conflict audit in your organization simply by estimating the number of hours employees and managers spend each week miscommunicating or engaging in conflict and multiplying that figure by the number of staff and their hourly salaries. The figure you come up with will be enormous. Then ask yourself, what are the full consequences of this lack of listening? How many customers, valued employees, fresh ideas, and creative insights has the organization lost as a result of conflict and miscommunication? How much have these losses cost? What would be it reasonable to do in order to stop paying that price?

To conduct a more detailed audit, we find it useful to bring together a cross-functional team with members drawn from every department and level within the organization. The team develops a set of questions to reveal the true cost of unresolved conflict in the organization, then designs a collaborative process for disseminating the results of the audit, and reaches consensus on what to do in response. Here are twenty illustrative questions you can use to begin creating a conflict audit:

- How much does the organization spend on lawyers, litigation, and human resources time related to conflict?
- How much time does the average manager spend each week trying to prevent, manage, or resolve conflicts? At what salary?
- What is the cost of stress-related illness and conflict-related turnovers?

- How much employee time is spent on rumors, gossip, lost productivity, and reduced collaboration due to conflict?
- What is the impact of conflict on staff morale and motivation?
- How many conflicts recur because they are never fully resolved?
- What customers, creativity, and opportunities have been lost due to conflict?
- Where might the organization be now had it not experienced these conflicts?
- What are the core values of the organization regarding conflict?
- What are the main messages sent by the organizational culture regarding conflict?
- How are negative conflict behaviors rewarded?
- How do leadership and management typically respond to conflicts? How might they respond better?
- Have employees been trained in conflict resolution?
- What do people do when they have conflict? Where do they go for help?
- Is there an internal mediation process? Who is allowed to use it? How often is it used? Do employees know about it?
- How satisfied are employees with existing resolution processes?
- How skilled are managers in using these processes?
- What obstacles hinder the use of existing resolution processes? How can employees be motivated to use them?
- What skills do employees and managers need to resolve conflicts successfully?
- What systems changes would reduce or help resolve conflict?

Clearing the Decks for Listening

In addition to conducting a conflict audit, it may also be useful for you to initiate a conversation among your coworkers to identify the elements of effective communication. Nearly everyone lists as the first element in communication the ability to listen. But what makes someone a good listener? How can people learn to become better listeners? Here is a personal exercise you can use to clarify what is involved in listening.

Recall a leader with whom you have worked or someone in your life who was an active, empathetic, and responsive listener, perhaps a manager or team leader who made you feel you were valuable and had worthwhile things to share or a favorite team member who spent time trying to find out more about you. It may have been a boss who mentored you or asked hard questions that helped you understand how to become more successful. Or it may have been a colleague who always seemed to be there when you needed to talk, nodding and making eye contact to let you know you were understood. What did these listeners do that made you feel heard?

It will soon become clear that effective listening is an essential element in the operation of any workplace. As people reflect on their experiences, they recognize that responsibility for effectiveness in any communication rests not only with the speaker to be clear in what they say but also with the listener to genuinely pay attention and hear what is being said actively, empathetically, and responsively.

But how can you help yourself and others improve their skills in listening? Clearly, everyone listens, but not everyone listens in the same way. Effective listening does not begin with listening but with the listener clearing the decks and focusing his or her attention on the person who is about to speak.

To begin, empty your mind of all the thoughts competing for your attention—including what you are planning to say in response—and surrender your ideas about what the speaker should or should not do or be. This means being fully present and focused on what is being said, not just on the surface, but underneath as well, with all your senses, including your posture, body language, eye contact, emotions, intentions, heart, and mind. It means working interactively to clarify whatever you have not completely understood.

Ways of Listening

There are many ways you can become a more active, empathetic, and responsive listener. Most people think of listening as a passive activity in which they sit quietly and take in whatever is said. But the best listening is highly active and interactive and requires energy, openness, awareness, and an application of initiative and curiosity on the part of the listener.

There is a crucial difference, for example, between hearing, which is physiological, and listening, which is psychological, between listening *at* people and listening *with* them. Anyone who has a teenager will recognize this distinction. There is a difference between listening only to what we want to hear and listening to discover what is important to the speaker; between listening in a role—as, for example, when people listen as managers or school principals—and when they listen as human beings. Fundamentally, no one wants to be listened to by a manager or a school principal. Everyone wants to be listened to by a human being.

Listening, like speaking, is largely a matter of *intention*. Its effectiveness depends on how important we think the information is to us. When we listen, we can do so in a variety of ways. We can listen only to the details of what someone is saying but not to their deeper meaning. We may listen only for openings or holes in other people's arguments—picking out what is wrong with what they are saying so we can use it against them. We can listen while waiting for them to finish so it will be our turn to talk next.

There is a significant difference between listening passively and listening actively, listening guardedly and listening openly, listening sympathetically and listening empathetically. We know when someone is listening for facts and when they are listening for feelings, when they are listening collaboratively and when they are listening adversarially. We know when they are listening not merely to words but to meanings, not just to problems but for solutions. In sum, we can tell when people are merely participating in listening and when they are actively committed to understanding what we want to communicate.

Committed listening is what we do when we believe what is being said is vital to us or when we are being told a fascinating story that on the surface may have nothing to do with us—but on a deeper level is about issues that are important to all of us. Committed listening is a reflection of the openness of our hearts and minds, our willingness to act on what we hear, and our integrity in the face of answers we do not like.

We once observed a committed listener in action in a workshop we conducted for teachers who were selected to be leaders in a large urban school district. The district had hired a new superintendent, and we invited him to meet with a number of teacher leaders. We were surprised at the brevity of his opening remarks, expecting a speech full of campaign promises.

Instead, he sat in the audience with a pen and paper, taking detailed notes and inviting the teachers to tell him about the conditions in their schools. He asked open-ended questions and gave unguarded responses. He listened for feelings, meanings, intentions, and solutions, and the message he sent was clear to everyone. He genuinely valued their ideas, wanted their participation and partnership, and was available to them as an active, responsive, committed listener. As a result, his debut was an instant success.

You can become a committed listener simply by choosing to be committed to hearing what another person is saying at the deepest level of your being and by listening as though it were *you* who was speaking. When you do so, especially with your opponent in a conflict, the quality of your participation and understanding of the communication will shift, as will your body language, facial expressions, eye contact, and presence. Your questions will deepen and become more risky, your comments will become more empathetic, and your relationship with the speaker will improve as you gradually increase your dedication to the task and the speaker perceives you differently.

Effective leadership is always a result of committed listening, not just to those who agree, but those who criticize, distrust, and attack. The best leaders recognize that criticism, distrust, and even

personal attacks represent caring about outcomes and consider criticisms as invitations to learning and improved outcomes. Successful leaders listen as though their effectiveness depended on listening
not only to what is being said but also to what is meant and not said
and letting people know they have been heard.

Setting the Stage for Listening

To increase your skills and become a more committed listener, you
can begin by focusing on the physical and emotional environment
in which the communication is about to take place. Effective listening starts with arranging the physical environment to encourage
genuine listening. The sketch that follows illustrates how most
managers arrange their offices, which is where most of their listening takes place.

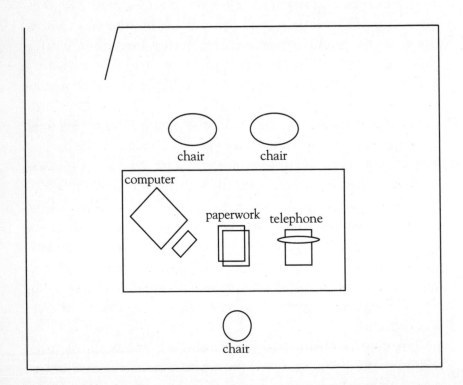

There are several problems with this way of configuring your space. First, some conversations should not be held in a manager's office at all because, for many employees, being called to the manager's office portends discipline or rebuke. Second, in many offices, the manager has a distracting screen saver running on the computer; a telephone, cell phone, or beeper that has not been turned off; and piles of paperwork calling for attention.

Third, the arrangement of the chairs signifies who is in power and who is not. It establishes the person sitting behind the desk as an authority, judge, and decision maker, rather than as a coach, mediator, or facilitator. Fourth, the desk separates people from each other and obscures much of their body language, which may communicate more about what they are feeling than the words they are using.

The next illustration shows two alternative arrangements for the same office, in which communication is likely to take place more effectively.

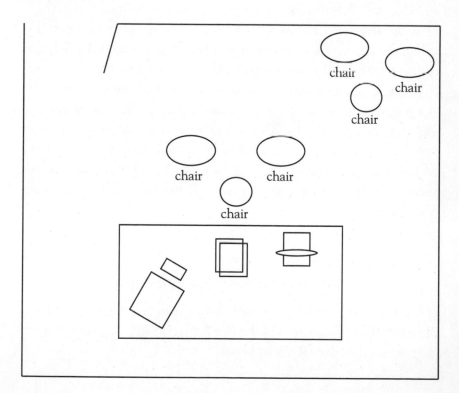

In either grouping of chairs shown in the second layout, communication is more likely to take place on an equal footing between participants. Telephones, paperwork, and computers are less likely to get in the way, and responsibility for problem solving is shared in more of a team atmosphere. The manager is seen as more of a participant and facilitator, and employees are able to speak more openly and naturally, allowing the listener to monitor body language for signals of consensus or resistance, without having a desk prevent their full communication.

Placing the chairs close to one another in a circle at a distance that encourages intimate communication, but far enough apart to respect everyone's personal space, conveys a message that communication is welcome and boundaries will be respected. Try this in your office and experiment to see what works best. Make sure to arrange your chair so it does not communicate favoritism by being closer to one person than another.

Communication, of course, does not consist primarily of arranging desks and chairs; yet, setting the stage correctly can improve the mood of a conversation. The atmosphere and ambiance of the setting can be improved by natural or indirect lighting, refreshments, plants, art, and other details that create a friendly, open atmosphere and an environment that conveys a message of welcome and receptivity. You may not have enough space or room for these amenities in your office, in which case you may want to move your conversation to a different location, such as a restaurant, park, or living room where everyone can listen in a relaxed atmosphere.

The Elements of Communication

It has been suggested that all successful communication consists essentially of a combination of the five fundamental elements that are diagrammed in the following chart.

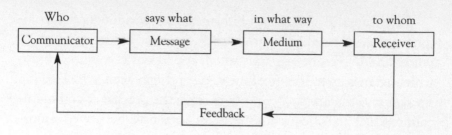

The difficulty with this typical description of communication is that we have all had the experience of being articulate, expressing our message clearly and accurately, using a medium that conveys our ideas appropriately, and having a receiver who is awake and listening; yet, the communication fails. Most communications that end in employee discipline or termination, divorce, or claims of racial or sexual harassment are excellent examples of how simply being articulate, using an appropriate medium, and reaching an awake listener can still be ineffective in communicating unwelcome meanings.

On the other hand, we have all had the experience of being in love, perhaps speaking incoherently, using a clumsy, ineffective medium—even speaking a foreign language to a listener who is half asleep—yet, somehow our communication is able to get through. How do we explain these anomalies?

Hidden Frameworks for Communication

Clearly, something else is at work in addition to the five elements cited in the diagram. That "something else" is the hidden framework, the context, culture, environment, system, or setting in which the communication takes place. These often include the real-life roles, responsibilities, histories, needs and desires, and expectations of the speaker and listener; the messages that are communicated by the medium and by the organizational culture; and the deeper meaning and importance of the communication.

There are three important hidden frameworks for conflict communications. First, there are the words, symbols, metaphors, tone of voice, and body language that we all use in our communications, which often convey their true meaning and significance both to the speaker and the listener. Second, there is the process of communicating, which includes how respectfully, responsively, actively, empathetically, appropriately, and reliably the message is communicated. Third, there is the relationship between the speaker and the listener, which includes each person's unspoken interests, needs, emotions, and expectations of the other and the degree to which each person has let go of past conflicts.

Each of these hidden frameworks defines our communications more reliably than the literal definitions of the words we are using. Yet we focus most of our attention on the meaning of specific words and their dictionary definitions—which make up a part, but by no means all, of our communication. The larger part, to which we pay less attention, consists of the framework of our communication: the subtle, symbolic significance of the words, gestures, and body language we use; the process, style, or way we communicate; and the impact our conflicted relationship is having on the listener's willingness to hear what is being said.

Even an innocuous word like "hello" can be interpreted in many different ways depending on the context, tone of voice, phrasing, speed, timing, location, personal history, and emotional relationship between speaker and listener. Just a simple sentence can communicate rage, lust, friendship, enmity, admiration, disrespect, happiness, or sadness. For example, consider the range of subtle variations produced by changing the emphasis on different words in the same statement, offered by mathematician Rudy Rucker:

I'm glad to see you.	(Even if no one else is.)
I'm *glad* to see you.	(What made you think I wouldn't be?)
I'm glad to *see* you.	(Instead of talking to you by phone.)

I'm glad to see *you*.	(But not the schlub you came with.)
I'm glad to *see you*.	(It's wonderful to be with you.)
I'm glad to see you.	(So stop asking me if I am.)
I'm . . . glad-to-see-you.	(Are you glad to see me?)
I'm . . . glad . . . to . . . see . . . you.	(I'm drunk or don't really mean it.)
I'm glad . . . to see you.	(But only as an afterthought.)
I'm glad-to-see *you*.	(Me Tarzan, you Jane)

As you listen to your words and observe your gestures and emotions in conversation with your opponent in conflict, search for the hidden frameworks that are giving added meaning to your message. Consider, for example, what metaphors, body language, and tone of voice are you using? What is your communication process and style? What is the relationship between you and the person to whom you are speaking? If there is tension or unresolved conflict between you, is it seeping into your communications? Do you have unmet, unspoken expectations that are blocking your efforts to convey meaning? Is there a perceived difference in your power or status? What is your history with each other? Is there an emotion, tone, or tension in your communication that is not matched by the words you are using? What does the listener think will happen as a result of your communication?

How Communication Gets Distorted

There is only one test for the effectiveness of any communication, and that is what the listener understands. If we consider communication from the point of view of the person on its receiving end, we can see that there are many opportunities for distortion that can easily arise between speakers and listeners.

Communication behaves like a wave or ray of light that is bent each time it passes through a different medium. Messages in organizations pass through many different layers as they travel from the speaker's intention through a hidden framework of symbols, processes, expectations, and relationships that translate them into meaning for the person receiving them. Whether we are speaking or listening, we can learn to take account of these ways communication can be distorted and adjust for their negative effect on meaning by noticing what happens to the communication and correcting for it. In organizations, for example, a message is altered by being

- Refracted or bent, just as light is distorted or refracted by passing through water
- Diffused, by passing through so many people that it becomes less focused or reaches someone other than the person for whom it was intended
- Amplified, expanded, or magnified by each layer or departmental barrier it is forced to pass through
- Interfered with, as conflicting messages, needs, and agendas alter or confuse its path or add or subtract meaning before it reaches the listener
- Diluted, as the message passes through multiple people who pass it on, causing it to lose some of its meaning with each one
- Canceled, as conflicting messages can block it completely

Some of these forms of interference are displayed in the chart on the following page. In response, as speakers, we can be clear and strategic about what we say, how we say it, and why we say it and by tailoring what we say to the ears of a particular listener. We can be alert to what is likely to distort our meaning and endeavor to avoid these distortions.

As listeners, we can be skillful in understanding what the other person means—or means to say—taking account of the ways the communication is being distorted and testing the accuracy of our perceptions by asking questions. Yet some of these distortions originate not with the speaker or listener but with the hierarchical structures and bureaucratic cultures of many workplace organizations.

The Influence of Hierarchy and Bureaucracy on Organizational Communications

As a way of understanding the distortions that inevitably take place whenever people communicate inside organizations, consider the miscommunications that are commonly generated by the hierarchical, bureaucratic environments in which most of our private and public sector organizations operate and by the power inequalities and imbalances that permeate these systems and structures.

Imagine, for example, a typical hierarchical, bureaucratic organization in the form of a pyramid with vertical levels corresponding to divisions between executives, managers, supervisors, and employees and horizontal functions, stovepipes, or silos corresponding to different departments. You may have spent a considerable part of your working life inside such an organization. If not, try to imagine for a moment how any communication inside such an organization is likely to work, as illustrated in the following chart.

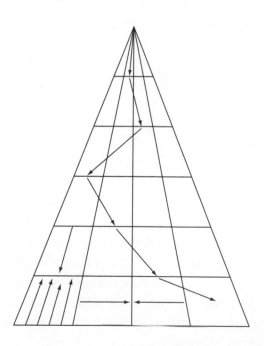

Any communication that takes place inside this hierarchical structure is likely to be distorted in a number of specific and predictable ways. For example, if a communication comes from the top down, there is a strong likelihood that it will be twisted, diluted, and reinterpreted at each level of management and staff. If the communication comes from the bottom up, it will have to be simplified and compressed simply in order to reach its final destination higher up the chain of command, and most of these messages will never arrive because there are too many of them to do so.

Each level will be likely to add its own special spin to the communication, which will result in some messages being magnified in importance while others are minimized or nullified. Each department, as it battles with others for budget, staff, and resources, is likely to cancel, distort, suppress, or contradict information that emanates from other competing departments.

Competition within the organization is likely to encourage people to see each other as adversaries, rather than as members of the same team. Because their relationship is structurally adversarial and superficial, communication is likely to become aggressive, defensive, blaming, responsibility-averse, conflict-avoiding, insular, self-promoting, and difficult.

An incident occurred recently in the midst of a major corporate change initiative that brought these distortions to light. The organization in which we were working was attempting to transition to self-managing teams and a flattened hierarchy. During this process, the chief financial officer (CFO) decided to meet with the people who report directly to him to let them know about a predicted shortfall in revenue. He assumed that because they had started a team initiative, these managers would discuss the problem with their teams, brainstorm solutions, and let him know what they recommended in order to respond to the problem. They, on the other hand, assumed that because the team initiative was not complete, he would decide what to do and tell them or ask them to brainstorm solutions at the meeting. As a result, no one was prepared to deal with the problem, everything ground to a halt, and the department could not respond to the crisis.

The context of their communication was that there was a conflict between two sets of expectations. The first, appropriate to a hierarchy, was that the CFO would make the decisions and tell them what to do. The second, appropriate to self-managing teams, was that they would all work together to define the problem, identify and implement solutions, and move the process forward. Either the CFO should have been more explicit in his request that the teams take the ball and run with it or the teams should have sought clarification and taken initiative in solving the problem.

Contradictory messages and interpretations proliferate in hierarchical structures unless messages are simplified by translating them into a bureaucratic language to the point that all the subtlety and complexity is removed from them. As a result, official organizational messages tend to be formal, obvious, impersonal, and meaningless. A lot of time and energy is then spent by listeners trying to fill in the gaps using informal communication devices such as gossip and rumors, which are highly volatile, damaging, and inaccurate.

Hierarchical structures that are intent on getting their messages across generally place a higher value on uniformity than on diversity in communications and on standing behind messages that are handed down from the top, rather than on raising questions or admitting that they are inaccurate. For these reasons, hierarchical communications tend to limit creativity and individuality and raise suspicions and distrust, which have a profound impact on organizational cultures and lead to further separations of speakers and listeners, perceptions of incongruence and lack of integrity, inconsistencies in official communications, and distrust of those at the top.

The Leader's Role in Conflict Communications

Leaders can play an important role in preventing this kind of damage, not only by designing less hierarchical and bureaucratic organizational structures, but by modeling how to take the time to listen and risk surfacing conflicts; by creating opportunities for effective communication across organizational lines; and by listening actively, empathetically, and responsively to those who work for them, especially their critics. As long as leaders sweep conflicts under the rug, suppress dissent, reward "yes-men," and prefer settling disputes to resolving them, employees will naturally follow suit.

Leaders can also play a role in listening for and analyzing internal tensions, identifying the preconditions of conflict, being sensitive to stresses in relationships, and moving proactively to predict and prevent conflicts before they occur. When environmental changes, pressures, and demands threaten organizational stability and create the preconditions for disputes to arise, leaders can clarify the "big picture" issues, identify strategies for intervention, and transform the context in which work takes place.

When leaders listen actively, empathetically, and responsively to employees at every level of the organization, it becomes easier for them to head off potential conflicts and design effective, appropriate actions to resolve them when they occur. This leadership style, described by Tom Peters as "managing by walking around," allows leaders to feel the pulse of the organization and identify issues that are likely to foment or exacerbate conflict.

Leaders can also help resolve conflict by listening to how others perceive them and being aware of their own vulnerabilities, miscommunications, and conflict styles. They can avoid adversarial assumptions and seek assistance in resolving conflicts they cannot face or resolve themselves. When conflicts arise, they can be aware of their blind spots and use reflective feedback to reveal unseen and unheard sources of tension within the organization.

Leaders derive their mandate less from their titles than from the relationships of trust they develop with employees. Trust arises only when leaders act with integrity and engage in actions that are consistent with their values. Leaders who encourage open communications, who listen not only to those with whom they agree but to their opponents, critics, and those with whom they have difficulty speaking, engender trust in their followers.

When conflicts occur, trusted leaders make it a point to listen for deeper meanings and common interests, to take responsibility for what they contributed to the conflict, to speak honestly and act with integrity, to participate fully in dialogue and negotiation over issues, to collaborate in creating solutions, and to consistently push for lasting solutions.

In addition, trusted leaders are committed to translating their intentions into action. If their intention is to create an organization in which conflicts are prevented and resolved, a trusted leader will take action to surface hidden conflicts, investigate their sources, encourage mediation and similar dispute-resolution processes, and continue dialogue until "win-win" agreements are reached.

Thus, listening for conflicts and surfacing them, addressing big-picture stresses that create chronic disputes, being at the heart of the day-to-day workings of the organization, having sufficient self-knowledge to be aware of their own vulnerabilities, and having the integrity to commit to resolution and transformation as desired outcomes are qualities that leaders can use to build organizational cultures in which conflict can be seen as an opportunity and a journey.

Creating a Commitment to Communicate

To become a more effective communicator, it will be important for you to learn better ways of speaking and listening that communicate your commitment to genuine, honest communication with your opponent and your determination to seek a fair resolution of the conflict.

Being a committed communicator means taking responsibility for observing and managing the context of your communications, improving your skills, and eliminating negative and ineffective communication behaviors. It means proactively seeking feedback and not waiting for others to volunteer it. It means asking your coworkers, family, friends, and colleagues to support you in making good on your commitments and calling you on them when you do not.

For example, we worked with a small operations unit in a large corporation that helped us understand some of the ways even minor miscommunications can lead to serious misunderstandings. Mike, the manager, was described in interviews we conducted with the people who reported to him as follows:

> Mike's style is too much micromanaging and detail oriented. We get paralyzed if he isn't available.
>
> Mike's style is talking and not listening.
>
> Mike is unwilling to delegate to his managers.
>
> Management needs to be less negative, political, and confrontational.

Mike's aggressive, personalizing, controlling, and disrespectful behaviors and speaking style were getting in the way of his staff's ability to listen to him. As a result, a number of conflicts arose in the organization that made him look ineffective as a leader. We gave Mike some strong, empathetic, yet honest feedback about the feelings of his staff. We persuaded him to work on becoming more open and improving his effectiveness as a communicator.

We asked the people reporting to Mike to anonymously identify to us in writing some specific, concrete actions he could take to improve his communication style and create greater trust in their relationship. They gave him some painful, risky feedback. We prepared a written document summarizing their feedback. Mike was able to take their comments not as personal observations from his enemies, but as a group picture revealing how his communications were not working.

Before our intervention, no one was willing or able to give Mike honest feedback out of fear that he would retaliate against them. Yet, by their silence, they condemned him to continue making the same mistakes and themselves to continue misunderstanding his intentions. By ignoring the problem they paid a stiff price, until their demoralization and inability to solve ongoing problems demanded their attention.

As a result of their feedback and our coaching, Mike was able to dramatically improve his communication skills. He started the next meeting by thanking everyone publicly for their honest feedback. He then met one-on-one with every member of his staff to gather more information about how he could improve. He took all their suggestions seriously, and while he did not do everything everyone asked and had several failures, he demonstrated a genuine commitment to changing his behavior. The group responded by giving him the support he needed to improve and acknowledging him when he did.

Only by reality-testing your intention to change and requesting feedback from those who do not understand what you are trying to tell them can you learn whether you are making good on your commitment and effectively communicating. If your listeners do not recognize your commitment, it is *not* real. Making a clear commitment to yourself and an open declaration of commitment to others is the first step in this process. The second step is learning the skills necessary to make good on your commitments and actually implementing them. The third is requesting feedback, making corrections, and generously acknowledging others for contributing to your growth and learning.

Effective Communication for Speakers

Effective communication includes not only listening but speaking as well. Even in extremely hostile confrontations, if you are the speaker, you can defuse misunderstandings through a variety of active, empathetic, and responsive speaking techniques.

The difference between a communication that is felt by the listener to be authentic and believable and one that is felt to be inauthentic and unbelievable is the listener's interpretation, not only of the words you use and their dictionary definitions, but the congruity of your communication, subtle indications of your intentions, and the integrity of your commitments as measured by what you do afterwards.

If these elements in your communication are weak or inappropriate, your questions—no matter how polite—will strike the listener as prying. Your statements of feeling will appear self-righteous, your assertions accusatory, your declarations egotistical, your requests manipulative, your contracts empty, and your commitments inauthentic. Here are some methods you can use to encourage other people to listen to your true meaning when you speak:

- Before you speak, draw out the other person's ideas. Start speaking by listening, so your ideas can be targeted and presented to your listener more effectively. This does not mean watering down what you want to communicate, but recognizing there are a multitude of ways you can say what you mean so the other person will feel engaged.

- Discover and manage your listener's unspoken expectations. Make sure you do not base your comments on false expectations regarding what the other person wants or is willing to do. Do not encourage others to have false expectations of you.

- Choose an appropriate form of speaking. Decide what you want to communicate, and choose the form of communication that best supports your intention. If you want to make a declaration, make it an "I" statement rather than an accusation. Make sure your questions are genuine and not disguised statements. Be clear when you make a promise that you mean it and will follow through.

- Speak respectfully, empathetically, and responsively. Make sure you speak respectfully to your listeners, especially if you disagree with them or disapprove of their behavior. Make sure you are responsive to the issues they have with you, and speak to them as you would want them to speak to you.

- Put the listener at ease. Speak informally or in a way that relaxes your listeners and encourages their trust in what you have to say.

- Demonstrate that you have heard the other person's deeper needs and feelings. Make reference as you speak to the listener's issues and feelings, which may not be apparent at first glance. Demonstrate that you are paying attention to what they have been telling you by summarizing their remarks without watering them down and, if anything, making them stronger.

- State your interests rather than your positions. Rather than repeating what you want, explain in a personal way the reasons why you want it.

- Anticipate objections and address them before they are raised. Try to anticipate what the other person is likely to say in response. Address those issues before the listener does as a way of demonstrating that you understand his or her concerns.

- Acknowledge differences and restate issues positively. Acknowledge your differences openly and state them neutrally, then restate the main issues positively so that they can be resolved. Afterward, test for understanding and for agreement or disagreement with what you said, so you can respond proactively to the other person's concerns.

- Clarify and emphasize your agreements. Do not lose sight of what you actually agree on. Start by thanking the other person for agreeing to discuss issues openly with you. If the person has done so, emphasize earlier points of agreement, whatever they may be. There will always be something you agree on, even if it is only an agreement to talk directly with each other rather than ignore the problem or take it to someone higher up.

- Focus on developing solutions. Address problems that can be solved rather than trying to assign blame or citing conditions that are beyond your or their control. Ask the other person "What solution would you suggest?"

- Ask questions of the listener. Asking questions is nearly always more powerful than speaking. Or, at the end of your comments, turn the conversation over to the listener by requesting a response to what you said or formulate a more profound question that, if answered correctly, could actually result in your changing your mind.

- Compliment the other person for listening. Give positive reinforcement for listening and indicate your willingness to listen in return with an open mind.

Phrases for Miscommunication

Some of the miscommunications that trigger our conflicts lie hidden in the words and phrases we use. As speakers, our communications are more effective when we take time to reflect strategically on the exact message we want to communicate and eliminate the words and phrases that are likely to trigger miscommunications and conflicts.

For example, do you use the words "always" or "never" to describe other people's behaviors? If so, you might want to consider substituting phrases that convey the same meaning, yet without encouraging the other person to respond with "No, I don't" or "Yes, I do," thereby triggering endless, pointless arguments. Instead of "always," try saying "You do that too much for me," "Please do that less often," or "That bothers me." And in place of "never," try saying "You do not do that enough for me," "Please do that more often," or "I really appreciate it when you do that."

Try to recall the words you used in a recent conflict or miscommunication or the words someone else used in a conflicted conversation with you. Was your communication successful, or did misunderstanding, disagreement, and conflict result? What could either of you have said differently? Here are some examples of words and phrases that often lead to miscommunication and conflict:

- *Ordering:* "You must . . ." "You have to . . ." "You will . . ."
- *Threatening:* "If you don't . . ." "You'd better or else . . ." "You'll pay a big price . . ."
- *Preaching:* "It's only right that you should . . ." "You ought to . . ." "It's your duty . . ."
- *Interfering:* "What you should do is . . ." "Here's how it should go . . ." "It would be best if you . . ."

- *Judging:* "You are argumentative (lazy, stubborn, dictatorial . . .)." "I know all about your problems." "You'll never change."
- *Blaming:* "It's all your fault." "You are the problem here."
- *Accusing:* "You lied to me." "You started this mess." "You won't listen."
- *Categorizing:* "You always . . ." "Every time this happens you do the same thing . . ." "You never . . ."
- *Excusing:* "It's not so bad." "It wasn't your problem." "You'll feel better."
- *Personalizing:* "You are mean." "This is your personality." "You are the problem here."
- *Assuming:* "If you really respected me, you would . . ." "I know exactly why this happened."
- *Diagnosing:* "You're just trying to get attention." "Your personal history is what caused this to happen." "What you need is . . ."
- *Prying:* "When?" "How?" "What?" "Where?" "Who?" "What are you hiding?"
- *Labeling:* "You're being unrealistic (emotional, angry, hysterical . . .)." "This is typical of you . . ."
- *Manipulating:* "Don't you think you should . . ." "To really help, you should . . ."
- *Denying:* "You did not . . ." "I am completely blameless . . ."
- *Double binding:* "I want you to do it my way, but do it however you want."
- *Distracting:* "That's nothing, listen to what happened to me . . ."

Effective Communication for Listeners

As we have indicated, it is rare, in our initial approaches to conflict, that we sit down with our opponents and engage in open, honest, problem-solving dialogue and actually listen to each other and learn from our problems. Instead, we spend most of our time trying unsuccessfully to win or defend ourselves, make our opponents understand our point of view without really understanding theirs, not lose or suffer or look bad, or make the problem go away. As a result, we spend sleepless nights obsessing over emotional slights, focusing on superficial issues, and planning responses to our opponents' statements without being curious about their deeper truths.

If this is how we behave, we are likely to experience little more than the anger, fear, and shame that come from feeling attacked; the loneliness and sadness of not being listened to; the sadistic pleasure and guilt of attacking others; the pain and grief of lost relationships; and occasionally, the pyrrhic victory that comes from authoring our opponent's defeat.

As a result of these adversarial feelings, we fail to realize that, like all self-fulfilling prophecies, hostile attitudes generate hostile realities. When we believe our opponents are "out to get us," we naturally behave toward them with reciprocal hostility and defensiveness. Seeing our hostility and defensiveness, they naturally respond in kind, thereby proving to us that we were right in the first place! As a result, many people come to feel, as critic Gore Vidal once quipped, "It is not enough that I succeed—others must fail."

When we resist listening to our opponents or recognizing the legitimacy of their needs and interests, we become unable to participate in honest, empathetic dialogue and cannot communicate effectively to solve our problems. As a result, we are left with few alternatives, other than to surrender, engage in aggressive opposition, or paper over our disputes with temporary, inadequate, superficial settlements.

On the other hand, as Mahatma Gandhi, Mikhail Gorbachov, Martin Luther King Jr., Nelson Mandela, and countless others have clearly demonstrated, even an entrenched military opposition finds it difficult to sustain itself when a leader with sufficient courage refuses either to surrender or to become an enemy.

Listening is the first step in transforming our opponents into collaborative problem solvers. Active, empathetic, and responsive listening takes place when we genuinely care about what the other person is trying to tell us and actively reach out with questions, tone of voice, and body language. It arises when we participate in open, honest dialogue that moves back and forth, and both sides are authentic in their responses. It occurs when we search for creative solutions or work together to come up with fresh ideas and approaches to solving our problems. It happens when we listen as *we* would want to be listened to if we were the one who was speaking.

The deepest level of listening arises when we listen as though *our* lives depended on our understanding what our opponent is saying, when we are no longer even aware of our existence as listeners and have completely merged with the speaker and the story. When we listen in this way, with our hearts as well as our minds, we may even begin to feel love and affection for the one who is speaking.

Thus, there are many ways you can listen to your opponent, ranging from going through the motions to listening with your heart. As your listening moves deeper and further along this continuum, you will develop improved skills and discover increasing opportunities for problem solving, resolution, and transformation.

For example, we recently coached a client who made considerable progress on this journey. Tim was a well-meaning, much-loved leader in city government who became isolated as a result of his communication problems. His staff, who respected and valued him, felt blocked in their communications with him, which they described as follows:

> The volume of work is such and the number of crises and emergencies is so great that even if he were organized, Tim would be pulled off constantly. Tim's meetings get interrupted by calls all the time. His availability to hear what we have to say is missing. It's hard to get his time and attention to focus on issues.

> Tim is marvelous, smart, and a good people person, but he is disorganized and lacks follow-up. He never has time to hear our problems.

Tim is disorganized, and there often is no follow-up because his job is so overwhelming and challenging that no one can do it. Tim loses the points we are trying to make as we give them to him. He doesn't seem to hear us anymore.

We encouraged Tim to use the three steps that follow in each conversation with the employees who reported to him. His consistent practice using these steps over a period of several months paid off in better relationships with his staff. Tim found the three steps easy to articulate but difficult to consistently carry out in practice. Take a moment in your next communication to apply them one at a time and notice what happens as a result.

Step One: Let Go of Your Own Ideas, Roles, and Agendas and Try to Understand What the Other Person Is Saying. The first step in communication is not speaking. It is not even listening. It is *preparing* to listen by emptying yourself of your own preconceived ideas, dropping predefined roles, and letting go of agendas, assumptions, judgments, and expectations—of everything that might twist what you will hear into something other than what is meant.

The greatest enemy of learning is not ignorance but what you think you already know. Ask yourself, "What is going on in my mind when my colleague is communicating with me? Am I open to learning and poised to understand what he or she is saying, or am I thinking about what I am going to say in response? Am I listening as a human being or as a manager or employee or teacher?" Possibly the greatest challenge you will face in listening is letting go of what you think you know is true and realizing that *your* version of the truth may be preventing you from hearing or understanding theirs.

Step Two: Search Behind the Words for the Other Person's Meaning, Especially If He or She Disagrees with You. After you empty yourself and let go of your judgments, genuinely listen to the words used by the other person, try to sense the deeper issues, and hear the assumptions, expectations, and hidden meanings that lie beneath what is being said. Ask yourself, "What does my opponent really want?" "What are his or her real intentions?" "What is going on beneath the surface?" Are you aware of the subtlety hidden in the words being spoken? Are you listening to what is *intended* and not just to the words that are being used?

Step Three: Respond Respectfully and Nondefensively, Acknowledging and Addressing the Other Person's Concerns First. Respond by addressing the speaker's point of view, rather than immediately countering with your own and ignoring most of what was said. When people feel they have not been heard, they repeat their comments over and over and become frustrated, strident, and angry. Try saying, "Thank you for giving me that information. I really appreciate your willingness to tell me what you saw and heard and how you experienced it."

When you respond seriously to what other people say, they *feel* heard and can then relax and make an effort to listen and understand you. Put yourself in their shoes and walk a while along the path of their perceptions before you disagree. Speak to them in ways that could make a difference, rather than simply replacing their ideas with your own.

Active, Empathetic, and Responsive Listening

Being a committed listener includes being active, empathetic, and responsive during the listening process and participating actively in the communication. Using the following techniques can assist you in becoming a more committed listener and encouraging others to listen when it is your turn to speak. These techniques can open up your communications, invite people to share their feelings and points of view, and allow you to discover what is being said beneath the surface. In doing so, remember that the point is not to substitute technique for intention, but to make them consistent.

Encouraging. Encouraging questions and comments invite speakers to share their feelings, perceptions, and attitudes. Comments such as "Please tell me more," "I'm interested in what you are saying/thinking/feeling," "I would like to know your reactions," "I hear what you are saying" are inviting statements. You can even say, "Tell me more about why you disagree with me," which will elicit more open conversation and dialogue. What statements could you make to your opponent in a conflict you are now experiencing that could be encouraging?

Clarifying.   As the discussion unfolds, ask questions that clarify the points being made by the speaker. Send a signal that you are interested in the speaker and the content of what is being said. Questions like "When did this happen?" "Who else was involved?" "What did it mean to you?" elicit detail and meaning. Clarifying questions de-escalate emotions by focusing the speaker on facts rather than feelings. Be careful not to interrogate the speaker with prying questions. Your tone of voice and intention mark the difference between prying and clarifying. What are some clarifying questions about a confusing or ambiguous situation you might ask?

Acknowledging.   You can encourage greater openness by recognizing, naming, and acknowledging the feelings being expressed. Comments like "I can see you are pretty upset about that. Can you tell me why?" or "I can appreciate now why you might feel that way" give permission for greater depth of communication. Be careful not to assume you know what the other person is feeling. You can also use these expressions to give someone permission to say what they are feeling. Avoid popular catchphrases such as "It sounds like you are very angry right now" because they convey an impression that you are trying to manipulate the speaker and betray a lack of empathy rather than a presence of heart. What acknowledging statements might you make when a coworker or friend gets upset?

Normalizing.   As feelings are expressed and opinions offered, you may want to communicate to the speaker that it is natural or normal to have these feelings. Statements like "I think I might feel the way you do if that happened to me" allow the person to feel accepted while expressing difficult emotions or critical thoughts. These statements will encourage the speaker to go deeper in the conversation with you. Can you think of a way of normalizing the feelings of someone with whom you are in conflict?

Empathizing. Put yourself in other people's shoes to better understand their perceptions and feelings. Look inward and find a time when you had a similar experience, reaction, or feeling. You might say, "I think I can understand why you might feel so strongly about this subject because I experienced something similar in my own life." Or, "I can appreciate why you might feel that way." Or just, "I understand." Do not say, "I know exactly how you feel." You do not. What are some empathizing comments you might make?

Soliciting. Ask questions to solicit advice and identify possible solutions, such as "I would like your advice about how we might resolve this." "What do you think we should do?" "Tell me more about what you want." "What would you like to see happen?" "Why do you think that would work?" What questions could you ask to solicit advice about a disagreement or conflict you are having?

Mirroring. Mirroring reflects back the emotions, affect, demeanor, body language, tone of voice, metaphors, even breathing patterns used by the speaker as a way of encouraging the speaker to feel you are a companion in whatever he or she is thinking or feeling, rather than a dispassionate observer who does not really understand. If the speaker takes a defensive posture, you can try initially taking one yourself, then moving to a more open one. In doing so, do not make it appear that you are mimicking or being disrespectful.

Agreeing. If you disagree with a speaker about a topic, it does not mean that you have to disagree about everything in life. It is useful in the course of your disagreements to remember and identify the issues on which you feel you are in agreement. You might say something like, "What I like about what you just said is . . ." or "I really agree with you about that." You can then add, "What I think we disagree about is . . ." What might you say to someone with whom you disagree to let the person know you share areas of agreement?

Supplementing. Instead of "yes, but," say "yes, and,"—and instead of thinking of others as adversaries, convert them into allies. You might say something like, "Let me build on that and see if we are on the same track," or "Let me support what you are saying with another point," or "Not only that, . . ." What could you say to add to what your opponent said or to supplement the other person's basic points and distinguish them from your disagreements?

Inviting Elaboration. Asking open-ended questions that do not have a fixed answer lets the speaker know you respect his or her point of view. You can ask wide-open questions, such as "Why?" "What would you like to see happen?" "Why is that important to you?" Or you can ask more directed questions, such as "I'd like to ask a question about that" or "How would you . . ." or "Help me understand why you . . ." What do you really want to know from or about the person with whom you are in conflict? What might you ask that could get you that information?

Reframing. Reframing or rephrasing consists of preserving the basic content or message of a communication, but altering its form so that it can be heard nondefensively and result in dialogue. For example, you can reframe by transforming "you" statements into "I" statements or by identifying the reasons for your disagreement. As an illustration, you change the statement "You are incompetent!" into a genuinely curious question, such as "Why did this happen?" Or, "What did I say that created that expectation?" Or, "What did you think you were supposed to do?" One format for reframing is, "I feel . . . when you . . . because . . ." How might you reframe a statement in your conflict to suggest a solution? Can you think of a way you could ask a question to focus on a behavior you do not like?

Responding. Listening respectfully also means responding authentically to what is said and not using listening techniques to manipulate the speaker. The speaker is entitled to a response that comes to terms with what was said. One approach is to say, "If I understand you correctly, you see the problem this way—[summarize]. Here's how I see it." Or, "Would you like to know how I see it?" Try to respond without being defensive or angry while still making your point clear. If your main purpose is to learn from your disagreement, you will not do so either by backing away from the conflict or getting drawn into angry, defensive responses. What could you say to someone with whom you disagree that would allow you to achieve both these goals?

Summarizing. If you want the other person to feel heard, summarize what was said in your own words, for example, by saying, "Let me see if I understand what you just said—[summarize in your own words]. Is that correct?" This feedback helps the speaker feel heard and provides an opportunity to confirm, correct, or improve your understanding of the other people's communications. It demonstrates your interest in what was said and your desire to grasp the essential meaning of the communication. It is useful to summarize at the end of a conversation to see if you have the same perception of what was said. In doing so, you risk making a mistake, but it is better to be mistaken and receive clarification than to continue based on a false assumption of what was meant. How might you do this?

Validating. Recognize the speaker's contribution and thank the person for communicating with you. Validate specific points the speaker made that you found useful in the conversation. You can make comments such as "I appreciate your willingness to raise these issues with me." "I learned a great deal from what you said, specifically . . ." "I know it took a lot for you to be as open as you were, and I want to acknowledge you for taking that risk." "I appreciate your willingness to talk to me about this." "I didn't know you felt that way before." What comments might you make to validate the speaker in a way that communicates your interest and authenticity?

We hope you do not feel overwhelmed or daunted by this list of techniques. Obviously, you do not always have to do everything we list in order to communicate effectively. The most important way of improving your listening skills is by becoming conscious and aware of how you are communicating, identifying what got you into trouble or triggered a defensive response in the listener that you did not intend, being open to feedback, and working to continually improve the skills you presently possess.

None of these methods will guarantee a successful communication, and each can be used by an uncommitted listener to give the appearance of listening while holding firmly to a private agenda. We call this "New Age manipulation" because all the words and techniques are right, but the listener really does not care about the speaker or the message being delivered.

Finally, it is important to understand that you can have every one of these techniques down perfectly, but if your heart is not in it, your opponent will know. Conversely, you can never use a single one of these techniques, but if your heart is in it and you are genuinely interested, your opponent will know that as well.

Your challenge is to be as deeply honest and empathetic as you can; to become sincerely curious about your opponent; to listen with your heart for other people's unspoken needs, interests, desires, and intentions; and to search for the words and communication techniques that will clarify your communication, improve your relationship, and reinforce your integrity and authenticity.

Empathetic Listening

The most important organ in listening is neither the ear nor the mind but the heart, and it is within your own heart that you will discover the true meaning of any communication. When you listen with your heart, you become one with the speaker and discover your opponent's truth inside you.

Empathetic listening, for this reason, is much deeper than merely active or responsive listening. It requires you to focus your awareness not merely on the words being used but on what the speaker may be thinking or feeling without words. It means asking yourself what it might feel like to walk in your opponent's shoes or what would cause you to make that statement or to communicate or behave as they did.

When you listen within a role—the way, for example, that a manager typically listens to an employee, a teacher listens to a student, or a government clerk listens to a member of the public—you are likely to be listening primarily to determine the *facts* that can help you decide what to do. But in addition to the facts or what you should do, you can also listen for subtle information about the speaker, how he or she perceives the world, and what is really important to them.

Thus, in addition to the facts, you can go deeper within yourself, access your empathy, and when listening to your opponent, you may also be able to hear faint indications, for example, of

- Emotions and feelings
- Wishes and desires
- Interests and positions
- Dreams and visions
- Intentions
- Humiliations
- Denials and defensiveness
- Openings to dialogue
- Similarities
- Cries for help
- Desire for forgiveness

- Distortions of perception
- Prejudices
- Family patterns
- Role confusions
- Stereotypes
- Self-esteem
- Resistance
- Apologies
- Differences in style
- Admissions of guilt
- Requests for acknowledgment

In truth, all of these elements are present in all our conversations, except that we generally do not really listen for them. So the next time you listen to a colleague or family member, and especially to your opponent in a conflict, see if you can hear these and other elements in what your opponent is saying. See if you can hear more accurately by listening with your heart, with empathy and intuition, and imagine what might cause you to make similar statements or behave in similar ways.

Where Do We Go from Here?

After becoming active, responsive, and empathetic listeners and learning to speak and act with commitment and integrity, the next challenge in resolving your conflict is to work through the powerful, intense, negative emotions that can keep you from listening to your opponent with an open heart and an open mind.

If you can find ways of working *through* your emotions—both those you feel and those you experience from others—you will develop a new and powerful strategy for resolving your conflicts. All your work on listening can be lost in a moment when a firestorm of feeling overwhelms you.

To learn how to embrace and acknowledge the powerful emotions that fuel your conflict and reach deeper into the center of conflict where profound transformations take place, read on.

Strategy Three

Acknowledge and Integrate Emotions to Solve Problems

By embracing the inescapable, I lost my fear of it.
I'll tell you a secret about fear. With fear, it's all or
nothing. Either, like any bullying tyrant, it rules
your life with a stupid blinding omnipotence, or
else you overthrow it, and its power vanishes in a
puff of smoke. And another secret: the revolution
against fear, the engendering of that tawdry despot's
fall, has more or less nothing to do with courage. It
is driven by something much more straightforward:
the simple need to get on with your life. I stopped
being afraid because, if my time on earth was
limited, I didn't have seconds to spare for funk.

—*Salman Rushdie*

What do you do when your efforts to listen result in emotional outbursts instead of calm and reasoned conversation? What options are available to you when you feel caught up in intense emotions like anger or fear or when others react emotionally and your efforts to communicate disintegrate and slip out of control?

To begin, it is helpful to recognize that expressing intense emotions can be constructive or destructive, pleasurable or painful, positive or negative. Emotions can distort or clarify our communications, escalate or de-escalate our conflicts, encourage us to act collaboratively or prevent us from doing so. Having strong feelings can blind us or allow us to see others as they really are and leave us feeling exhausted or fulfilled.

Most people experience their most intense emotions during conflict and perceive the intense emotions of their opponents as exclusively negative, destructive, painful, blinding, and exhausting. Yet expressing, acknowledging, and integrating your emotions can also be a powerful positive force for problem solving, resolution, and transformation, depending on how you understand, approach, and express them.

Just as conflict routinely triggers negative emotions such as hatred, fear, shame, depression, and grief, *resolving* conflict routinely triggers positive emotions such as affection, courage, pride, elation, and joy. Every emotion has a negative and positive pole, making it possible for us to shift suddenly from negative to positive feelings based on how people respond to us at the time. Our feelings are not fixed states of mind, but are in constant motion and capable of moving slowly or rapidly from one extreme to another and anywhere in between.

How we respond to our own powerful emotions affects our capacity to hear and respond to those of others, making us more or less available for relationships with people who express similar emotions. It is useful to think of emotions as teachers to be learned from, rather than as devils to be suppressed. Despite the ambivalence and uncertainty of our emotions, we can all become more skillful in how we handle them when they arise, whether in ourselves or in others.

Every conflict triggers an intense emotional reaction, and these reactions are probably the most important element keeping us locked in impasse. Yet most of our workplaces and organizational cultures require us, either overtly or covertly, to "check our emotions at the door," "leave them at home," and suppress them whenever possible.

While we can temporarily hold our emotions in check, we cannot eliminate them or keep them permanently on hold, and trying to do so simply makes them surface somewhere else. What is worse, doing so prevents us from learning from our conflicts, integrating our emotions, and using them constructively to help solve our problems.

The primary reason for this repressive attitude toward emotions in the workplace is our general lack of skill in handling intense emotional communications and our low level of what professor Daniel Goleman has labeled "emotional intelligence." Emotional intelligence is often described as consisting of a combination of self-awareness, self-regulation, motivation, empathy, and social or relational skills, as depicted in the following chart:

Components of Emotional Intelligence.

	Definition	*Hallmarks*
Self-Awareness	The ability to recognize and understand your moods, emotions, and drives as well as their effect on others	Self-confidence Realistic self-assessment Self-deprecating sense of humor
Self-Regulation	The ability to control or redirect disruptive impulses and moods The propensity to suspend judgment, to think before acting	Trustworthiness and integrity Comfort with ambiguity Openness to change
Motivation	A passion to work for reasons that go beyond money or status A propensity to pursue goals with energy and persistence	Strong drive to achieve Optimism, even in the face of failure Organizational commitment
Empathy	The ability to understand the emotional makeup of other people Skill in treating people according to their emotional reactions	Expertise in building and retaining talent Cross-cultural sensitivity Service to clients and customers
Social Skill	Proficiency in managing relationships and building networks Ability to find common ground and build rapport	Effectiveness in leading change Persuasiveness Expertise in building and leading teams

Source: Daniel Goleman, *Harvard Business Review*, November-December 1998.

Goleman argues not only that each of us can significantly increase our emotional intelligence, but that emotional skills can be highly useful in making even ordinary workplace decisions and that "passions, when well exercised, contain wisdom; they guide our thinking, our values, our survival."

Indeed, recent scientific research has shown that more accurate assessments can be made of the meaning of words and phrases by people who are able to access the emotional processing centers of their brains than by those who are not.

In our experience, the people we have observed who possess the hallmarks of emotional intelligence cited in the chart above are able to respond to other people's negative emotions more skillfully, experience fewer conflicts, and resolve them quicker, with fewer repercussions.

We invite you to examine your emotional life at work; to look at how your feelings influence your experiences, motivation, communications, and relationships; and to consider what you might do to improve your overall emotional intelligence. It is always useful to become more conscious of the role emotions play, not only in escalating your conflicts and shaping your view of yourself and your opponent, but in limiting or expanding your ideas about what it is possible for you to do to resolve your conflicts.

Emotional Responses

We all pay a heavy emotional price for unresolved conflict. This price includes not only emotional aggravation but physical pain and illness. Howard Friedman, a psychology professor at the University of California at Riverside, has analyzed a hundred studies connecting people's states of mind with their physical health. He found that being chronically pessimistic, irritated, cynical, depressed, and anxious doubles the risk of contracting a major disease. Subsequent studies bear out this result.

There are strong neurological connections between the emotional centers of the brain, the immune system, and the cardiovascular system. When stress hormones and brain chemicals produced during negative emotions flood the body, they hamper the ability of the immune system to fight disease, making us more susceptible to cancer, raising blood pressure, increasing cholesterol, and rendering us more vulnerable to diseases of all kinds.

Emotions are always present in all our relationships, even when they do not appear on the surface or reveal themselves in obvious ways. The only real questions are whether we are capable of acknowledging them and whether it is possible for us to learn how to respond more skillfully and intelligently in their presence.

There is always a risk of opening a floodgate of repressed emotions whenever we communicate openly and honestly with our opponents or directly address the emotional issues in our conflicts. This is because there are two fundamental ways of responding to any emotion, whatever the type of conflict, and whether the emotions are ours or our opponent's. We can either

- Tighten up and turn away or
- Relax and turn toward

It may initially appear that if we relax and turn toward our emotions, we will sink into a morass of negativity, become angry, and retreat from resolution. Yet the opposite is true: relaxing and moving toward our emotions help unlock our disputes, while moving away from them keeps us stuck.

When we withdraw from our emotions, we end up learning little or nothing about what gave rise to them or how to experience them fully, respond to them more skillfully, or recognize what lies beneath them. When we relax, let go of our fear of expressing emotions, and engage them openly and honestly, we release ourselves from their grip and increase our clarity, creativity, and opportunities for learning, problem solving, resolution, transformation, and healing.

Suppressing, denying, and avoiding our emotions lead us away from solving the problems that caused them to surface in the first place. These strategies block us from releasing what lies beneath our emotions and therefore from understanding what they mean, both to us and to our opponents. Our emotions surface for reasons, and we need to discover where they come from and what they mean in order to realize that it is possible to communicate about what led to them in rational and constructive ways.

How Unexpressed Emotions Create Conflict

We were asked to mediate a bitter conflict in the payroll department of a large public sector organization. The atmosphere was so angry, rude, tense, and hostile that over the last two years, every employee in the department had applied for a transfer! They had been experiencing intense negative emotions for *eight years*, and the price they paid had become enormous.

We started by asking how the conflict began and were met with total silence as each employee tried to remember. Finally, Blanche said that eight years ago Frieda had made an insulting comment about her husband when he was dying of cancer. The anger, pain, grief, and guilt connected with her husband's death added to Blanche's injured feelings, leaving her so upset that there was no easy way to communicate her intense emotions. She felt that the workplace did not allow her to express these feelings and, as a result, slipped into a cold, punishing, seemingly irrational anger.

Frieda was visibly shocked to hear that this was the reason behind their enmity. She told Blanche she had not known her husband, had not known he was dying of cancer, and had no reason or desire to insult him. We asked her, "Since Blanche believes you insulted her husband when he was dying of cancer, what do you want to say to her right now?" There is only one appropriate answer to this question, and Frieda immediately and sincerely said she was sorry for any insensitive remarks she might have made.

We then asked Blanche, "Since Frieda has apologized to you, did not know your husband or that he was dying of cancer, and had no reason or desire to insult him, what do you want to say to her in response?" Again, there is only one appropriate answer, and Blanche also apologized, admitting that she should have gone to Frieda and told her of the emotional pain her remark had caused. Both women began to cry, releasing their anguish and pent-up anger, and realizing the price they and their colleagues had paid for eight years of emotional miscommunication.

Everyone in the department was shocked and speechless at the realization of how such an innocent mistake could have created such enormous anguish and pointless suffering. We asked the group, "Is there anything anyone else wants to apologize for or any other mistaken communications you want to discuss?"

Since they had kept this conflict alive for eight years, they all had something to say. As they spoke about related incidents and apologized for their role in the conflict, relief began to fill the air. Several staff members apologized for having been complicit in spreading rumors and gossip, remaining silent, or supporting their friends and not telling others what they only assumed was true. They were able to see that they had jointly created a culture of avoidance and emotional hoarding that had prevented resolution and healing.

At the end of the session, the two former archenemies tearfully hugged each other, and everyone agreed to communicate more openly in the future. Within six months, the performance record of the department increased by 200 percent, and the staff was much happier. They became so united that they even went on a "wildcat strike" when management tried to change their work rules!

These women were not alone in their inability to express their emotions in conflict. Most of us have difficulty expressing intense emotions because we are afraid we will not be able to communicate them constructively or skillfully enough to contain their destructive potential. Many of us feel inadequate listening to other people's intense emotions, fearing we could be hurt or lose control over our responses. Yet the result of not confronting these fears can lead, as in this case, to years of unnecessary pain and anger.

Unfortunately, the unwritten policy of "no emotions allowed" followed in most workplaces is based on a false premise: that human beings can function successfully while suppressing deep emotions over long periods of time. In our experience, successful work teams are defined in part by their ability to acknowledge and discuss emotions and support team members who are in distress. By contrast, in organizations where emotions are suppressed, so are creativity, open communication, problem solving, and morale.

More to the point, it is nearly impossible to resolve many of the conflicts that arise in the workplace without delving into the emotional lives of the participants and discussing their emotional responses to the events that are fueling their conflict. For this reason, managers who try to resolve conflicts between coworkers often get stuck in impasse and feel inadequate as conflict resolvers. This is not surprising because they have been asked to perform a task they have neither been trained for nor allowed to complete.

By attempting to sweep disturbing emotions and conflicts under an imaginary rug, these managers, employees, and organizations pay a steep price for their avoidance of conflict and suppression of emotional expression. They postpone authentic communication, dialogue, and certain kinds of problem solving, often making the underlying emotions and conflicts worse, and encouraging suppressed rage, emotional withdrawal, and litigation.

The real reason many organizations discourage emotional expression and favor settlement over resolution originates in the traditionally masculine idea that emotions reflect weakness or the fear that if we appear vulnerable before our opponents, they will seize the advantage and crush us.

In truth, expressing emotions makes us stronger, but suppressing them makes us more fearful and brittle. Nobel prize–winning Japanese novelist Kenzaburo Oe has written eloquently about his own reluctance to face deep emotions and what lay beneath them: "What was he trying to protect himself from . . . that he must run so hard and so shamelessly? What was it in himself he was so frantic to defend? The answer was horrifying—nothing! Zero!"

Instead of trying to protect ourselves and our organizations by suppressing the honest expression of emotions or avoiding them, we need to move toward and through our emotions, responsibly express them, give permission for people to openly reveal their real hidden feelings, and use emotional intelligence as an adjunct to creative problem solving.

In saying this, we are not advocating that organizations countenance out-of-control tantrums in the workplace. Instead, we are suggesting that the responsible, empathetic, honest expression of feelings, together with the strategic development of emotional intelligence skills, can help us escape from impasse and lead us beyond conflict suppression and settlement to better problem solving, genuine resolution, and transformational outcomes like forgiveness and reconciliation.

By creating work environments that reflect and acknowledge our real human natures, we allow people to be present as whole human beings who have emotions as well as intellects. We believe it is possible to create organizational cultures in which employees can express their emotions and clear the air without being destructive or losing sight of the main goal, which is both to resolve our conflicts and to learn from them.

In emotionally intelligent organizational environments, coworkers are able to support one another in satisfying each other's emotional needs in ways that improve their ability to work together, solve problems, and produce better results. To learn how to achieve these ends, we return to the cauldron where emotional responses and attitudes were forged: our families of origin.

Families and Emotions

We are all born with an innate capacity for experiencing pleasure and pain, desire and repulsion, satisfaction and frustration. As young children, we gradually increase our capacity to communicate our emotions and closely observe the emotional behavior of our parents, siblings, and peers while they model for us how to engage in conflict.

By doing so, we learn how to express our feelings, what roles they can play in our conflicts, and what succeeds or fails in getting us what we want. These patterns are reinforced over time by relatives, teachers, and friends and become nearly automatic, like the default setting on a computer. As a result, we become imprinted with emotional patterns that we carry with us for the rest of our lives and that influence our initial response to conflict in the workplace.

For the most part, we communicate our emotional patterns to coworkers and opponents unconsciously, without responsibility or scrutiny, and accept them blindly, without awareness, choice, or intelligence. Indeed, entire generations can develop ways of expressing anger, fear, sadness, addiction, guilt, panic, manipulation, and withdrawal and pass these lessons on to their children. This especially occurs to the extent that they are unconscious or unaware of them, inviting the next generation to do the same. In this way, the conflicts of the parents are visited on the children.

In our families we learn not only how to express our emotions and engage in conflicts, but how to suppress and avoid them. In the process, we come to accept a set of ideas, myths, and assumptions about emotions that shape our responses to conflict. We use these myths and beliefs to justify our feelings about ourselves and others and create self-fulfilling prophecies—sometimes of inadequacy, paranoia, and victimization.

We learn to limit our expression of emotions, to construct intellectual defenses and explanations that rationalize our behaviors, and to avoid honestly owning and communicating our feelings. We learn how to respond to a narrow range of conflict behaviors and little or nothing about how to respond to behaviors that we did not experience.

Each of us brings these unconscious emotional patterns and conflict experiences into the workplace and operates out of them, as though our coworkers were our parents or siblings, or silently assuming that they will result in similar outcomes and responses in others. We may even express our emotions and behave in conflict in an unconscious effort to elicit from other people the emotional responses and conflict behaviors we became familiar with in our family of origin.

Overlaid on this legacy of family responses are a set of strategies learned in childhood from friends, peers, team members, and classmates. Our need for acceptance and approval from friends and peers begins in early childhood and extends into our adult lives, guiding us toward a different set of emotions and patterns in responding to conflict. Here again, we accept these experiences for the most part without conscious choice, in automatic response to our school, neighborhood, and peer environments, and bring them into the workplace.

Once we have developed a successful strategy for responding to powerful emotions in conflict, we tend to repeat it over and over again and to use it even when it clearly cannot be successful. We stop learning how to develop other, potentially more successful, approaches and rely instead on what we perceive as our strengths. As a result, we ignore our weaknesses, thereby creating the possibility that they will turn into tragic flaws.

Yet what we may even correctly perceive as a successful emotional response or conflict behavior based on many years of experience with our parents, siblings, or peers can suddenly be turned into a failure when we try it with our managers, colleagues, and team members at work.

Thus, one possible strategy for moving from impasse to resolution lies in your willingness to conduct a conscious, critical, nonjudgmental examination of your own emotional history and repertoire of conflict responses. In the process, it may be helpful for you to research your family history, cultivate a capacity to listen and learn from others, make a determined effort to choose your own emotional path at work, and become responsible for your own emotional life and conflict behaviors. To do so, it may be helpful to reexamine some common myths and assumptions about emotions.

Common Myths and Assumptions About Emotions

In every organization, whether as employees, managers, customers, or vendors, we encounter cultural myths and assumptions that profoundly influence how emotions are viewed and handled. In most organizations, these myths and assumptions result in suppressing emotions and avoiding conflict. Yet, as a result of doing so, more and more issues and feelings get swept under the rug, causing people to blow up, shut down emotionally, or leave.

Here are some commonly held myths and assumptions about expressing emotion that may be influencing your organizational culture:

- It's not proper to express emotions at work.
- Emotions are irrational.
- Emotions are negative.
- Emotions can't be controlled and will escalate if released.
- Emotions can safely be ignored.
- Emotions are not helpful in making decisions.
- Emotions are unnecessary.
- Emotions are for children, women, or the helpless.
- Good, nice people don't feel emotions.
- It's okay to express emotions if I can justify my feelings logically.
- I shouldn't feel emotions immediately but save them for later.
- I'll lose control or go crazy if I express my emotions.
- People will go away if I express my emotions.
- Other people have no right to express emotions to me.
- I'm responsible for fixing other people's negative emotions.
- If I express my anger to someone, it means I don't love or respect them. If they express their anger, it means they don't love or respect me.

Most of these myths and assumptions encourage us to suppress our feelings, discount our emotional experiences, and avoid communicating what we actually feel. As we have pointed out, these feelings do not go away as a result but emerge elsewhere, often in the form of unresolved conflict, depression, suppressed anger, distrust, fear, self-doubt, loss of motivation and morale, and illness.

Do these myths and assumptions sound familiar to you? Have they hindered your communication with people who are important to you? Have they supported or undermined your relationships at work? Have they affected your family or others in your life? What have you done to understand, counter, or change them?

Many options are available to you when you experience intense emotions in conflict and you choose to overcome dysfunctional family patterns and cultural dictates in the workplace. You can change your responses any time you choose. To do so, you need to bring a deep level of awareness and acceptance to your emotional experiences, dissecting and distinguishing the jumble of elements that constitute your feelings.

Elements of Emotion

We often experience emotions as a muddle and feel powerless to shape or control them. As a result, we resist or repress their full meaning and are unable to learn from them. Yet if we can learn to experience our emotions as separate, distinct elements that combine to produce what we feel, we can also begin to manage, integrate, and exercise them for constructive purposes.

The first step in doing so is to accept your emotions and experience them as fully as possible without resisting or suppressing them. This does not mean venting, dumping, or passing them on to others, but simply paying attention and allowing them to move freely inside you. When you block your emotions, they tend to congeal and harden or camouflage themselves and achieve a distorted expression. But when you experience them fully and completely, they tend to break up, become more manageable, and disappear.

The second step is to bring a sense of awareness to your emotional experiences and try to isolate and identify exactly what it is you are feeling. As you become more precise in your awareness of each of the separate elements in your emotions, you may find it easier to observe them as they ebb and flow, without feeling controlled by them.

As you consider the following list of emotional elements, reflect on the questions we have included after each element to help you gain insight into your responses, become more accepting of your emotions, and increase your moment-by-moment awareness as they are happening.

- *Quality:* Is the emotion you are feeling depression, anger, guilt, pain, shame, love, fear, or some other reaction?
- *Intensity:* Is it mild or intense? Barely noticeable or gripping?
- *Direction:* Is it inner-directed or outer-directed? Toward a specific target or generalized toward no particular person or situation?
- *Duration:* Is it momentary or long lasting? Does it come in cycles? How did it start? How long has it lasted?
- *Location:* Where is it felt in your body? Where is its impact strongest? Is it a wave or a spot? Does it radiate? What is its shape?
- *Origination:* When have you felt this way before? What triggers or causes it? What is it linked to? What makes it disappear?
- *Resistance:* Is any part of you resisting the full expression of the emotion? What part of you is doing so? Why are you doing so? What are you afraid will happen if you let it go? What makes you think that will happen?
- *Meaning:* What does the emotion mean to you? Why does it have that meaning? Where did you learn the meaning? What else could it mean?
- *Awareness:* How aware are you of each of these elements? Can you detect subtle movements in each? Are you blocking or impeding your awareness? If so, why? What would happen if you did not?

- *Change:* How often and easily do your emotions change? Are they increasing or decreasing? Are they fixed or flowing?

- *Patterns:* Take a few moments to review your emotional responses. Do they fit together in any way? Do you notice any patterns? How might you consciously alter your patterns?

The Stages of Emotional Response to Conflict

You may have noticed that your emotional responses extend over time. If you watch the flow of your conflict emotions carefully, you can discern a number of discrete triggers and stages in their formation. You may also notice that some of these stages are over within seconds while others can last months or even years. It is possible to intervene consciously at any point to transform what you are feeling and open up the possibility of resolution by moving to a different stage in the process.

As you review the following stages in the development of your emotions in conflict, reflect on the times and circumstances when you have lost awareness and an ability to choose in your emotional responses to conflict or when you have slipped into "automatic pilot" and resorted to old patterns:

- *Triggering action or event:* An action or event takes place and is communicated to you, becoming a fact in your life.

- *Perception of emotional tone or intent:* You perceive an underlying adversarial intention, perhaps through body language, tone of voice, quality of action, context, or style of communication coming from your opponent.

- *Stimulation of memories and subjective associations:* These perceptions trigger and connect with conscious and subconscious memories and associations with conflict, which have their own emotional content.

- *Interpretation or attribution of meaning:* You attempt to explain or interpret the action or event together with its emotional tone in a way that makes sense of your experience, according to your emotional patterns and prior experiences with conflict.

- *Rise of an emotional response:* Based on the meaning or interpretation you have given to what happened, you begin to feel fear, anger, sadness, shame, guilt, hate, grief, or similar emotions.

- *Suppression, repression, intensification, and neutralization of response:* You become uncomfortable with your own emotional response and decide to push it down, or it triggers a memory and you build it up, or you try to neutralize or turn away from it.

- *Action or inaction based on emotional response:* You then respond to whatever triggered the emotion, either by taking some action or failing to take it.

- *Internal consequences of action taken:* You experience internal consequences and feelings that reflect your perception of whether you acted or failed to act properly and how you feel about yourself as a result.

- *Reflection and reinterpretation:* You reflect on what happened and what you experienced and did or did not do in response, then reinterpret it after the event and the pressure of the moment subsides, reconstructing it to fit and reinforce a coherent pattern of response to conflict.

- *Learning and transformation:* As a result of what happened, you may learn something from your emotional response, or from the conflict, and either be transformed as a result or become more skillful in processing your emotions in the future.

As you reflect on these stages in your emotional responses to conflict, consider the following questions: Are these the stages you go through in responding emotionally to conflict? If not, where and how do you differ? In which stage do you first get stuck in responding to conflict? What happens to you as a result? What keeps you from having a complete experience of your emotions? What would it take to be able to learn and become more skillful in your conflicts?

In organizational conflicts, these stages are frequently distorted by unspoken messages in the culture regarding the expression and experience of emotion. For conflicts to be transformed within organizations into sources of learning, change, and transformation, it is necessary to expand the level of permission to discuss and express emotions; increase emotional awareness, skills, and intelligence among managers and employees; acknowledge the presence of emotions in the workplace; and openly identify ways of responding more skillfully to emotion through dialogue, coaching, and informal problem solving.

Human resource managers, mediators, and other conflict resolvers can use these elements, stages, and a variety of similar analytical techniques to refocus people who are in conflict on their own internal emotional responses and find more skillful ways of responding to other people's intense emotions. Yet, as we have pointed out, it is only by openly and honestly addressing emotions that it becomes possible to unlock these conflicts, acknowledge the human character of emotional experience, and reorient people to problem solving.

Some Ways of Managing Intense Emotions

If you have worked in an organization, you have probably noticed undercurrents of intense emotion that lie hidden just below the surface, yet powerfully define and shape people's relationships, coloring all their interactions. These undercurrents accumulate over time as colleagues store away and nurse deep emotional injuries they can neither express, release, nor resolve.

When intense emotions accumulate, the pressure to release them can become so strong that we feel we cannot do so safely or that doing so could trigger consequences we are not prepared to face. When opportunities for release suddenly arise in the course of conflict, the temptation of release may be so great that the emotion emerges with more power than if it not been suppressed. An outsider who only witnesses the release and does not understand the accumulation of injuries behind it may interpret the resulting explosion as an overreaction or irrational response.

Yet emotions are not irrational or illogical. They are *non*rational and *non*logical, or rather, they are successful adaptations we have adopted for reasons we may not immediately or entirely understand. They are shaped by our experiences in the families, organizations, and cultural systems in which we grew up and are *strategies* that at some point succeeded in getting us what we wanted or needed, even at the expense of pride, self-esteem, and love. More important, they are useful sources of information about the world and, when integrated and communicated positively, can assist us in solving a wide range of problems.

In organizations, expressing emotions in conflict is often seen as reducing the chances for resolution. Yet when we are roused and our most intense emotions are triggered, we notice more; are finally able to say what we really think, feel, and need; and feel more authentic as a result. Expressions of emotions can help clear the air and make it possible to move beyond ancient grievances. Yet they can also prove destructive, trigger escalations and counterattacks, and end in impasse. Simply expressing emotions without altering the *way* they are expressed just reinforces and strengthens them.

In our experience, it is possible for people to express intense emotions, even in the workplace. They can channel the destructive potential of their emotions in more constructive directions by transforming the *way* they are expressed and shifting from destructive "venting" and "dumping" to constructive forms of owning our feelings, discovering their deeper meaning, and encouraging empathy with others.

You can do so, for example, by making "I" statements rather than accusations, by explaining your emotions rather than exhibiting them, and by asking questions that move the emotion in the direction of problem solving, as in: "What would you like me to do differently in the future?" Or asking questions that turn the emotion inward toward increased vulnerability, as in: "What would you like me to know about you that you think I do not adequately understand?" Or asking questions that reframe the emotion by pointing to what is underneath it, as in: "Are you angry at me because you feel I don't respect you?" Then asking, "What did I do that caused you to feel that way?" And finally, "What is one thing I can do to encourage you to feel I do respect you?"

By examining and openly expressing your feelings, you will be led to their sources, which are often hidden from view. If you can learn to open these gateways skillfully and easily—in ways that do not cause damage to others—and allow whatever you have kept penned up, perhaps for years, to emerge in ways that are constructive and vulnerable, you will be able to integrate your emotions with logical analysis and use them to lead you to a deeper understanding of the issues, your opponent, and most of all yourself.

Letting go and turning toward your intense emotions, as opposed to tightening up and running away from them, is the first step in learning to control them. When you cannot take this step as a result of having suppressed your feelings, you will more easily get stuck in emotional conflicts, allow the level of intensity to build until it is too high for you to manage, and move into an unending cycle of conflict in which you become blind to your deeper feelings and act irrationally.

For these reasons, it is important for everyone in the workplace to improve their emotional skills by learning to manage their intense emotions and develop ways of expressing them clearly, calmly, constructively, and quickly so that resolution can be achieved. Here are seven methods you can use to manage your own intense feelings:

- *Experience your emotions fully, without suppressing them.* Start by giving yourself permission to experience whatever you are feeling completely, without slipping into myths and assumptions that discount or suppress your feelings. When you experience your emotions completely, they tend to relax and release their hold.

- *Turn a spotlight of awareness on what you are experiencing and how you are experiencing it.* Monitor and observe your emotions carefully over time, trying to understand and be aware of their elements more, and see them more clearly.

- *Accept your feelings nonjudgmentally, and see them as sources of information.* Accept your deepest feelings without shame or suppression. Your ability to accept these feelings without being agitated by them will help you become more accepting of the emotions of others.

- *Turn a floodlight of analysis on underlying causes.* Recognize broadly what caused your emotions, understand their origins in your family patterns and past experiences, and recognize what makes them tick and stop ticking so that you can communicate them rationally and calmly to others.

- *Communicate your emotions to others not as judgments or "you" statements but as information and "I" statements.* Honestly communicate even your strongest emotions to others and reveal what you are feeling without feeling ashamed, guilty, or pushy. Own your emotions, and do not present them as other people's responsibility.

- *Ask for what you really want, and let it go.* Consider what you would deeply like the other person to do or say that would make you feel better, and ask if he or she would be willing to do it. Before doing so, in your heart give permission to refuse.

- *Integrate your emotions, and channel them into problem solving.* Understand that your emotions are an integral part of who you are. Consider how you might further integrate them to create a deeper sense of authenticity, and use them to identify, clarify, and solve problems.

By adopting this process of experiencing, observing, accepting, analyzing, communicating, and problem solving, you will find it easier to release your emotions and use them as sources of learning, intimacy, creativity, and personal and organizational transformation, rather than as triggers for loss of control, venting, and negative self-esteem.

Using these methods can also help your opponent manage and communicate his or her emotions by modeling a different way of expressing them. For example, by asking a series of calm, empathetic, poignant questions like those listed above, you give someone who is yelling at you permission to experience what they are feeling completely, become more observant and accepting of their feelings, discover their sources and causes, realize that they can communicate their needs or wants without yelling, and plumb their feelings for information that can help solve their problems.

Simply by asking these questions, you subtly shift your focus away from the emotion-processing parts of your brain and toward the parts that observe, accept, and analyze experiences. If you are able to accept yourself and your feelings nonjudgmentally, be completely aware of what you are feeling, and experience your feelings as useful sources of information, you will be able to communicate what you feel and make the transition to problem solving without becoming overwhelmed by their intensity.

For example, in a conflict resolution session we conducted between a female manager and her male subordinate, we noticed a pattern in the words and phrases he was using to describe her: she was "controlling," "punishing," "a bitch," and "bossy." He was unable to solve problems because "she won't let me," "I have to ask for permission," and "she micromanages me."

When we read these words back to him and asked if they reminded him of anyone, he immediately said, "Oh my god, it's my mother!" In that moment, the conflict literally disappeared. This allowed him to recognize his subconscious family patterns and his manager to recognize that she was unknowingly behaving like his mother. They were then able to reach a number of useful agreements on how they could work together in the future that successfully freed them from the grip of ancient, seemingly irrational emotions. They reached a resolution—and a real transformation—by moving *through* their emotional responses to an analysis of their actual origins.

It is often the case that what is really upsetting us has little to do with the other person, but is flowing from anger we have toward ourselves or is connected with unresolved issues from our distant past. Through analysis, we can reach a deeper understanding of why these emotions are so powerful. Strong emotions that do not seem to flow logically from what just happened are a strong indicator of a conflict pattern we have not yet fully recognized or resolved.

We once consulted in an organization where the director requested feedback on her leadership skills by asking staff to provide her with anonymous feedback on 3 × 5 cards. When she read their responses, she felt attacked and became angry and defensive. We spent considerable time listening to her pain and anger. When we asked whether she felt she was in the right job, she started to cry. She said she knew she was in the wrong job and could not seem to do anything to please her staff or her superiors. Her tears revealed her hidden sadness, loneliness, and shame. She admitted that she had chosen the wrong career, was desperately unhappy, and resented having had to move from a city she loved to one she intensely disliked.

Once she revealed her true feelings to us, rather than being defensive and angry toward her staff, she was able to thank them for their honesty and admit that they had accurately described what she was feeling. We reviewed several ways she could manage her strong emotions while looking for a new position, and she was able to drop her anger and defensiveness and defuse her emotional responses to her staff.

As a result, unnecessary conflicts began to dissipate or were quickly resolved, and a problem-solving process was initiated that resulted in her being offered a more appropriate position in the same organization in the city she loved. She became happy when she learned she was going to return home, and her staff grew in understanding, courage, teamwork, and emotional intelligence as a result of working through their emotions and the underlying problems to which they were pointing.

Behind the Mask: Hidden Markers in Emotional Communication

As conflicts escalate, emotions tend to spiral out of control, so much so that one of our clients, in describing his boss's anger, said that listening to him was like "trying to drink from a fire hose." We can all learn to manage our intense emotions, minimize angry outbursts, and respond more skillfully when they occur. We can all learn to sidestep powerful streams of emotion or let them pass around or through us. We can then see who is really behind the fire hose, where it is twisted or kinked, and why it is emerging now with such force. We may then be able to act more strategically and find a path toward problem solving and resolution.

When we are confronted with intense emotions, we tend to lose track of what is going on beneath the surface. Indeed, this is partly the purpose of intense emotional outbursts. When we feel stunned, frightened, or trapped in an emotional drama, we become unable to see what is going on behind the other person's mask. We allow expressions of strong emotion to camouflage what is really taking place and distract us through bluster and intensity from seeing what our opponent has carefully hidden, thereby preventing us from doing anything strategic about it.

Many people express intense emotions because they are afraid that otherwise we will see them as they believe they really are and that their true, intimate, vulnerable feelings and inadequacies will be exposed. In this way, anger and sadness can be used as diversionary tactics, like a mother bird who feigns injury to draw a potential predator away from her nest.

To help you discover the hidden messages that are usually significantly different from the ones people present, we offer the following glimpse behind the emotional masks people sometimes wear. See if you can recognize the masks you wear, and those worn by your opponent, by searching behind the facade for what is really happening in emotional communications:

- *Accusation as confession:* It is often the case that people who feel guilty about something they have done accuse others of having done it. This is a way of diverting (and sometimes even attracting) attention. Have you ever accused others of something you did yourself? How did it feel? Why did you do it?

- *Insult as denial:* Every insult is a choice that says more about the insulter than the one insulted. For example, if X says that Y is lazy, it is likely that X is hardworking and does not give *himself or herself* permission to take time off or relax. The insult, therefore, says more about the jealousy of X than it does about the character of Y. Think of the insults you have used to describe your opponent, or vice versa. What do these insults reveal about the one who used them?

- *Anger as vulnerability:* Anger is partly a request for communication or connection and partly an effort to create distance or boundaries. Both are a result of being extremely vulnerable, either to the person or the message. Are you vulnerable when you are angry? To what and whom? Why? What might you do instead?

- *Defensiveness as egoism:* Often people become defensive when they mistakenly assume that the conflict or disagreement is directed at them or they are unable to separate their ideas from their identity. Have you ever thought someone meant something personal, only to discover it was not about you at all? How can you take responsibility for your role in conflict without making it be about you?

- *Withdrawal as rage:* Those who withdraw from conflict often do so to silence their own uncontrollable rage, based on an assumption that they cannot communicate what they deeply want so there is no alternative other than withdrawal. Have you ever withdrawn in a silent, punishing rage? Can you think of a safe way of communicating what you deeply want without withdrawing?

- *Passivity as aggression:* Public compliance often masks private defiance. Passivity does not always mean agreement but may instead be an aggressive form of inaction or a use of inertia to block momentum. Sometimes the victim role is used to disguise a power play. Have you ever played the victim? Have you ever used passive behavior to gain power over others? Has this created a satisfying relationship? What might you do instead?

- *Attack as smoke screen:* Sometimes people attack others to draw attention from their own failures. Children sometimes initiate arguments or make blunders to draw their parents' attention away from conflicts with each other. Have you used an attack as a smoke screen to hide your vulnerabilities? Why? Why not admit your failures instead?

- *Apathy or cynicism as caring:* Apathy and cynicism sometimes "protest too much," revealing injured feelings as a result of deep caring or a sense of frustration that so little has been accomplished. Have you ever been cynical when what you really wanted was the opposite? What would happen if you became vulnerable and showed you cared?

There is a strong connection between intense emotional energy that is opposed to a person or idea and a secret attraction to the very thing that is being fought against. As novelist Thomas Mann noticed, "We are most likely to get angry and excited in our opposition to some idea when we ourselves are not quite certain of our position and are inwardly tempted to take the other side."

Thus, we have often observed managers who are intensely angry and accuse their employees of "goofing off," yet are profoundly unhappy at work and would secretly like to goof off themselves. We have also observed employees who are strongly opposed to a supervisor's arbitrary use of power, but would secretly love to exercise it arbitrarily themselves. We have often watched as people become highly emotional and argue dogmatically over an issue when they secretly know there is something true in what the other person is saying.

Do you ever feel drawn to the ideas or behaviors of people you oppose? What masks do you use in your conflicts? Are you using emotions or arguments to achieve a result you have not communicated to others? Are you using a mask to hide your deeper emotions? How have masks helped or hindered you in your conflicts? What would it take for you to drop them completely?

Taking Off the Masks and Revealing Hidden Emotion

When you hide behind masks or send confusing signals about your true desires and intentions, you send distorted, double messages to others. This can cause considerable damage, both to yourself and your relationships. It is difficult for others to hear or understand your innermost voice or to respond to your request when you mask what you mean or who you really are.

We don masks and engage in distorted behaviors in part because we are afraid we are not good enough or that others will not like or accept us and believe we need a thick skin constructed out of ego to protect our deepest vulnerabilities. Once we assume a mask, we become accustomed to its safety and frightened to take it off. After a while, we get used to it and think it is who we really are. We cannot then remove it without creating confusion within ourselves and others as to who we actually are and are forced to keep it in place at all times and at all costs.

For example, Jim, one of our favorite clients, had a brusque, blunt style—almost like a street fighter, with a quick wit and willingness to call things as they were. He asked his organization to become more empowered and self-managing and said he was willing to give up his top-down, command-and-control management style. But his frustration with the team process increased as his staff expressed their unwillingness to accept responsibility and "step up to the plate." As a result, he yelled at people, telling them to "get it or get out." He raised his voice to a fever pitch and delivered ultimatums, shouting that if they did not get empowered, they would be fired!

After a devastating meeting in which he blew up and yelled angrily at everyone, we told him he was sending mixed messages, that angry ultimatums were not likely to encourage his staff to do what he wanted them to do, and that he could not force them to be empowered. He listened carefully to what we said, but did not respond.

A week later, we received a call from a team member who was in a state of shock. Jim had called a special meeting to apologize for his outbursts and angry statements. In a softened, gentle voice, he told them about his passion for what they were doing, his fear of letting go, and his desire to do so now so that he could move on to more challenging work.

Jim's mask of anger was a projection of his fear that his staff would fail if he released control. By opening up and becoming more vulnerable, he communicated his desire to turn control over to the teams. His willingness to take off his mask and stop blaming others set the tone for what followed. His staff took the reins and designed a series of meetings for the leadership group and then for the entire organization to make sure there were no failures. This initiative dramatically shifted responsibility for leadership, decision making, and results to the teams. Jim played a key role in these meetings, acting as an equal participant and fellow team member but also as a leader rather than a boss.

Jim broke through his anger by using "I" statements instead of "you" statements or accusing "them" of misdeeds. "I" statements help communicate strong emotions while labeling feelings as belonging to the person who has them, rather than blaming them on the person whose behavior accidentally or intentionally triggered or inspired them.

There is a vast difference, for example, between "You are a filthy slob!" and "Leaving dirty coffee cups in the lunch room makes me feel you don't respect me or my need to work in a clean environment."

Both statements express real emotions, but the second opens the door to negotiation, dialogue, and possible solutions. The first, by contrast, simply dumps the speaker's frustrations on someone else and triggers denials, counteraccusations, and defensiveness. "You" statements sometimes succeed in causing the listener to wash the cups, but they also undermine the other person's self-esteem, stiffen resistance, and encourage defensiveness, perhaps leading to a few broken cups and placing the whole relationship at risk.

On the other hand, using "I" statements provides opportunities for speakers to be released from feeling controlled by their emotions. They allow listeners to hear the reality of how their behavior affected the speaker without feeling compelled to respond defensively or aggressively. They encourage everyone to put all their cards on the table and not scatter them chaotically or attribute blame for what they are feeling to others. They encourage everyone to take responsibility for their emotions and search for joint solutions to shared problems.

Virginia Satir, one of the founders of the field of family therapy, delved deeply into the problem of masks and identified a series of behaviors she called "power plays." Power plays are surface actions intended to distract others from self-doubts others want to hide, both from themselves and others. Satir identified the deeper levels of emotion underlying each power play. She pointed to outward behaviors, indicated the inner feelings that lay on their surface, and speculated on the deeper feelings that lie hidden beneath the mask. For example:

What Lies Beneath the Mask

Behaviors	*Expressions*
Placating	
Outward expression	I'm always doing everything wrong!
Inside, surface	I must keep everyone happy so they will love me!

| Inside, deeper | I'm really unlovable. If I don't placate others, they won't love me. |

Blaming

Outward expression	You never do anything right!
Inside, surface	Nobody gives a damn about what I care about. Unless I keep yelling, nobody will do a thing!
Inside, deeper	I'm really unlovable . . . I'm the one to blame.

Superreasonable

Outward expression	One needs to face the fact that one makes errors in one's life!
Inside, surface	I must let everyone know how smart I am. Logic and ideas are all that count!
Inside, deeper	I'm really unlovable. If I were not so logical, I would get lost in my emotions.

Irrelevant

Outward expression	Hey! Anybody got a joke?
Inside, surface	I will get attention no matter what extremes I have to go to!
Inside, deeper	I'm really unlovable. If I don't keep changing the topic, people will notice my faults.

In each of these examples, the deeper feeling is one of being unloved and unlovable. This is the core, hidden belief we hold about ourselves that drives our need to create masks and engage in power plays in the first place. This core belief fuels innumerable conflicts, driving us to use emotions—and the masks and power plays we create to disguise them—to justify our failed relationships and placate ourselves with excuses we subconsciously know are phony and unsatisfying. This knowledge leads us to anger—not only at others for not loving us, but at ourselves for being unlovable.

Behaviors That Trigger Anger

Anger is often difficult to fathom, partly because it is often used as a mask or power play as described above, and partly because we do not always recognize its true source. For example, we once interviewed a manager of a small entrepreneurial company who was well known for being angry and disgruntled. He quickly raised the temperature of his responses, becoming more and more angry for reasons we could not identify and that seemed unrelated to our behavior or comments and to anything that had recently happened.

We tried to respond logically, but—as you may have discovered—logical behavior sometimes paradoxically triggers an increase in anger rather than reducing it. We tried to uncover the source of his anger, but he would not reveal it. Finally, we told him we would not continue the conversation if he could not control his anger. Once we set clear limits, he relaxed and calmed his voice. We then probed again to discover the source of his anger, and he recited several incidents in the business that had left him feeling isolated, besieged, unappreciated, and a complete failure.

As a result, we were able to initiate a group conflict resolution process that brought the management team together to agree on a set of ground rules for their future interactions with each other, identify what was not working in their relationship and communications, and jointly focus on rebuilding the company. In the ground rules, they all agreed to not yell at each other in the future; to offer honest, supportive feedback to anyone who did; and to assess a penalty on anyone who did that required them to contribute $20 to a fund to purchase pizzas for the rest of the team. As a result, the yelling stopped completely.

It is inevitable that people will engage in behaviors that push your buttons or trigger your anger. Yet anger is a choice because you own your buttons and are ultimately responsible for how you react when they are pushed. Thus, no one can actually "make you angry." You always have a choice, as was the case in our conversation with the manager we mentioned previously. We could have become angry ourselves and stormed out of his office, but that would have encouraged him to think we were the ones who were being hostile and unwilling to listen.

Instead, we surfaced his anger, expressed our discomfort with it, helped him calm down, established ground rules for our conversation, asked him respectfully what upset him, listened empathetically while he spoke, and brought his colleagues together to discuss the underlying issues that had aggravated him in the first place and agree on ground rules and consequences for the future.

The Many Reasons for Anger

There are many excellent reasons for getting angry that are legitimate and understandable, several of which we have mentioned. For example, it is reasonable to become angry when our personal space is invaded and we feel violated, or when our needs are not being recognized or met by others, or when we are treated disrespectfully. Anger creates a protective boundary between us, commands people's recognition, and even encourages their respect.

Sometimes anger toward others, as Virginia Satir recognized, is simply a projection of our own low self-esteem, anger at ourselves, or false expectations of others. When one of these reasons is at the core of our anger, instead of openly and honestly communicating what we expect or recognizing that our expectations are either unjustified or hidden and therefore unattainable, we more commonly suffer silently and blame others for not meeting them.

When employees are fired, they often use anger and anger-creating behaviors as a way of releasing the pain of losing their job, surrendering the false expectations they had created about their possible future career, processing their grief and shame, and avoiding responsibility for their failure to meet other people's expectations. Paradoxically, anger is sometimes a way of giving other people permission to leave when they would not otherwise have the courage to do so.

Whenever anyone involuntarily leaves a place where they have worked for many years, anger and emotional distancing are likely to occur. Employees are likely to feel mistreated, misunderstood, and betrayed; to blame the organization for being unfair; to feel their colleagues did not support them; and to think their manager was out to get them. Often they are right.

Yet these employees pay an additional, hidden price for not critically examining their own skills and performance, for failing to accept responsibility for what they did and did not do, and for their complicity in what occurred. As a result, it will become more difficult for them to learn from their experiences and to continue learning, growing, and improving in their next job, especially if they want to believe it is secure.

One powerful motivation for anger is that it creates intensity and intimacy. It strips away other people's masks and forces them into the present moment. It demands their attention, and while it is a deeply intimate emotion, it produces only *negative* intimacy, which is preferable to indifference once positive intimacy has become impossible.

Another motivation for anger occurs when we feel bad or worthless and decide to relieve our misery by reassuring ourselves that we are no worse than others. As a result, we may subconsciously try to get them to become angry at us so that we will feel less guilty or look better to others. Sometimes when we speak judgmentally about others, it is because we have already judged ourselves, cannot accept the negative opinion we have formed of ourselves, and want to bring others down to our level so they can directly experience and understand our pain and frustration.

In the workplace, anger is often simply a way of pointing out what needs to be improved or what is not working for someone. Sometimes we use anger to gain attention, recognition, acknowledgment, affection, or other outcomes we feel we are unable to obtain through achievement.

Anger can also be a compensation for being paid or treated unfairly and is routinely used to create alliances, friendships, and cliques with others. In place of sharing positive interests, which requires us to become vulnerable to being rejected, we use gossip, rumors, and anger against others to cement alliances, under the theory that "the enemy of my enemy is my friend."

Anger can also be a distorted expression of fear, guilt, shame, or humiliation. For example, when children do something dangerous, their parents usually respond initially with anger, instead of frankly acknowledging their fear or pain, as a way both of forcing the child to pay attention to safety and of releasing their fear and pain or guilt, which originate in caring. Thus, beneath anger is fear, beneath fear is pain or guilt, and beneath pain or guilt is love. These feelings lead to four entirely different conversations.

For example, we can yell angrily at the child, "Don't do that!" But it is equally possible for us to speak from our fear, saying, "That scared the heck out of me!" Or, we can speak from our pain or guilt, saying, "I would feel terrible if anything bad happened to you." Finally, we can speak from our love, saying, "I love you so much I would feel awful if anything bad happened to you." While these conversations are significantly different, they are also essentially the same, yet elicit vastly different emotions in the person to whom they are directed.

Anger is also sometimes a cry for help, a need to be heard when no one is listening. It is often used to cover weakness or divert attention from a sensitive subject or vulnerable topic. Getting angry is useful as a tactic in trying to get one's own way. Aggressive negotiators, for example, use it to throw the other side off balance, and command-and-control managers use it to secure a subordinate's compliance or divert attention from their own failure.

Anger can also feel cleansing and help us release negative feelings and the shame of victimization, either by expressing them constructively, venting them, or dumping them destructively onto others.

Exploring Anger

Unless the true reasons for anger are recognized, acknowledged, and addressed, it will prove difficult to discover or solve the underlying problem that gave rise to it. Moreover, until we address these underlying reasons, surrendering our anger will feel like surrendering our issues and right to respect. This will make it more difficult to resolve the reasons that gave rise to our conflict, encouraging it to spiral out of control or remain at impasse.

We encourage you to explore your anger, including the triggers or flash points that get you angry. Doing so will allow you to say to yourself, "Here comes a trigger for my anger. I don't need to react immediately. I have a choice. I can choose to respond by discovering the reason for my anger, which I may be able to communicate successfully to the other person without becoming angry, use it to clarify and develop solutions to the problem I need to solve, and become more skillful in expressing anger in the process."

Once you understand the reasons for being angry, you can successfully identify the behaviors that are triggering it. You can then communicate the feelings that lie beneath your anger to your opponent—such as fear, pain, and caring—along with a request for changed behavior and a proposal for how you both might solve the problems that gave rise to it. As you do so, your anger will begin to dissolve automatically, and your conflict will turn into a source of learning and change.

Subconscious Beliefs and Assumptions About Organizational Anger

Behind the angry responses of people working in organizations lie a set of largely unexamined beliefs, feelings, and subconscious assumptions. As you consider these underlying issues, notice which ones may be fueling your anger and whether you are willing to give up the assumptions they rest on, question their validity, or change the conditions that created them.

For example, you may become angry because you believe you have been treated unfairly or unjustly by a coworker or manager. You may subconsciously assume that the person with whom you are angry has caused you to be treated badly and that your unfair treatment was not natural, inevitable, or a result of your own actions but reflected a conscious choice made by them. These actions may seem wrong, or even evil to you, because you assume they had a clear alternative, which was to treat you fairly.

Or when they claim they do not understand why you are angry or how they could have caused or contributed to your problems, you may subconsciously assume they are lying or that if they really understood these things or cared about you, they would have acted differently. You might then assume that because they did not, they must be evil, insensitive, or ignorant.

Yet it is equally possible that the people who treated you unfairly are simply obeying orders or conforming to the mandates of the organizational culture and context in which they are working. By understanding the organizational culture and context in which the conflict arose and using active, empathetic, and responsive listening to explore your opponent's underlying experiences, assumptions, feelings, and realities, you may discover that your assumptions are false, one-sided, and unwarranted.

For example, your opponent may not have had a choice in how he or she responded, or the choice may not have been apparent, or you each may have had a different set of interests, experiences, or feelings, which have been misunderstood completely. Or the organization's structures, systems, and culture may be driving the conflict, offering few choices about how to act.

When we feel certain that others have acted deliberately against us, we use anger as a way of trying to get them to understand, through direct experience, what it feels like to be treated unfairly. Anger is therefore an effort to communicate what we feel and to encourage others to change their behavior and mitigate or correct the unfairness as a result. Yet, by doing so, we end up treating them unfairly and recreating the behavior we found objectionable.

It is rare that we are able to honestly communicate our objections in ways and words that encourage the other person to hear.

We also have a hard time expressing our anger to someone who is superior to us in an organizational hierarchy. Therefore, when we express our anger, we indirectly and subconsciously communicate that the other person is not our superior but an equal or inferior to us. If the others express their anger back to us, they reinforce our point of view.

Most of us accept the idea that anger that originates at home or in our families should not be allowed to intrude in the workplace. But if we are angry at a spouse, partner, or family member, or at life in general, and have no means of communicating our emotion, we are likely to find covert, subconscious ways of releasing it. For example, we may engage in gossiping to coworkers, sabotaging the success of a project, or undermining the reputation of an opponent.

Sometimes we feel we have no right to express our anger to certain people and that others have no right to express their anger to us, based on a lack of depth or reciprocity in our relationship. When they cross this invisible boundary, we become even angrier, marking a subconscious perception that our boundaries have been violated or signaling to others that we desire their attention or affection, even as we drive them away.

We sometimes use anger to test our relationships, as a way of deepening, solidifying, or breaking them apart. We subconsciously assume that if people respect us they will accept our anger, that their anger toward us confirms the existence and importance of our relationship to them and shows us that they care.

The closer the relationship, the more we believe we have a right to get angry without breaking the relationship apart, as can be seen in many families. Yet we may also use anger to drive away the people who care about us—usually so we will not be hurt—but in the process, do not often see how much we have hurt them. Thus, we experience anger as a barometer of caring and feel that as long as the anger is there, so is the caring.

For example, when we are in a relationship that is in the process of ending, most of us would rather that the other person feel anger toward us, rather than indifference. But once the relationship has really ended and we have met someone new, we feel the other person no longer has a right to express anger toward us, and we no longer want that person's caring. Yet, as long as we feel angry at each other, a caring connection exists between us. When we stop feeling angry, we release ourselves from caring.

When we feel powerless or helpless or that we have no right to express our anger directly, we find indirect, ambiguous ways of expressing it. Edgy jokes, satire, emotional withdrawal, passive-aggressive behavior, resistance to change, and noncooperation are all ways of expressing anger without admitting to it. Each of these indirect methods communicates the anger while making it impossible to address the reasons that gave rise to it.

When we are angry, we receive attention from others and are sometimes more likely to get what we want. We may also feel powerful because others changed their behaviors in response to our feelings. If they become angry in response, we feel less guilty about being angry at them and secretly glad that they did not made us look bad by being the only one who is angry. If they do not become angry in response, we feel guilty or become even angrier because they seem to be saying they are superior to us, that we do not have a right to express our anger, or that they do not care about us and how we feel.

Our anger subconsciously makes us feel righteous and important. It justifies our failures and diverts attention from our faults. It allows us to express our pain and fear indirectly without feeling vulnerable in the presence of someone we do not trust. It motivates us to be true to our cause and blinds us to the price we pay or the ways it makes us less effective in achieving our goals.

While these subconscious beliefs and assumptions fuel our anger, few of them have anything to do with the *person* with whom we are angry. Mostly our anger is self-anger that flows from our own issues. We may become angry, for example, at people who engage in behaviors we would secretly like to engage in ourselves, behaviors we do not like in ourselves, or behaviors we would like to discourage ourselves from engaging in. Or we may grow angry at others when the one we are really angry at is ourselves for tolerating their continued disrespectful behavior toward us.

Releasing anger feels better than keeping it locked up inside. The anger we hang on to turns against us and destroys us. Expressing anger directs our pain outward; yet it ends up hurting ourselves as well as others we care about or desperately want to reach. In the process, we fail to realize that we have an alternative, which is to release our anger without inflicting it either on ourselves or others. To do so, we need to understand not only the deeper reasons for our anger, but the reasons why we should let it go.

Letting Go of Anger

There are dozens of paradoxes regarding anger. For example, just as anger creates intimacy, it also creates boundaries. Just as it helps focus attention on solving problems, it also is a destructive force that leaves greater problems in its wake. Every positive payoff that comes from anger can be achieved more skillfully, lastingly, and constructively without it.

We need to recognize that there is a dark, destructive side to anger and refuse to surrender to it. Our challenge is to find ways of getting people's attention, achieving results, creating intimacy, and securing assistance by asking for what we want and need directly. Just as there are many reasons for anger, there are an equal number of reasons for giving it up, letting it go, and using a more effective tactic. Here are some good reasons for giving up your anger:

- Anger is a form of ongoing connection with someone you dislike and probably do not want in your life.
- Anger is a double-edged sword that always injures both its target and the one who directs it.

- Anger is often an externalization of anger against yourself. As a result, forgiving the other person means forgiving yourself.

- Anger creates the "other-as-enemy" and does not allow for empathy or the "other-as-friend."

- Anger converts the person who uses it from a victim to a perpetrator and undermines the sympathy that would otherwise be due as a result of the original injury.

- Anger can be released without giving up what we want; all we surrender are ways of getting what we want that are destructive to others.

- Anger is paradoxically a reflection of weakness and vulnerability to others. When we rely on our internal strength, others' actions need not bother us.

- Anger creates a barrier against our own vulnerability, a defense against the most intimate and important parts of ourselves.

- Anger undermines successful collaboration among team members and blocks efforts to reach consensus on important decisions.

- Anger in organizations forces bystanders to take sides for fear of being injured themselves. It promotes the formation of cliques and factions that fuel the conflict and keep the anger flowing.

- Anger is sometimes used to force changes, increase productivity, and attack the competition, but ultimately erodes well-being and decays the results that flow from internal unity, morale, and trusting relationships.

- Anger is a kind of energy that lives in us and destroys our souls from the inside.

- Anger saps the energy we need to live in the present and plan for the future to be available for change and personal transformation. This energy is reclaimed when we let anger go.

In organizations, anger nearly always destroys trust, reduces morale and motivation, undermines collaboration and team relationships, sabotages strategic planning, and creates a culture of shaming and blaming. This turns customers away, increases employee turnover, fuels grievances and litigation, obstructs creative problem solving, deepens frustration, and adds to the already enormous cost of unresolved conflict.

Methods for Managing Anger

Being able to manage anger is an important life skill that can help you dissipate its self-destructive effects and move toward resolution in your conflicts. Here are some techniques you can use to manage your anger:

- *Own it.* Don't blame anyone else for your anger. Be responsible for your own intense feelings and for openly and constructively expressing them.
- *Discover the underlying reasons for it.* Ask yourself why you are angry, what triggered your emotion, when your anger began, and what deeper emotions or prior experiences are connected to it.
- *Share your feelings and perceptions nonjudgmentally.* Drop all the self-justifications, defenses, stories of wrongdoing, accusations, and judgments you are using to support your anger. Avoid statements such as "you are wrong" and clearly indicate what the other person *did* that caused you to become angry. Use "I" statements, report your feelings constructively, and identify what triggered your emotions.
- *Ask questions to discover whether your perceptions are accurate.* Without making judgments or fixing blame, ask questions to find out more about what happened so you can get to the bottom of what caused your anger. Ask if the other person meant to treat you disrespectfully and, if so, why.

- *Focus on solving the problem rather than blaming others for it.* Define the problem as an "it" rather than a "you." Brainstorm possible solutions with your opponent. Take a problem-solving approach to the underlying reasons for your emotional response to the conflict.

- *Avoid responding defensively.* Do not fall into the trap of defending your behavior. Consider the possibility that you may have been wrong or that you and your opponent may both be right and wrong at the same time. Explore these possibilities openly. At the very least, if the other person does not understand, recognize that you did not communicate your feelings skillfully.

- *Ask clarifying questions.* Ask the other person—keeping your own tone nondefensive and avoiding hostility—to clarify what was meant. Ask if your assumptions about what was said or done are correct and allow the person to explain. Listen more carefully if you were not correct the first time, summarize, and ask if you are correct.

- *Clarify your expectations.* State specifically and in detail what you expect and why. If the other person cannot meet your expectations, you can always negotiate more realistic expectations so he or she will be clearer next time about what you really want.

- *Take a time-out.* Step away from the interaction for a few moments to reflect on whether it is getting out of hand. Determine whether it is possible to say the same things in a way that the other person can hear.

- *Ask for help.* Ask a third person to mediate or facilitate your communication. People are often more polite when company comes to dinner.

- *Apologize and start over.* An apology is merely a declaration of responsibility for whatever is not working, along with a request for improvement. It is an effort to overcome impasse and return to collaboration and problem solving by overcoming the arrogance of anger with humility.

As you consider these methods and possible ways of using them in your conflicts, notice which ones are the hardest to swallow. The ones where you balk may require more long-term focus and dedicated effort. The last method listed, apologizing and starting over, takes considerable skill. What would it take for you to apologize to the other person in your conflict? What do you think would happen if you did? Consider the following alternative ways of doing so.

Alternative Ways of Apologizing

A little apology can go a long way. Often the best way of defusing anger is to apologize for any misunderstandings or miscommunications that occurred and for any discomfort your opponent may have experienced as a result of your anger. An apology does not have to mean you were wrong or a bad person. It can mean you understand what the other person experienced and are sorry for whatever you may have done that contributed to his or her pain or discomfort.

An apology is simply a way of saying, "I value our relationship more than I value being right." An apology signifies a willingness to take responsibility for your behavior and what you contributed to the conflict. Your acknowledgment of responsibility will encourage your adversary to follow suit, which may lead to a resolution of the dispute and a melting away of the anger that kept it going.

Here are a number of different ways of apologizing, together with representative phrases from which you can choose:

- *Make your regrets about what happened completely clear.* "I am very, very sorry for what I did to cause the problem." Include specifics.
- *Take full responsibility for what happened.* "It was totally my fault."
- *Specify the behaviors that were wrong or offensive.* "I really apologize for having . . ." Again, be specific but neutral. "I'm sorry I

embarrassed you in front of your staff" is a statement that works; "I'm sorry I let everybody see what a horse's ass you are" does not.

- *Focus on the events and results that you regret.* "I'm sorry you weren't told about this in advance. It must have upset you."
- *Indicate your understanding that there was an alternative.* "I should have handled it differently."
- *Acknowledge the feelings that resulted.* "I'm sorry for the pain this must have caused you."
- *Ask for forgiveness, and wait until you receive it.* "Can you forgive me?"
- *Indicate what you could have done to prevent the problem.* "I wish I'd spoken to you before this happened."
- *Recognize the positive results of the error.* "This has been a real learning experience for me."
- *Make good on your promises quickly so the other party will see an immediate result.* "I will see that your name is put on the distribution list today so this doesn't happen again."
- *Ask what they need from you.* "What can I do to make it up to you?"
- *Negotiate an agreement for future forgiveness.* "What would it take for you to forgive me?"

Once you have chosen a method, consider why you chose it over the others. Then rate it on a scale of one to ten, with ten being the highest in authenticity, humility, and forgiveness. If you did not choose an apology that was a ten, ask yourself why it is so difficult for you to make an apology that is strong and unambiguous and what it would take to make it a ten.

The only way out of an intense emotion is through it. By running away or suppressing our emotions, we create internal knots that sap our energies, keep us focused on the past, and diminish our capacity to live in the present and plan for the future. We then get locked into behaviors we do not like and are unable to transcend, and become stuck in impasse.

The primary purpose of working through our emotions is not to settle or resolve them, but to accept, acknowledge, integrate, and thereby transcend them. Genuine transcendence comes when we own our emotions and, by owning them, simultaneously invite them to become our teachers and release ourselves from their iron grip.

Transcendence means no longer being subservient to our emotions, but integrating them into a coherent, constructive part of who we are. It means using our emotions to expand our awareness and the awareness of others. It means applying our emotions, in conjunction with logic and analysis, to assist us in solving our problems. Fundamentally, it means overcoming, rising above, and becoming greater than the sum of our problems.

As Milton Glaser has eloquently written, transcendence is the primary task we are each given in life: "All life is about transcendence. If you're ugly you have to transcend your ugliness; if you're beautiful you have to transcend your beauty; if you're poor you have to transcend your poverty; if you're rich you have to transcend your wealth. . . . You get nothing at birth except things to transcend."

If you want to learn to transcend your emotions, realize life's lessons, improve your skills, solve your problems, and take on a more advanced level of conflict, you will need to release yourself from the grip of intense, negative emotions. Once you have become free of their fiery control, you can use them to probe more deeply beneath the surface of your conflicts and, in the process, uncover their hidden meanings—as you will discover in the next strategy.

Strategy Four

Search Beneath the Surface
for Hidden Meaning

An autobiography is the truest of all books, for
while it inevitably consists mainly of extinctions of
the truth, shirkings of the truth, partial revealments
of the truth, with hardly an instance of plain straight
truth, the remorseless truth is there, between the
lines.

—*Mark Twain*

Resolving conflict is a bit like peering beneath the surface of the ocean to imagine the size and shape of an iceberg, most of which cannot be seen; or unearthing an archeological treasure and painstakingly brushing away the surface to reveal deeper layers that have lain hidden under centuries of dust and mud; or reading an autobiography, as Twain describes, in which we are able to find the truth, not primarily in but between the lines, hidden well beneath the surface of what is being said and done.

We rarely take time to search out or excavate these deeper truths in our conflicts, mostly because our attention is concentrated on the mistakes and misdeeds of our opponents or on our own victimization and emotional upheaval. Yet the center and core of our conflicts, what they really mean to us, are far more profound and important than the relatively superficial issues we are passionately arguing and debating over. In conflict resolution, the deeper we look, the more there is we can discover.

There is a vast difference in any conflict between what appears on the surface and what lies hidden beneath it, what we speak about publicly and what we secretly think or feel, the issues we openly address and those we conceal or avoid. And it is less the superficial, surface, openly argued-over issues than the deeper, more mysterious, hidden ones we rarely discuss that have the power to unlock our conflicts and catalyze our transformations.

When we search below the surface to discover the true source and center of our conflicts, when we finally understand how and why they happened, when we are able to listen to our opponents empathetically and see them as human beings, our conflicts begin to open up like flowers, revealing their hidden truths and allowing us to resolve and break free of their grip.

For example, few of us take the time before responding to accusations or criticisms to understand the emotions and experiences that must have fueled them or to search beneath their surface for what our opponent must have actually meant. More often, we launch a defense or counterattack that, by its force and outward direction, blocks us from understanding how and why the dispute happened and what we might have done to resolve it.

When we become highly irritated over trivial issues, such as when a manager blames us for making a mistake, it is a clear indication that we are actually concerned about something far more consequential, such as the distrust or disrespect communicated by the way the mistake was described. In actuality, we may be responsible for the error, yet respond defensively because our manager is being hypercritical or disrespectful, or has asked us to do something we feel is demeaning, or failed to ask for our version of what happened before blaming us.

On the other hand, our manager may actually be responsible for the error yet feel we are being dishonest or disrespectful by denying any responsibility for what happened, humiliated because we are not listening, or be too embarrassed to admit having made a mistake. Or we may both be responsible, yet remind each other of difficult family members, or trigger memories of similar unresolved disputes in the past, or be acting in ways that make each other angry or uncomfortable.

Regardless of which of these versions is true, we will have become involved in an argument over a relatively superficial issue and missed an opportunity to engage our manager in an open, honest conversation over more fundamental issues. Our arguments may seem silly even to us because we know the issues we are arguing over are petty, superficial, and pointless compared with what is really bothering us that neither of us is talking about.

What is usually at stake when we are in conflict is not just a simple mistake, or a few dirty coffee cups, or who gets what kind of office space to work in. Rather, it is whether we are being treated fairly and respectfully; whether we are able to trust our opponents; whether we are acting defensively or aggressively; whether it is possible for us to have an open, honest, empathetic, collaborative relationship with each other; and similar issues.

Yet what is also at stake in our conflicts is our own capacity for listening, learning, and growth; our ability to treat our opponents empathetically with complete integrity and unconditional respect; our level of skill in responding to other people's difficult behaviors; and the possibility that we might use our conflicts to transform our personal and organizational lives and transcend the conditions that gave rise to them.

The Iceberg of Conflict

One way of understanding the hidden layers and complexities of what lies beneath the surface of our conflicts is through the metaphor of the iceberg, which we have depicted in the following chart.

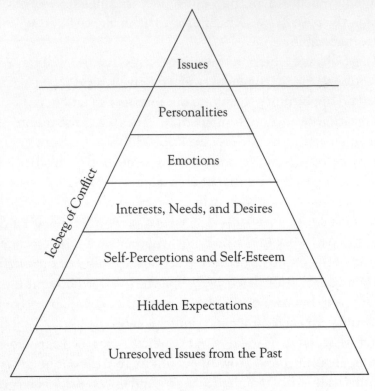

Awareness of Interconnection

Each deeper layer of the iceberg of conflict represents something that does not appear on its surface, yet adds weight, immobility, and hidden meaning to our arguments when we are in conflict. Beneath the iceberg, there is an "awareness of interconnection," meaning that we all have the capacity, when we go deep enough and do not become stuck on the surface, to experience genuine empathy and awareness of our interconnection with each other—including the person who is upsetting us.

We were recently asked to mediate a dispute at a university in which Isabel, a faculty member, claimed she was being sexually harassed by Miguel, her department chair. Isabel was highly respected by the president and provost of the school and was valued for making significant contributions to the academic program, and Miguel was respected as a distinguished faculty member and responsible department chair.

Everyone was perplexed by Isabel's repeated insistence that Miguel was stalking her, spying on her, and harassing her. We first met with Isabel alone to learn more about her experiences and discovered that she was not accusing Miguel of any of the usual sexual harassment invasions that involve touching, offensive language, or suggestive displays, but of watching her, standing outside the door of her classroom, and making her feel uncomfortable in faculty meetings.

When we met with Miguel, he was not only perplexed by her accusations but angry. He explained that of course he sometimes stood outside the door to her classroom because his office was right there, and he would meet students at the door when they came to see him. He felt he had not treated Isabel differently than other faculty members, although he acknowledged that he had not scheduled her classes for the time slot she requested and knew she was unhappy about it.

As the seriousness of the allegations and intensity of their emotions did not seem to match the facts, it became clear to us that we were seeing only the tip of an iceberg, and decided that our only recourse was to probe beneath the surface to uncover the hidden layers of their conflict. To pursue this strategy, we asked Isabel and Miguel to meet with us in a mediation session in which we would discuss the problem and search for solutions.

In our first joint session, we discovered that they had been colleagues during the early days of forming the department when there were few other faculty members around. They had worked closely together, and their friendship had been important to them. As the department grew, the faculty were asked to give each other peer evaluations.

Miguel was concerned about Isabel's habit of missing classes, arriving late, and not submitting student grades in sufficient time to meet university deadlines. He invited Isabel to lunch to discuss his concerns with her before putting them on paper in an "official" peer evaluation. True to form, she failed to show up, leaving him fuming and waiting at a restaurant for several hours. In response, he submitted his evaluation without discussing it or informing her beforehand, and as a result, it took her two extra years to make tenure.

Isabel, on the other hand, said she had always admired Miguel and looked to him for support, protection, and friendship. When she found he had "betrayed" her in his evaluation, she distanced herself from him and vowed to never trust him again. Five years later, when he became department chair, her distrust escalated, and when he did not give her the class schedule she had requested, feelings of betrayal and abandonment that she had never expressed to him reappeared.

As a result of uncovering these deeper elements in the iceberg of their conflict, Isabel and Miguel were able to recognize the pain they had caused each other and apologize for not having been better communicators. We suggested that they set a new date, have the lunch they missed, and come up with a plan for working together more effectively. They did so and presented a joint proposal at the next faculty meeting in which Isabel publicly withdrew her sexual harassment allegations, Miguel agreed to rotate class schedule assignments, and both indicated their desire to create a more collegial relationship.

A still deeper element in the iceberg was revealed only a year later, after Isabel had completed treatment with a psychotherapist we had recommended. She called to tell us that during therapy she had recalled a childhood experience of being sexually abused by a third-grade teacher who also happened to be named Miguel. As a result of discovering this deeper layer, she became less obsessed with Miguel's comings and goings. While their friendship never returned, their collegiality continued, and their conflicts became more manageable.

To understand the deeper layers of your iceberg and get to an awareness of deeper interconnection, consider a conflict in which you are now engaged. Try to identify the specific issues, problems, and feelings that exist for you at each level of the iceberg. As you probe deeper, notice whether your definition of the conflict changes and how it evolves. You may want to identify additional layers besides the ones we have cited, to reveal what is below the surface for you. Notice any emotions that emerge as you begin to look deeper.

Fear or resistance to these feelings can keep your conflict locked in place and prevent you from reaching deeper levels. Allow yourself to experience these feelings, whatever they are, and identify them so you can understand them and let them go. Try answering the following questions, first for yourself and then for your opponent:

- *Issues:* What issues appear on the surface in your conflict? What issues lie beneath the surface that neither of you are discussing?

- *Personalities:* Are differences between your personalities contributing to misunderstanding and tension? If so, what are they, and how do they operate?

- *Emotions:* What emotions are having an impact on your reactions? How are they doing so? Are you communicating your emotions responsibly, or are you distorting or suppressing them? What emotions is your opponent experiencing?

- *Interests, needs, desires:* How are you proposing to solve the conflict? Why is that your proposal? What deeper concerns are behind your proposal? What do you really want? Why do you want it? What needs or desires, if satisfied, would allow you to feel good about the outcome? Why is that important to you? What does getting what you want have to do with the way you are communicating?

- *Self-perceptions and self-esteem:* How do you feel about yourself and your behavior when you are engaged in conflict? What do you see as your strengths and weaknesses? Is any part of the conflict connected to your sense of self-esteem? If you were completely self-confident, would your opponent's behavior bother you?

- *Hidden expectations:* What are your primary expectations of your opponent? Of yourself? Are your expectations realistic? Have you clearly, openly, and honestly communicated your expectations to your opponent? What would happen if you did? How might you release yourself from your own unrealistic expectations?

- *Unresolved issues from the past:* Does this conflict remind you of anything from your past? Are there any unresolved or unfinished issues from the past that are keeping you locked in this conflict? Why? What would it take for you to let them go?

Notice whether your understanding of your conflict changed as you moved through these different levels and how your feelings about it, yourself, and your opponent might evolve further if you continued to probe them more deeply. Now ask yourself, "How many of my answers to these questions have I shared with my opponent?" If there are any that you have not shared, why have you chosen not to share them? Is there any way you might share them? Is there anyone who could help you do so?

Applying Your Knowledge of the Iceberg

The past is powerfully present in all our conflicts and communications, yet we are hardly objective historians in describing our own conflicts. We frequently do not even know in the beginning what we are angry about, which may have originated in some incident that happened years ago. We may become angry at others when in reality we are frightened, in pain, or trying to protect ourselves. We may be using our conflict to divert attention from some shameful incident in our past or to heal our wounds by inflicting them on others.

These emotional experiences can hypnotize us, making it difficult to know or say what is on our subconscious minds or what lies beneath the surface of our dispute. Instead, we operate semiconsciously when we are in conflict, reacting to unseen forces that are detectable only because our reactions are completely out of proportion to what caused them.

For this reason, it is often difficult to know exactly what is going on below the surface, particularly if you have already become defensive or angry and are operating in a highly emotional, semiconscious state. In your confusion, you can easily become hypnotized and attached to superficial issues. Your best option then is to listen to your own inner truth and be willing to reveal these deeper issues to your opponent. By revealing yourself, you invite similar behavior in return and can thereby break the conflict system.

Even then, you may not succeed. Each of us is so well defended that the information needed to resolve the conflict may be unknown or unavailable, and you cannot describe what you do not know. You may have hidden this information even from yourself because it is connected to some highly charged issue or unresolved conflict from the past that you do not want to face. You may think you are in touch with what is going on, yet be completely offtrack. The only way you can know for sure is by breaking the hypnosis, getting below the surface, and opening a deeper conversation with your opponent.

Picture a conversation, however difficult, in which you decide to share your deeper thoughts and insights with your opponent. Practice both parts of the conversation in your own mind, or with a colleague, or write them down on paper. Notice any shifts in your feelings as you envision each part of the conversation, and imagine how the other person might respond. After rehearsing, try it in reality, and see how close the actual conversation gets to the way you imagined it.

Most people who are stuck in conflict have never met with their opponents or had an open, honest discussion—even of the superficial issues in their dispute, let alone the deeper issues that are keeping them at impasse. When we ask people why they have not communicated important information about the deeper levels of their conflict to their opponents, they often say it is because their opponent is unwilling to listen, would not be interested in the information, or is untrustworthy. We then ask how they can know their opponent will not listen or is uninterested or untrustworthy if they are unwilling to speak.

We may also ask whether they are withholding important information about the conflict, not because of who their opponent is, but because of their own fear of being vulnerable in the presence of someone they do not trust. Most often, it is ourselves we are protecting by keeping our conversations superficial, either because we are afraid of being vulnerable in our opponent's presence or because we know in our hearts that what we reveal could change everything, including how we define ourselves and others.

Yet, at a still deeper level, this kind of honesty and openness is precisely what we most want and need. We cover our fear and vulnerability with rationalizations of lack of interest or lack of trust, but in the end, deprive ourselves of the opportunity to have an authentic, honest communication with someone who is probably as afraid of being vulnerable as we are.

Consider also, how will they ever begin to listen or become interested or trustworthy, if we do not provide them with real information that will help them understand who we are and why we are upset?

Getting to the real issues has to start with someone, and it might as well be you because you are the only one whose actions you can control. When you do so, the other person will usually start to listen, become interested, and behave in a more trustworthy way. If they do not, at least you will feel better and become more self-confident because you will know you have acted with integrity and courage.

Steps to Get Below the Surface

Novelist Ursula Hegi chronicled the rise of fascism by detailing daily life in a small village in Germany before and during World War II in her novel, *Stones from the River,* in which she describes the difficulty of telling the truth when silence is the norm: "It took courage for the few, who would preserve the texture of the truth, not to let its fibers slip beneath the web of silence and collusion which people—often with the best of intentions—spun to sustain and protect one another."

How do we break this web of silence and collusion to discover what is beneath the surface when everyone is behaving emotionally and no one is willing to risk honestly discussing what is going on? Here are some ways of getting below the surface of your conflicts:

- Start by focusing on yourself and understanding more about your own iceberg of conflict.

- Use curiosity, open-ended questions, and active, empathetic, and responsive listening as probes to take you beneath the surface.

- Take a risk by bringing a deep level of emotional honesty and vulnerability to what you see, hear, and observe, recognizing that the more honest and vulnerable you are with yourself, the deeper you will be able to go with others.

- Be willing to accept whatever you find beneath the surface without shame, anger, or judgment.

As you gain more perspective on your own subterranean issues, along with those of your opponent and the culture in your organization, you will become more confident and skillful and feel ready to take the next step: which is to ask questions of your opponent so you can move together to address the issues that lie below the surface of your conflict.

A simple way of doing this is to become curious and willing to ask naive, honest, even silly questions—the kind that three-year-olds ask. You have probably been trained to avoid asking questions that could make you appear stupid or that seem to have obvious answers, but these are often the most powerful questions, and posing them can dramatically alter your conflict.

We suggest that you not censor yourself, but let your questions flow, with only one caution: a probing, attacking, prying style of questioning will communicate not curiosity but a closed mind and will prove counterproductive. Begin by asking permission; use a gentle, respectful, empathetic approach; ask questions you would like to be asked by your opponent; and listen actively and nonjudgmentally to the answers. Invite your opponent to join you in exploring deeper, underlying issues; welcome the resulting insights, and thank your opponent for his or her responses.

Here are some questions you can ask to deepen the dialogue and turn your opponent's attention toward solutions. These questions can be asked by managers or employees, teachers or principals, parents or children, neighbors or officials, and anyone who wants to get below the surface of a conflict:

- "What do you think I did or failed to do that contributed to the conflict?"
- "Can you give me a specific example?"
- "How did you feel when I did that?"
- "Can you tell me more what bothered you about what I did?"
- "What do you think you did or failed to do that contributed to the conflict?"
- "Would you like to know how that made me feel?"
- "What did you mean when you said . . . ?"
- "Why does what I said create a problem for you?"
- "What is the worst part of what happened for you?"
- "Why don't you tell me about your experience and I'll listen to you, then I'll tell you about mine."
- "I hope you can hear what I'm saying without getting upset or angry or confused. Will you let me know if what I say starts to bother you so I can communicate with you better?"
- "If you had it all to do over again, what would you do differently?" "Why?"

- "Would you be willing to start over again right now and do it differently?"
- "What is most important to you in solving this problem?"
- "What would you suggest I do to solve my part of the problem?"
- "Can you think of any solutions that might be acceptable to both of us?"
- "What would it take for you to let go of this conflict and feel the issues have really been completely resolved?"
- "How would you like me to communicate with you in the future if there are any more problems?" "What should I say if I experience a problem?"
- "Would you be interested in hearing how I would like you to communicate with me in the future?"
- "What kind of relationship would you like to have with me?"
- "How would you like this conversation to end?" "Why?"
- "What can we do to make our next conversation go more smoothly?"

Notice that each of these questions allows you and your opponent to become more honest and authentic with each other, to search further beneath the surface of your conflict for its deeper meanings, to share responsibility for having caused it, and to move toward joint responsibility for resolving it.

Discovering the Invisible

One of the side effects of not searching beneath the surface of your conflicts, especially in conflict-avoidant organizations, is that not only can you become hypnotized and stuck in conversations over relatively superficial issues, but that by continually avoiding communications about deeper issues, you can learn to ignore them, so after a while they become invisible.

Then later, when you are locked in conflict, you may actually hear and see only what supports your position in the conflict and ignore everything else, as though it were invisible or nonexistent. You may even pretend the other person does not exist and look right through them, as if you were passing a stranger in the street. This lack of awareness of what we call "invisibles" occurs in small ways in everyone's conflicts, organizational cultures, and daily work lives.

As an illustration, right now take your eyes off the page and take a moment to look at the things that are around you, then return and read further. What did you see? Perhaps you saw a table and chairs, a desk and telephone, or grass and trees. But here are some things you may not have noticed, a set of elements, forces, and connections that are largely invisible, yet nonetheless link you to your environment, your opponents, and your conflicts:

- *Empty space:* the open spaces around you that allow you to move freely, the spaces between your words that allow their meaning to be understood, and the emptiness in your mind that allows you to hear your opponent
- *Processes:* the process of reading in which you are engaged right now or the process of communication or negotiation with your opponent
- *Relationships:* the relationship between you and the subject matter of this book or between you and your partner in conflict
- *Culture:* the myths, expectations, and largely unspoken assumptions that define how we speak, dress, and interact with each other; how we succeed or fail; and whether we avoid, become aggressive, or try to resolve our conflicts
- *Emotions:* the pleasure of reading or the fear of searching below the surface of your conflict or of trying out some of the ideas we are suggesting
- *Ideas:* the idea that something might exist in a room and yet be invisible or that there may be more to your conflict than proving you were right and your opponent was wrong

- *Intentions:* the intention to read or not let anyone get away with treating you this way, to resolve your conflict, or to become a better communicator
- *Expectations:* the expectation that this book will be useful, that the other person will listen to you calmly, or that they will not be receptive
- *Symbolic meanings:* the hidden meanings you associate with the word "invisible," with what your opponent did or said, or with being in conflict
- *Values:* the value of respect or honesty in communications, of aggression in responding to someone's insults, or of collaboration in solving problems
- *Histories:* the past associations you have with invisible issues or the personal, family, and organizational histories associated with your conflict
- *Opportunities:* the opportunity to try out new techniques in your conflict that might lead in a new direction
- *Time:* the time that passes as you read this page; your memory of the past, vision of the future, or sense of the present; and the influence these have on your conflict and communications
- *Changes:* the changes that have taken place in you since you started reading this passage, since the conflict began, or since you started thinking about what you could do to communicate with your opponent

None of these elements is visible, yet each is present wherever you are and has a powerful influence on your life and conflicts. You probably behave as though many of them are not really there, even when their impact leaves an identifiable mark. So how can you enter the invisible world where these forces are created, shaped, and resolved? Here is an example of how we located an invisible issue and used it to unlock a conflict.

Sally was vice president in charge of programs, and Ted was vice president in charge of operations for a large hi-tech company. They were embroiled in a bitter conflict that was threatening to cause the company to lose customers. In interviews with us, they blamed each other for starting the conflict, as did the employees who worked for them. Each group identified the other group as the source of the problem, causing communication between the groups to freeze and the entire organization to become polarized.

Sally felt she was undervalued by the president of the company, had little or no voice in executive decisions, and was constantly stuck with the responsibility of making Ted's bad operational decisions work. Ted felt he was losing the president's favor, was not respected or trusted by Sally, and that his only recourse was to resist or sabotage Sally, who was his main competitor for the president's attention. Each was convinced that they were completely right and the other one was completely wrong.

We began our intervention by asking them about their family backgrounds. Sally said she was the youngest girl in a family with three older brothers, and Ted said he was the oldest boy in a family with three younger sisters. We asked them to describe what it was like growing up in their families, and they suddenly realized they were reenacting ancient sibling rivalries and behaving like children who were competing for the attention of their parents.

We told them that in our interview with the president, he had agreed with them and told us he felt they were behaving like little children and that he was considering firing both of them. We also told them we had asked the president whether he felt he had been playing favorites, and he admitted that he had been rewarding Sally and Ted for their hyperaggressive, competitive behavior and would stop doing so in the future.

As a result, Sally and Ted agreed not to personalize each other's behavior and to act like they were members of the same organizational family. They agreed to meet once a week, discuss what could have worked better the week before, and plan for the week ahead. Once they began discussing their ongoing issues, the conflict ceased, they rapidly reached a number of side agreements on how they could support each other, and went together to thank the president for no longer playing favorites.

The president agreed to include Sally on the executive decision-making team and reassured Ted of the vital role he was playing in the organization. He told them he was thrilled that they were now getting along, would treat them fairly in the future, and told them how impressed he was that they were taking the initiative to resolve their conflicts. While Sally and Ted continued to have disagreements, they began treating each other as allies and were able to contain their conflicts and see them as a source of creative energy.

Using Empathy and Honesty to Probe the Iceberg

Empathy is one of the most powerful methods available for resolving conflicts. With empathy, we are able to access deeper layers of the iceberg; develop an "awareness of interconnection" with our opponent; and realize that we all share a common set of emotions, interests, issues, and perceptions. With empathy, we discover that we can all understand and identify with each other, even when we differ in languages, cultures, and personalities.

Empathy is a skill you can exercise and improve in all your interactions, although it is not as easy as it may appear. To start with, you need to give up all the negative characterizations and judgments you have formed about your opponent. Judgments are defenses against empathy. They merely convince us that we already know the truth and consequently do not have to ask any more questions.

To exercise empathy, we need to be able to hold two opposing ideas at the same time. First, we need to recognize that our opponent is a separate, unique, complex individual whose ideas, feelings, and experiences we can never fully know or understand. Second, we need to try to walk a while in our opponent's shoes; understand his or her ideas, feelings, and experiences; and realize that we share an enormously rich set of human frailties, strengths, desires, and expectations.

Empathy is different from sympathy, which is feeling sorry for someone. In sympathy, we are absorbed in the other person's feelings whereas, in empathy, we are using our own feelings to understand what the other person *might* be feeling, then asking a question to find out whether we are on the right track. In a strange way, sympathy ignores the real person and, by offering consolation to someone as a victim, places him or her in a power-down position.

Empathy treats other people as separate individuals who are entitled to their own feelings, ideas, and conflict experiences and, in that respect, is equal to us. In sympathy, there is often a kind of consensual boundary violation that paradoxically leaves the "victim" feeling less secure than before. There is no violation of emotional boundaries in empathy, which leaves other people feeling more secure than before because they feel respected as unique individuals.

Most of us have engaged in role-playing at some point during our work lives. Empathy is a part of all role-playing and acting experiences in which, by vividly imagining someone else's life, we start to feel what it might be like to actually be in their shoes. While we know we are pretending, the emotions we feel still ring true. They feel genuine—and are often accurate for the person whose experience we are role-playing. To find out, we need to ask a question based on what we would be feeling if we were in experiencing the same problems.

One reason you may find yourself at an impasse in your conflict is that you are unable to empathize with your opponent or imagine what it might be like for someone to be on the receiving end of your communications and behavior. One way of getting unstuck is to reach out to your opponent with understanding and empathy. It is possible, for example, to use role-play to understand how your opponent might feel, then ask a question to find out if your empathy is accurate, and imagine how you might build a bridge between you.

Empathy takes us deeper into ourselves to find the internal places where we recognize and understand each other. We are all capable of feeling anger, fear, and pain and can discern what lies beneath the surface of the conflict for our opponent by considering what would lie beneath the surface for us.

The best way to practice empathy is to consistently follow a simple golden rule: speak and act as though *you* were the one who is about to hear what you are about to say, or experience what you are about to do, and are not some faceless, aberrant, misunderstood opponent.

Creating Empathy Through Role-Reversing Dialogue

To practice empathy as a strategy in resolving your conflicts, try the following exercise. Get a sheet of paper and a pen or pencil, pick someone with whom you are in conflict, and complete the following steps either alone or together. You can also do this exercise orally by shifting from one chair to another and saying what you think the other person might say or role-playing your opponent's part in the conflict and asking a friend to role-play you. Then,

1. Write down or state orally what you would most like to say to this person.

2. Write down or state what you would say back if you were the other person.

3. Write or state your response to what "they" wrote or said to you.

4. Write or state their response back.

5. Now consider what it would take to bridge these two sets of statements and make them into one. Write or state a single, internally consistent, composite version that captures the essence of both.

Look at what you wrote or said, first to see whether you honestly expressed both sides of the conflict and presented them equally. If not, start over again. If so, did you learn anything you did not know before you started about what the other person might have felt or thought? To make the exercise more powerful, try it in real life with your opponent. You might even suggest that your opponent take your side in the argument for a few minutes while you argue their position, just to see what it feels like to be on the other side.

In organizations, you may want to do a "reverse role-play" and temporarily redistribute roles, titles, or positions in a team or organizational hierarchy or sides in a dispute. Afterward, debrief the participants to see what everyone learned. The results can be profound, and we have found that participants in this exercise often come away with lasting empathy for each other's roles.

While consulting with an information technology (IT) organization, we observed that staff members were engaged in a number of conflicts with a business unit over what they perceived as unrealistic demands while the business unit complained about the IT bureaucracy, unreasonable rejection of their requests for help, poor quality of customer service, and chronic miscommunication.

We asked both groups to participate in a strategic planning session where it was agreed that some staff members would exchange work locations to better understand the conditions in each other's offices. In each business unit, one person was assigned to work in an IT office, and one IT person was assigned to each business unit team to act as a liaison.

After a year, their conflicts were over, and both groups of employees who had changed locations asked to remain where they were so they could continue coordinating the delivery of services. As their empathy increased, they were able to develop an integrated strategic vision for the company as a whole that reduced conflicts and improved service for other customers.

The Connection Between Empathy and Honesty

Empathy alone is not enough to routinely produce resolution. Once we have successfully placed ourselves in another person's shoes and discovered something about what may be important to them, we need to have the courage to honestly communicate what we have learned. Empathy that is not combined with honesty tends to become sentimental, cowardly, and ineffectual, while honesty that is not tempered with empathy tends to become brutal, aggressive, and excessively judgmental.

If empathy consists of discovering the other person within ourselves, honesty consists of communicating what we discover so the other person can reach a similar level of self-understanding. This can be done through a process of asking questions and offering responses. Honesty means not turning away from what we see, but speaking openly, fearlessly, yet empathetically about it so others can learn the lessons that lie hidden in what they have *not* communicated.

In this way, empathy and honesty are always intertwined. To reach a deeper level of honesty and successfully communicate what you believe is taking place beneath the surface of our conflict, you will require a deeper and more profound level of empathy. As you reach new levels of empathy, you will require still deeper levels of honesty.

Honest communication is not easy. Most of us have learned to "play it safe" at work. You or your opponent may even be participating in a "conspiracy of silence" based on an unspoken agreement to communicate superficially and avoid honestly saying what is true for yourself or your colleagues. If so, it would be easy for you to guard your communications, withhold critical information, and mistake your internal conflicts for conflicts with others.

Worse, by not being honest, you are probably cheating yourself, your opponent, and the organization out of opportunities for learning and improving by being required to honestly confront a deeper set of problems and recognize and accept what you actually think and feel.

There are high risks associated with the use of honesty as a conflict strategy. Yet honesty is what differentiates conflict *resolution* from conflict suppression and settlement. Suppression takes place when we are afraid to tell or hear the truth. Settlement occurs when we want to avoid addressing issues that lie beneath the surface of our conflict. Resolution, on the other hand, requires us to bring out into the open the issues that are actually driving our dispute and work our way through them.

While honesty can give people the impression that we are escalating or intensifying the conflict, it is difficult to resolve the hidden reasons for a dispute without being open and honest. Indeed, to settle our dispute without reaching the underlying reasons for it; to maintain distance through denial, defensiveness, and self-justification rather than risk honest self-examination; and to allow the downward spiral of rage and shame to block our ability to communicate authentically is to settle for meaningless, safe, static, shallow relationships.

Yet, when we are able to be deeply honest and empathetic with our opponents, we simultaneously become more authentic within ourselves and encourage our opponents to participate in open and honest communications that can lead to problem solving. In the end, we are able to live more comfortably with ourselves and improve the quality of our work lives only by addressing the issues that are important to us and learning from our conflicts.

By discouraging honesty, we run the risk of creating organizational cultures that keep us in impasse and encourage communications that are civil, superficial, and characterized by meaningless politeness. This is why the greater risk is *not* being honest, as opposed to the lesser risk we face when we discuss our conflicts openly and engage in conversations that can lead to increased understanding, resolution, and change.

Real Honesty Is Real Difficult

Real honesty is difficult and can easily backfire. By a single comment, we can lose the empathetic connection we need to create deep listening in our opponent. We can escalate the conflict to the point that it becomes more difficult to resolve. We can even convince ourselves that we are being honest when we are actually being brutal or aggressive.

Real honesty is difficult primarily because we want to be kind more than we want to be honest, because we want to protect ourselves and each other from the harshness of the truth, and because we think honesty will make us more vulnerable to our opponents or cause people in power to dislike us and negatively impact our organizational career.

It is especially difficult for us to be honest with those we dislike or who dislike us. This is because superficiality, silence, secrets, and lies seem less risky and more powerful to us than vulnerability, honesty, shared responsibility, and open communication. Aggression and self-defense give an appearance of honesty and are more readily accepted in organizational environments because they are instinctual, seemingly strong, grounded in distrust, and difficult to control.

Yet honesty requires vulnerability and self-honesty, which are the opposites of aggression and self-defense. Moreover, aggression and self-defense are weaker than honesty because they are self-protective and based on a falsehood, which is that our opponents are actually out to get us, as opposed to simply looking out for themselves. In truth, our opponents are merely using aggression and self-defense as tactics to avoid being vulnerable with us!

When we hide our true thoughts and feelings from others, we condemn ourselves to silent suffering and self-doubt. In this state, we may repress our most vulnerable thoughts and feelings because we feel they are too frightening or powerful to discuss openly. Or we may externalize them, see them as characterizing our opponents, and experience them from the outside-in rather than the inside-out. At the same time, our need for self-protection, sympathy, and uncritical support from others makes us less willing to take responsibility for our aggressive or defensive actions and further reduces our self-esteem.

Real honesty is also difficult because we want to avoid being blamed for the conflict and to make ourselves appear good and right by making others appear bad and wrong. Yet the negative consequences we direct at others ultimately and inevitably return to us.

If we make our opponent lose, feel bad, or accept blame for what went wrong, our relationship and communication will suffer as a result, and everyone will pay a price.

It is also dangerous to speak honestly because to do so is to accept the possibility that the other person will speak with equal honesty to us. Hence, we are reduced to silence, banality, or nonengagement, fueled in part by a fear that honesty will not be held in check by the other side and that we either lack the willingness to be honest with ourselves or sense that we do not have the skills to manage the chain reaction of anger that could cause our conversation to spiral out of control.

There is a deeper reason honesty is dangerous, which arises when we take deliberate steps to protect ourselves from hearing the truth because we know that it is true and that serious life consequences will occur as a result. We suspect that these consequences could force us to change our behaviors, or redefine our lives and identities, and compel us to leave the comfortable—albeit dysfunctional—ruts we have created for ourselves. We know intuitively that honesty is a precondition for transformation.

Rationalizations for Not Being Honest

Although we are not always honest, we have all become highly skilled at rationalizing our behavior. Each of us can easily present a list of perfectly good reasons for avoiding honest communications with bosses, colleagues, family, and friends, not to mention our opponents in conflict. As a result, entire organizations find that they have become committed to cultural norms that permit dishonesty and encourage self-serving communications.

For example, in one organization with which we worked, the staff were so focused on customer sales that they treated each other with unflagging, superficial, jovial banalities and never communicated their deeper truths. They asked us to help them figure out why, despite their superficial camaraderie, there was such low morale in the organization.

As the conflicts they had kept beneath the surface began to emerge, they realized that suppressing honest communication does not make it disappear, but actually makes it more powerful and at the same time more difficult to resolve. By creating happy-face, have-a-nice-day norms for communication, they had prevented themselves from addressing issues that have to be addressed in order to solve problems, improve morale, and ensure continued growth.

Here are some of the rationalizations the employees in this organization used to justify keeping their communications superficial and not risking honest dialogue. As you read this list, notice the ones you use when you want to hide honest feelings from your opponent or protect yourself from the risk of open and honest interactions.

- "I don't want to hurt their feelings."
- "They will misinterpret what I say."
- "They won't be receptive."
- "It will put our relationship at risk."
- "I will become open to retaliation or counterattack if I open up."
- "There's nothing in it for me because we can settle our issues without it."
- "It could escalate, and I should not increase the conflict."
- "I will be out on a limb and won't be supported."
- "Nothing will change anyway."
- "I always take the risks, and this time it's their turn."
- "In the past, I haven't found it useful."
- "I could lose my job or the respect of others."
- "It's not me; they're the ones who are stuck."

As you review this list of rationalizations, consider which of these rationalizations has discouraged you from communicating honestly? Why? Is it possible that you have been using a rationalization to defend yourself against a fear that could be better handled through communication and problem solving? Are your negative conflict

experiences actually a result of being honest or of not being suffi-
ciently empathetic in communicating what you think or feel? Ultimately, where do you think avoidance of honesty will get you? Is
that where you want to be? What impact do you think avoidance
of honesty is having on the organization? What would happen if
you abandoned them? What would it take to do so?

Rationalizations for Being Honest

If you are unwilling to abandon your favorite rationalizations for not
being honest, consider the following set of counter-rationalizations,
which match and negate the ones listed above. These counter-
rationalizations are equally valid, yet may encourage you to communicate more honestly.

- "It's possible for me to communicate honestly without hurting
  anyone's feelings if I do so empathetically."
- "It's possible for me to communicate accurately so there will
  be less possibility of misinterpretation."
- "They can't be receptive unless I give them something to
  receive."
- "Without honesty, there can't be an authentic relationship
  between us."
- "If I act collaboratively, they will find it more difficult to re-
  spond defensively."
- "I increase my own self-esteem and skill as well as their op-
  portunities to change through honest communication."
- "The problem will get worse if I don't communicate honestly."
- "If it escalates, I can use conflict resolution skills or mediation
  to resolve the conflict at a deeper level."
- "If I risk being honest, the other person may take that risk also."
- "Things will begin to change when I communicate honestly."
- "I can't live with myself if I don't speak my own truth."

- "I could improve my job and gain the respect of others."
- "We will both remain stuck unless I do something to end the impasse."

Consider asking a colleague, coach, or mentor in the organization to give you feedback on how honest you are being in your communications. Then consider asking your opponent to be completely honest with you, and respond to any rationalizations offered with counter-rationalizations and a request to be more honest in the future.

Finally, consider using these rationalizations and counter-rationalizations as a checklist to analyze the subtle, invisible messages regarding honesty that are being communicated by your organizational culture. Consider asking your coworkers to identify the rationalizations they hear or use most often, and develop strategies for encouraging more empathetic and honest communication, as described at the end of this chapter.

Taking Responsibility for Our Actions and Inactions

It does not matter how creatively we rationalize not being honest or deny and evade responsibility for the effectiveness of our communications and resolution of our conflicts. None of it could happen, or endure for long, without our active or passive participation. We can obscure but not eliminate the truth: that responsibility for conflict extends not only to those who spoke or acted and *should not* have but to those who did not speak or act and *should* have.

We recognize today that legal responsibility for war crimes extends not only to those who engaged in them but to those who proposed them, profited from them, supported them, defended them, rationalized them, and covered them up. It extends further to those who knew about them and did nothing to prevent them and those who ought to have known but chose to remain silent or ignore them—in other words, to everyone who was conscious and within reach of them. We could say the same about conflict.

The primary reason for empathy and honesty in conflict resolution is that they encourage each of us to become fully responsible for our choices. We can do so simply by asking profound questions, treating our opponents with empathy, giving ourselves permission to be honest, inviting mutual understanding, prompting others to communicate as though they were the ones receiving the information, applauding their willingness to hear difficult truths, modeling being honest with ourselves, and learning to accept, even embrace, the unpleasant things for which we are responsible in our lives.

Taking responsibility for what we have said and done or not said and done in our conflicts forces us to be honest with ourselves and allows us, at the same time, to be honest with others. It encourages us to experience our lives as within our control and to appreciate, learn from, and live with our conflict choices. This extends not only to what we think, say, and do but to who we are and whatever our lives silently stand for.

We work closely with a highly successful mediation project, Centinela Youth Services, in southern California. This program brings young people who have been accused of crimes face-to-face with their victims in mediation. Both sides are encouraged to be honest and empathetic about what happened. Thus, the juvenile offender is asked to accept responsibility and be honest and empathetic by admitting the crime, acknowledging its impact on the victim, and providing restitution. The victim is also asked to accept responsibility and be honest and empathetic by agreeing to mediate; describe the loss; seek fair restitution; and then release, forgive, reconcile, and hopefully redeem the offender.

This program and others like it produce extraordinary results by keeping adolescents out of prison, teaching them to communicate honestly and empathetically about their crimes and to be responsible for what they said and did or failed to say and do. Their recidivism, or rearrest rate, is substantially lower than that of juvenile offenders who have not gone through these programs, primarily because of the honesty, empathy, and responsibility encouraged by the mediation process.

Taking responsibility for your conflict choices starts with acknowledging what you have contributed to it and the pain of what you said and did, or failed to say and do, caused your opponent. Here are several steps you can take to accept greater responsibility in your conflict communications:

- Start by giving yourself an honest appraisal and identifying what you contributed or are responsible for in the conflict.
- Unhook yourself from judgments about other people's personalities and motives, and try to describe their behavior in nonjudgmental terms.
- Do not dismiss other people's critical comments or take them personally, but search for what is true about them.
- Listen to others empathetically, and acknowledge their honest responses.
- Tell the truth yourself. Speak the unspeakable, but in ways others can hear.
- Express a willingness to reassess your own statements, actions, or positions.
- Surface and discuss covert behavior, especially any you may have fostered, accepted, or supported.
- Be unwilling to engage in covert behaviors yourself.
- Search for alternative ways of achieving what both of you want or desire.
- Find honest forms of expression that allow others to listen and save face.
- Help others take baby steps toward honest, empathetic dialogue. Start by asking questions, responding, and acknowledging their contributions.
- Look for ways of forgiving, reconnecting, and reintegrating with your opponent.

By accepting not just 50 but *100* percent responsibility for your conflict choices, you will close the door on the possibility of blaming others. While no one is ever 100 percent responsible for their conflict, making the assumption that you are will magnify what you are able to learn as a result. It will allow you to discover hidden opportunities to correct your mistakes, become more skillful in resolving future conflicts, and free yourself from the feelings and behaviors that led you to impasse.

Making Organizational Cultures More Empathetic and Honest

Most organizational cultures generate rules, rewards, and sanctions that discourage honest communications; suppress intense emotions; and minimize risky, truthful, and authentic dialogue. They usually do so either to protect their internal processes and relationships from unnecessary disruptions and unanticipated changes or to create a positive public image of how the organization operates. While these restrictive cultures may seem to be necessary for success or survival, they add layers of dysfunction, disillusionment, demoralization, and despair to the lives of those who work in these environments.

The smiling faces these dysfunctional corporate cultures present to employees and the public often mask unhappy, repressive, conflict-avoidant realities. Indeed, it is rare in most organizations that employees feel completely free to openly and honestly discuss what is actually going on, especially with those above or below them in the hierarchy or with outsiders, customers, and those with whom they are in conflict.

All organizations generate unspoken informal rules for deciding when it is safe to be honest and when it could cost you your job. In some organizations, these rules contribute to the creation of dishonest, incongruent, unethical organizational cultures that encourage secrecy, covert behaviors, and silence, rewarding them and preventing employees from resolving their conflicts.

On the other hand, by encouraging empathy, honesty, and openness; identifying and calling attention to negative and covert behaviors; clarifying shared values; and encouraging managers and employees to act ethically and responsibly, these same repressive cultures can be transformed and the dysfunctional behaviors they generate discouraged.

We have worked with many individuals who have tried to change their organizational cultures to increase support for empathy and honesty, and these efforts have sometimes succeeded. But there is always an element of risk in these ventures. Culture change requires a concerted and conscious effort on the part of internal allies on all levels of the organization who are willing to stand and be counted and external consultants who are willing to support the development of new norms and the consolidation of new behaviors.

As an illustration, several years ago we worked with the facilities department inside a large Fortune 100 corporation whose leaders wanted to shift their culture from one of fragmentation, isolation, and competition to one of honesty, information sharing, cross-functional collaboration, and team-based, cross-departmental partnerships.

The leadership team initially met to define the characteristics of the new culture, identify the elements that needed to change, and communicate these new expectations, behaviors, and rules to the supervisors, who would have the job of communicating them to the employees and carrying them out. One member of the leadership team sent us this e-mail following their meeting: "After seeing the Leadership Team members interact and then the Supervisory Team discuss the proposed changes, I saw a clear difference. The Supervisors are far more driven and compassionate about what they are doing. I sense this has a lot to do with their commitment and desire to break out of the old mode of doing things. It is my perception that the Leadership Team, at this point, is not as developed and could have a hampering effect on the Supervisory Team's growth."

He got it exactly right, and the identical dynamic was taking place between the supervisors and line employees. Cultural transformation clearly required a leadership team with a clear vision and a strong commitment to making their own behaviors congruent with the new culture. Yet, for the cultural change to succeed and become sustainable, everyone in the organization needed to own the change, participate in defining it, and be willing to implement it in ways that were consistent with what they wanted to create.

In this organization, a strong sense of ownership was needed, not only among the leadership team and the supervisors but also among hourly staff, craftspeople, custodial employees, engineers, and secretaries. If they had been left out of the process, or failed to agree with and support the new behaviors, the leadership team's plans, no matter how brilliant, would have sunk without a trace.

The leadership team soon realized that their initial efforts had been guided by the old culture, which was encouraging hierarchical participation, competitiveness, isolation, divisiveness, fear of change, and tension between departments. They instituted a more honest, empathetic, collaborative approach to the change process in which everyone agreed to participate in transforming the culture by implementing the following collaboratively designed changes:

- Work on eliminating the feeling of boundaries between people, departments, and teams
- Break down preconceived notions of how to act and treat each other
- Recognize the baggage from the past and eliminate it
- Work together, argue, and still go to lunch
- Focus on specifics and not focus too wide
- Have better communications among ourselves, eliminate mixed messages and competition

- Build trust
- Do not keep going around roadblocks or ignoring them; instead, stop and do something about them
- Realize things can change and get rid of the negative
- Know what each person brings and value it
- Unify our division into one group
- Have fun!!!!!

Organizational cultures are essentially *holographic*, suggesting that every piece contains and reproduces the whole. This means that it is impossible to change an isolated element in a culture without also transforming the entire matrix of mutually reinforcing behaviors that interact with each other and give the culture its overall character. This aspect of organizational culture allows it to be transformed by strategically changing even minor, seemingly unimportant parts.

For example, we worked with a woman who had recently been selected to manage a cardboard box factory that was operated primarily by male employees. On the weekend before she began, she came to the factory and installed lace curtains on all the windows on the factory floor. This seems like a small change, but it *dramatically* altered the culture in the factory. She sent a signal that employees were respected. The curtains caused them to notice aesthetics, value their environment, and feel more proud of their workplace, as though they were invited guests in someone's home.

A first step in creating more honest, empathetic organizational cultures consists of inviting everyone in the organization to participate in the change process and asking questions about the elements in their existing culture that weaken honesty and empathy. Using the data from this analysis, it is then possible to introduce new norms, expectations, behaviors, and rewards that will encourage and sustain the new culture.

One way to begin is by conducting an informal "culture audit" in which the old culture is examined and the new elements employees want to introduce are identified. The following initial questions can assist in analyzing the old culture and defining the new one:

- What are the unspoken rules in the culture regarding honesty and empathy?
- How are these rules learned, communicated, and changed?
- When are these behaviors considered appropriate or inappropriate?
- Which behaviors are rewarded? Which are punished?
- What topics can and cannot be discussed?
- When is it considered inappropriate to be honest or empathetic?
- What do people do when there are problems or conflicts?
- Which problems or conflicts are swept under the rug?
- How do people finally end up resolving their conflicts?
- How are intense emotions expressed and responded to?
- How do people respond to difficulties, glitches, and failures?
- What messages do leaders communicate through their behaviors?
- What do people believe about their power to change behaviors?

A second step in creating more honest and empathetic cultures is to reach agreement on a set of shared cultural values. Employees may decide, for example, that their culture should encourage participation and play, increase everyone's ability to be honest about what is happening within and around them, be more open to receiving feedback, or do more to encourage trust.

A third step is to craft a long-term strategy for transforming the culture, including finding creative ways of supporting those who have already begun to be more honest and empathetic and developing processes and techniques that will encourage others to do the same.

A fourth step is to consistently implement and practice the new cultural behaviors and regularly and publicly monitor the change process to make certain it is congruent with the desired changes. It is important for those who consider themselves leaders or change agents to model the values they seek to instill in others, especially during the change process.

A fifth step is to redesign the structures, systems, processes, and relationships, including the rewards and punishments, evaluations and assessments that encourage old culture behaviors or cause people to blindly defend themselves against being more honest and empathetic.

To create meaningful and lasting changes in your organizational culture requires not only considerable clarity about what needs to be changed and a sharp, compelling vision of what needs to be introduced into the new culture. It also requires a great deal of honesty and empathy in the process or the way these changes are identified, agreed upon, and implemented. To do so and to assist you in resolving your conflict generally, it is useful to develop a strategy of separating what matters from what gets in the way, as described in the following strategy.

Separate What Matters from What Gets in the Way

Plantagenet: The truth appears so naked on my side
That any purblind eye may find it out.
Somerset: And on my side it is so well apparell'd
So clear, so shining and so evident
That it will glimmer through a blind man's eye.
—*Shakespeare*, King Henry VI,
Part 1, Act 2, Scene 4

In earlier chapters, we directed your attention toward understanding the culture and context of your conflicts, listening to their deeper meaning, and responding to the emotions that get stirred up by them. Above all, this requires you to move toward your conflicts, your opponents, and yourself.

In this strategy and those that follow, we now focus our energies on finding and implementing creative solutions to your problems. This includes learning to negotiate your differences collaboratively; plan strategically; respond to other people's difficult behaviors; live with paradox and dissent; overcome resistance; engage in committed action; and design organizational systems, structures, and cultures that can successfully implement these strategies and prevent future conflicts before they get out of hand.

This may sound easy, but the first step in creating a strategy for problem solving and committed action to resolve your conflicts consists of separating what is important from what gets in the way of resolution. This includes identifying and letting go of what is keeping you in impasse, including your need to be angry, "win," and be right. In the process, you will discover that what you think of as "The Truth" about your conflict can block you from discovering an even greater truth. But before we take two steps forward into insight and wisdom, we need to take one step back to consider our biases.

The Truth in Conflict

When we are in conflict, there is always at least one thing we share with our opponents: we both know we are right! We assume the truth will be clear and apparent to every unbiased listener, as Shakespeare's Plantagenet and Somerset claimed. Yet our opponents somehow have no difficulty at all in rejecting our ideas, any more than we do in rejecting theirs, despite the fact that we are both thoroughly convinced we are right.

Rather than claim our experience to be The Truth, we need to understand that our experience, while certainly true for *us*, is not necessarily true for anyone else, especially for our opponents. Everyone experiences life differently and therefore perceives different truths. What people see, recognize, and comprehend is always a combination of the truth of what they see, along with the angle of their vision, what they feel and think about what they are experiencing, and the emotional state, personality, and attitude of the person who is looking.

In this way, nonmathematical truths are rarely absolute and invariant, but relative and able to change with small shifts or rotations in the personal frame of reference of the observer and their relationship to what they are observing. Truth is therefore not a single entity but a composite, so that by combining and integrating diverse perspectives, experiences, and personalities, we are able to discover a greater truth than would have been possible with any single truth standing alone.

The idea that our experience is the sole and solitary truth automatically allows us to formulate a *position*, which represents what we want based on our exclusive version of what is true. Understanding that there are multiple truths allows us to shift our focus and identify *interests*, which represent the reasons that underlie and support our positions.

Interests allow us to combine our separate individual truths into a larger combined truth and create a composite perspective that acknowledges both our experiences. When we shift from a framework of single to multiple truths, we also shift our process from one of *debate* over who is right to one of *dialogue* and a creative search for solutions that could satisfy everyone's interests.

For example, we once advised a group of thirty sales representatives at a large commercial bank as they organized into self-managing teams. Before they began to work in teams, everyone was rated monthly on their individual sales performance. These ratings were published throughout the organization, stimulating intense, aggressive, sometimes destructive competition to see who could achieve the highest score.

The newly organized teams wanted to eliminate these individual monthly rating lists and report only team results in order to encourage the transition to teams. But the head of the organization refused and wanted to keep the individual lists in place. In a strategic-planning session, a conflict flared between a woman who spoke in favor of team-based lists and the head of the organization who defended individual reporting. Neither would budge from their position because each was certain they were right.

When we shifted our focus from positions to interests and from debate to dialogue, the team members discovered that the head of the organization wanted individual results reported because he was afraid that otherwise they would use their teams as places where they could slack off, become irresponsible, and blame other team members for their nonperformance. Everyone on the teams was able to understand and acknowledge his legitimate concerns, which allowed them to respond with alternative suggestions.

It also took the manager some time to understand that the reason the teams wanted their results listed as a composite was actually to motivate their members to collaborate—not give themselves room to slack off, become irresponsible, or blame others. They wanted to support each other in making their team efforts succeed and dramatically change the culture of the organization, which included how people would be rewarded, so as to encourage greater collaboration. The head of the organization could then see their goals as legitimate and realize that they all had similar interests at heart.

As a result, the manager and the teams were able to negotiate a compromise in which both sets of results were listed, along with an agreement to assess the sales they produced in the next quarter to see which approach worked best. This decision motivated the teams to produce extraordinary results, and on average, they produced 130 percent of their annual goals in only six months!

By being willing to listen to each other, separate what mattered from what was getting in the way, and acknowledge the truth of the other side's interests, they were able to reach a higher truth that supported the transition to collaboration and teamwork, acknowledged the need to make sure individuals did not slack off, and focused on producing outstanding results.

Another example of the damage caused by being certain of The Truth of your own position occurred when we facilitated a strategic-planning process for the senior staff of the mayor of a large urban city. The mayor's staff and city council were at loggerheads, with each side not only knowing they were right, but convinced that the other side was both mistaken and operating from a hidden agenda.

One staff member expressed the mayor's point of view: "The city council is our main obstacle. They've decided to defeat the mayor's programs so he won't get credit, to the point of being irrational. It's a power struggle." A city council staff member saw it differently: "There is an ideological war between the mayor and the city council. There is an issue of respect also, both politically and in terms of behaviors. We are criticized for not being consensus oriented in our relations with the mayor, but the mayor's office is far more isolationist than the council is. We don't have an independent way to accomplish our goals, and we need each other but they are too arrogant and don't want to work with us."

Everyone in this conflict was frustrated at the inability to reach agreement, so they continued holding on to their positions and refused to acknowledge the other side's point of view. When each group realized it could not achieve what it wanted without the cooperation of the other side, a change began. The mayor's office created a task force and assigned a staff member to work with each council member to build a closer relationship. They agreed to stop acting unilaterally and develop programs in partnership with the council, rather than coming in with fully developed plans and demanding instant approval.

In both these examples, the protagonists were locked in positions and prepared to defend them to the death, if necessary, because they knew they were right. Argumentation and debate solidified each side's stance and prevented them from listening to the truth on the other side or even trying to meet the other side's reasonable and legitimate interests. What was needed in both cases—as in every conflict—was to separate what would be useful in resolving their conflicts from what would not and was getting in the way.

Separating Elements in Conflict to Encourage Resolution

When we are in conflict, we tend to lump the issues that upset us into a mass of indistinguishable complaints. Yet as long as they are intertwined, it is difficult to negotiate, fix, or resolve them. As strange as it may seem, simply creating distinctions or separations between any of the elements in your conflict can produce a significant shift in your ability to approach them constructively.

These separations can transform your attitude toward conflict from passive, reactive, and powerless to self-possessed, proactive, and strategic. They will signal your readiness to transition from focusing on listening and emotional processing to focusing on problem solving and negotiation. With these separations, we are able to break seemingly monolithic issues down into easy-to-handle, bite-sized pieces using a set of uncomplicated tools. In doing so, we more easily discover solutions and increase our opponent's willingness to implement them.

The following "separations" should allow you to see your conflicts more clearly, identify strategies for tackling each issue separately, and make it easier to transform the whole.

- Separate positions from interests
- Separate people from problems
- Separate problems from solutions
- Separate commonalities from differences
- Separate the future from the past
- Separate emotion from negotiation
- Separate process from content
- Separate options from choices
- Separate criteria from selection
- Separate yourself from others

As you separate these aspects or elements of conflict, do so recognizing that, in an ultimate sense, nothing in conflict can be separated from anything else. By focusing on separating things that are actually inseparable, you can lose sight of their underlying unity and what they have in common. The deepest truth is that there is no separation between yourself and the people with whom you are in conflict, other than the illusion that what is separating you is unbridgeable.

When you discover that there are commonalities between you and your opponent and that you can unite elements you had previously thought of as separate, you may begin to see yourself and your opponent as parts of a larger whole. In those moments, you may realize that your conflict is actually an expression of a deeper underlying unity. Yet it is necessary to start with separations in order to come to a point where you can recognize this underlying unity, which is far more difficult to grasp.

While the separations we have listed may seem obvious, there are complexities and subtleties in each, and it is easy to lose sight of them when you are caught in a conflict. To apply them successfully and make the distinctions between them clear, we have provided an analysis of each one, followed by a set of questions to help you clarify your personal separations and unities.

Remember as you proceed that the basic idea is to move beyond simply settling your conflict to resolving the underlying reasons that gave rise to it. If you identify the deeper issues that are involved in your dispute and work through them completely, it will be easier to create solutions that prevent the conflict from resurfacing under a different guise.

Separate Positions from Interests

When we shift from debate to dialogue, not only does our process change, but the substance of our communications changes as well. In debate, we declare positions, whereas in dialogue, we recognize and satisfy interests. Positions are what you want, while interests are indications of why you want it or think the way you do about it. Interests are primarily based on needs, wants, desires, and feelings, while positions are based more on ideas and attitudes.

Roger Fisher and William Ury, in their classic book on collaborative negotiation strategies, *Getting to Yes*, develop the idea of interest-based negotiations. And Ury, in *Getting Past No*, shows how we can use interests to resolve disputes in a collaborative process that keeps people from getting stuck in mutually exclusive, positional arguments.

Here is an example: Imagine that you are meeting in a room with several colleagues in your organization and that some of them want the air-conditioning unit turned off, while others want it turned on. If we assume that the air-conditioning unit can only be on or off, there are only three fundamental bases for resolving this dispute:

1. *Power:* If you resolve the air-conditioning dispute on the basis of power, whether in the form of physical force, coercion, money, status, position, organizing ability, or political connections, each side will be pitted against the other, inevitably producing winners and losers and dividing the group against itself. The most powerful faction will be able to turn the air conditioning on or off at any time, regardless of what the powerless faction wants, permitting them to abuse their power. When accumulated power is used to gain personal advantages or protect a small group's privileges, it inevitably results in corruption, instability, and perceptions of unfairness. These trigger the use of negative forms of power by the powerless in order to prevent these negative outcomes, increase systemic fairness, and get their needs met.

2. *Rights:* If this dispute is resolved on the basis of rights, as through lawsuits, voting, or contractual negotiations, a compromise is likely to result in which the air conditioning is on, for example, from 10 A.M. to noon and off from noon to 5 P.M. There are still winners and losers in rights-based contests, although it is rare that victory and defeat are as absolute as when disputes are resolved using power. Corruption and abuses of power are reduced in severity but continue to exist, along with a new problem that rarely appears with the use of power: namely, bureaucracy. The group remains divided and adversarial, and no one has their interests met completely or is able to resolve the underlying reasons for the dispute.

3. *Interests:* If the same dispute is resolved on the basis of interests, we begin by finding out why people want the air conditioning on or off. If they want it off because they are unable to hear as a result of the noise, we can use a microphone or speak louder. If they want it on because they need fresh air, we can open a window or take a break. If they want it off because they are cold, we can bring in blankets, exchange sweaters and jackets, or find a directional heater. If they want it on because they are having trouble breathing

and the air is stuffy, we can use a fan. In the end, everyone is able to feel like a winner, no one loses, there are no abuses of power, no bureaucracy, and the group feels united. In short, there is no fundamental reason why anyone has to feel stuffy so that someone else will not feel cold.

For thousands of years, we have resolved disputes on the basis of power and proved the truth of Lord Acton's remark that "All power corrupts, and absolute power corrupts absolutely." As a result, for the past several hundred years we have shifted from power- to rights-based processes, relying primarily on law. Rights are limitations on the exercise of power. Indeed, every word in the U.S. Constitution can be considered a limitation on the power of an absolute monarchy to do exactly as he or she wishes. Nonetheless, rights originate in and depend on power, and we have only the rights we are able to enforce.

Only in the past several years have we begun to create effective mechanisms for making decisions on the basis of interests. Interest-based approaches such as creative problem solving, collaborative negotiation, and mediation define an arena within which there is an equality of power and rights because decisions are voluntary and based on consensus.

For this reason, interest-based approaches are the most time-consuming: *if* we ignore the time we would otherwise waste in petty squabbles and emotional tirades; the time spent resolving chronic conflicts that are generated whenever we use power- or rights-based processes; the time spent overcoming resistance; the time wasted on gossip, rumors, and being unproductive; and the time that is saved by increasing motivation and unity within the group.

The easiest way to separate positions from interests in your conflict is to ask your opponent why he or she has taken a given position. Here are some additional questions you can ask to elicit your opponent's interests or reveal your own:

- "Why does that seem like the best solution to you?"
- "If you could have any solution, what would you want?"

- "Help me understand why that is important to you."
- "What concerns do you have about this?"
- "What's the real problem here?"
- "What would be wrong with . . . ?"
- "Why not do it this way . . . ?"
- "What are you afraid would happen if we . . . ?"
- "What would you do if you were in charge?"
- "What are your goals for the future?"
- "Why not just accept my [or their] proposal?"
- "What would your proposal be if I was willing to meet your interests?"
- "What would it take for you to give up that proposal?"
- "What could I do to make my proposal more acceptable to you?"

Simply by asking these questions, you will automatically shift from assuming there has to be a win-lose outcome to assuming that both of you can win. By identifying interests, you make it possible to consider multiple options that are not mutually exclusive, do not result in anyone's defeat, and seek to satisfy everyone's legitimate needs.

To further explore the differences between positions and interests, consider the following example. Jim and Helen both work at the same level in a large accounting organization. Helen began at the company fifteen years before Jim and worked most of those years for Sarah, who is senior vice president for the unit. Jim arrived only two years ago and also works for Sarah, who hired him and recently recommended him for promotion.

The division moved to new headquarters, and each staff member was assigned a cubicle. Everyone was expected to move in and immediately start work. Sarah arrived at work on Wednesday morning, expecting to find all fifteen of the people who reported directly to her settled in their new office spaces, putting photos of their family members and pets on their desks and arranging their files.

To her surprise, she found Helen in her office in tears and Jim outside her door demanding an immediate conference. Perplexed and annoyed to be facing two disruptions so early in the day, she invited them into her office, hoping she could take care of the problem quickly because she had been asked to complete a report by noon for her boss, who was a tough taskmaster.

She quickly learned that a conflict had arisen between Jim and Helen over their new workspace. Through a misunderstanding or mistake by the maintenance crew that was handling the move, Helen and Jim had both been assigned to the same cubicle. When the movers realized their error, they offered to move one of them to a double space that was available across the hall, but that solution was not acceptable to either of them.

As it happened, the cubicle in dispute was the only one that was next to Sarah's office, and Jim and Helen both insisted on having it. In her haste and annoyance over this "childish" dispute, Sarah decided to take the cubicle away from both of them and assigned them to occupy the double cubicle across the hall, telling them to "share it until you get over this silly argument and learn to work together."

As the boss, Sarah clearly solved their problem, but what did her decision teach Helen and Jim about conflict resolution, leadership, or learning how to collaborate? With hindsight, Sarah was able to see that by accepting Jim's and Helen's positions at face value and failing to identify their underlying interests, she had missed an opportunity to create a win-win solution. Worse, her behavior communicated the following subconscious lessons about how they should go about resolving their disputes in the future:

- They do not have the ability to resolve their conflicts themselves.
- Therefore, they need someone else to intervene and solve them.
- The person who solves them will be someone in a position of power or authority.
- This person will not care what their real interests are.

- As a result, they will at best get only half of what they really want or need.
- This result will be imposed on them as a kind of punishment for disagreeing with each other.
- Conflict is therefore dangerous and pointless.
- There is no reason to think they can collaborate to get what they both want.
- There is no reason to think they can learn from their conflicts.

An alternative scenario would have been for Sarah to ask Helen and Jim to find out from each other why they wanted the cubicle near her office. If she had done so, she and they would have learned about a deeper conflict that had been simmering just beneath the surface.

When we met with Helen, Jim, and Sarah, we asked them why they wanted the cubicle. Helen told us she had worked with Sarah for a much longer time and needed to have daily contact with her in order to do her job. She also felt that Jim was trying to push her out and take her job. Jim responded by denying that this was the case. He felt Helen was trying to block him from communicating with Sarah and wanted to make him look inefficient, and that the other cubicle was too far away from the people he had to work with, which would make his job more difficult and take longer.

We asked Jim to tell Helen why he was not trying to push her out and take over her job. He said he had no interest in replacing her and was looking for promotion to a position in a different department. In fact, he said he thought Helen was doing a great job. We asked Helen if she was trying to block Jim from communicating with Sarah and make him look inefficient. She said she had felt hurt and jealous in the past and may have done the things Jim mentioned, but actually admired his work, was pleased to hear that he did not want to take over her job, and promised that she would stop doing those things in the future.

We then moved into joint problem solving and asked them to brainstorm solutions that would allow them to satisfy both their interests. As a result of their earlier conversation, Helen suggested that Jim take the cubicle since he needed to be closer to his coworkers. Jim, on the other hand, suggested that Sarah take it since she needed to communicate on a daily basis with Sarah.

When they brainstormed how to solve the problem together, they realized that Jim's coworkers could easily move across the hall allowing Jim to have the double-sized cubicle for himself and use it for team meetings. Both of them were extremely pleased with this solution.

Through this conversation, it became clear that their conflict had nothing at all to do with the cubicle. Clarifying and communicating honestly and empathetically about these issues made it possible for them to reach a far better outcome and satisfy both of their interests. Doing so also communicated an entirely different set of subconscious lessons about their ability to resolve their disputes in the future that differed from those listed previously, including:

- They do have the capacity to resolve their conflicts themselves.
- Therefore, they do not need anyone to intervene to solve them.
- They can find out themselves what their real interests are without relying on someone in a position of power or authority.
- The way for them to find out is to ask each other a "why" question or some other question that identifies their interests.
- It is possible for both of them to get what they really want or need.
- They can feel good about themselves and each other and create a successful partnership.
- Conflict can be creative, useful, and a source of learning and improved outcomes.
- It is possible to collaborate and get what they want.
- There are many reasons to think they can learn from their conflicts.

If we assume that Jim had continued to be upset that Helen ended up with the cubicle he wanted, Sarah could have asked him why he was so angry, in which case he might have said, "Helen has been here longer, she's part of the 'old guard,' and I never have a chance as the 'new boy on the block' to be included, appreciated, or have access to informal information that would help me do my job. In addition, you and Helen seem to share gossip and news and have a friendship that makes me feel excluded."

By doing so, Sarah would have revealed that the conflict was actually about the deeper problem of inclusion and exclusion in the informal network of the organization, as well as about her own leadership style, failure to provide sufficient acknowledgment and access for Jim to the information he needed to do his job, and playing favorites with Helen.

If Sarah had pursued her questioning still further and asked Helen why she had such a high level of emotion connected with the cubicle issue, she might have found a deeper level of tension on her part as well. Helen might have complained that while she had been with the firm for fifteen years and been a dedicated staff member and loyal supporter of Sarah, she had never been promoted. Jim, on the other hand, had far less experience than she did, but had been promoted to a position at the same level and received Sarah's recommendation for future promotion. This line of questions would have allowed Sarah to realize that she needed to evaluate Helen's skills and consider her for a promotion or raise during the next review period.

By mandating a solution to their conflict over the cubicle, Sarah could have quickly settled a superficial issue while pushing deeper problems under the rug where they would have festered and emerged in an endless series of new disputes until they were finally addressed and resolved.

By asking Jim and Helen to respond to each other's deeper fears, intentions, and interests in their careers, we gave them permission to talk about their real issues with each other, realize that they had been mistaken, acknowledge each other's contributions, brainstorm better solutions, resolve their conflict, and transform their relationship.

The important point is that separating their positions from their interests allowed them to finally begin talking openly, honestly, and empathetically about their real problems and identify better solutions. Indeed, Sarah might even have gone still deeper and asked detailed questions to encourage their future collaboration, such as:

- "Now that you've identified the real problem, what solutions would you suggest?"
- "Helen, could you put together a portfolio of your accomplishments so I can review them and consider you for a promotion or a raise?"
- "Jim, I'd like you to accompany me to a conference next month with the manager you want to work for. Could you look at the dates and let me know if you are available?"
- "I'd like the two of you to work together to develop a plan for addressing the issue of how we are assigning work space. Would you be able to present it together to a meeting with the leadership team next week?"
- "Now that we have solved this problem, can you both help me finish this report to my boss that is due in two hours and see what we can do together to make it shine?"
- "Great. After the report is done, I'd like to take you both out for a late lunch! How about it?"

This conversation, of course, would have taken more of Sarah's time than making an ad hoc decision to reassign their cubicles. But considering the amount of time she would have spent over the next several years intervening in petty disputes between Helen and Jim, the time invested in resolving their conflict was well spent. As a result of this exploration of interests and Helen's and Jim's discovery of their ability to find solutions themselves, they were able to improve their communication skills, make their relationship more collaborative, create a better solution for Jim's team, and save time in the long run.

Shifting from positions to interests automatically reduces people's perception that they have to compete aggressively to satisfy their needs. It helps them realize that they can collaborate successfully and get what they want. It allows them to directly address the issues that lie beneath the surface of their dispute and wakes them up by not forcing them to continue pretending they care about a cubicle when they both know there are more important issues at stake.

By separating interests from positions, it is possible for you to take the first step in taking charge of your conflict. Consider asking your opponent the following additional questions, which can help clarify your interests and those of your opponent:

- What is your position? What do you want? What are the points that you feel demonstrate you are right?
- Why have you taken this position? Why is it so important to you? What are your interests?
- What is my position? Why do I want it? What are the points that I feel demonstrate I am right?
- Is there anything about your interests that would prevent the satisfaction of my interests, or vice versa?
- If not, what could be done to satisfy both our sets of interests?
- What are some ways we both might win?
- Have you gained any deeper insights by having this conversation?

Bringing conflicting interests out into the open may run counter to your desire to deny that there are disagreements, minimize them, or sweep them under the rug. Or you may feel that if you accept the legitimacy of your opponent's interests, your own interests will not be met. In our experience, when people do not clearly distinguish positions from interests, they end up forcing solutions on others who feel resentful because their basic needs have not been met.

By openly eliciting and discussing interests, you will encourage dialogue about what is really important to your opponent. You can then identify interest-based alternatives, as in the examples of the air-conditioning or cubicle-assignment conflicts, that allow each side to drop their positions in exchange for satisfying a deeper set of interests.

Separate People from Problems

When we demonize our opponents, we also label and stereotype them; find evil in their hearts; and sincerely come to believe that they are unjust, dishonest, disagreeable, untrustworthy personalities. We personalize their behaviors toward us, even when their actions clearly have more to do with *their* perceptions, emotions, and unresolved issues than with us.

In our experience, it is rare that people actually intend to do each other harm. More often, they have personal goals that are important to them, and are willing to ignore others' interests or do harm to others in order to achieve them. While the harm we experience is the same in either case, the motivation is different. We do not need to take their actions personally or demonize their intentions to put a stop to them.

If you are able to separate the people with whom you are in conflict from the problems their actions or behaviors created, you will be able to focus your energy and anger on issues you can actually resolve. Doing so will allow you to recognize that your opponents—no matter how despicable their behavior—have redeeming human qualities that you should be able to recognize and appreciate. If you cannot, you will start behaving toward them as they behaved toward you, demeaning yourself and making it more difficult to find solutions to your problems.

The logic of personal hostility is circular and will always end up aggravating your conflict. It works this way: if others direct their hostility toward you, you will sooner or later become aware of it. When you detect their hostility, you will start to see them as your enemy, distance yourself emotionally, act aggressively in return, and become less willing to listen to their perceptions or negotiate collaboratively. When they detect your hostility, they do exactly the same in return, causing the conflict cycle to continue.

In this way, confusing people with problems inevitably creates a self-fulfilling prophecy. When you feel personally insulted, you naturally withdraw, which they naturally interpret as hostility, causing them to just as naturally withdraw from you. You see their withdrawal as a rejection, retroactively justifying your earlier withdrawal, and so the process continues.

Only by recognizing your opponents as multifaceted human beings, and at the same time refusing to accept or condone the part of what they are doing that you find unacceptable, can you open pathways to resolution, learning, and transformation. In the next strategy on difficult behaviors, we investigate this distinction in greater detail and suggest a number of methods for separating people from their actions. Notice, however, that if we follow this process to its logical conclusion, we will come to a place of forgiveness and reconciliation—not for what your opponent did, but for the human being who did it.

The truth is, no matter how much you hate someone, the person really is not the problem. The problem is what they are *doing*, together with your own lack of skill in separating the person from the problem. When you identify the problem as one of behavior and response, you position yourself to act more powerfully and effectively. You can then listen, which will encourage the others to listen to you in return. You can give them honest, empathetic feedback without provoking a counterattack or defensive response and learn ways of responding to them more skillfully in the future.

Paradoxically, you can become much harder on the problem when you are softer on the person. Otherwise, your natural compassion is likely to get in the way, and you will find yourself either being soft on the problem so as not to hurt the feelings of the person and leaving the conflict unresolved, or harder on the person than you have to be, feeling guilty or reducing your capacity for compassion and making the conflict worse.

With organizational disputes, you can start by meeting with the opposing group and agreeing on common goals for your relationship, or creating a vision for your work together, or defining a set of ground rules for your communications, or developing a set of shared values you both agree to live by in the future. You can ask them questions that may make them seem more human to you, such as why they originally wanted to work for the organization, what they feel most passionately about, what experiences they have had that led them to care so deeply about this issue, or what their hopes and wishes are for the future.

Doing so will remind you of some of the things you share and highlight the qualities you can genuinely appreciate in each other. It will also reveal that your opponent probably has the same fears and desires as you do. All our personal dislikes, personal attacks, and factional infighting start to melt away when we agree on what is important.

Try answering the following questions to identify the human qualities of your opponent. Notice the questions you find most difficult to answer, try to gain some insights into why, and consider how you might respond to your opponent's difficult behaviors more skillfully in the future.

- What do you like most about your opponent?
- What three admirable qualities does your opponent possess?
- What do you want or expect from your opponent? Why do you want it?
- Are you comparing yourself with your opponent? Why? Are you really comparable to each other?
- What is your opponent doing that is bothering you?
- How do you respond when your opponent engages in this behavior?

- Is your opponent's behavior succeeding? How?
- Why has your response not been successful in changing your opponent's behavior?
- Are you in some indirect way rewarding behavior you do not like?
- What are three things you could do differently to respond more skillfully to your opponent's behavior?

The fundamental premise behind these questions is that we are all responsible both for our own behaviors and how we respond to the behaviors of others. By separating people from problems and personalities from behaviors, you can shift the locus of responsibility from "me" versus "them" to "us" versus "it," both in relation to how the conflict started and how you go about resolving it.

You will always be more successful when you address your problems together, which you can do only if you identify the problem as an "it" rather than as a "you." Doing so will encourage you to take 100 percent responsibility for resolving your conflicts, make clear commitments, collaborate in finding workable solutions, and learn more as a result.

Separate Problems from Solutions

When you are in conflict, you are probably so busy focusing on your disagreements, bolstering your positions, and searching for quick solutions that you fail to listen to the conflict or involve your opponent in a collaborative search for answers that meet both your needs.

As a result, you are probably proposing solutions to the wrong problems, or your solutions are received with suspicion and distrust because your opponent did not participate in creating them. As a result, you will become locked in mountainous disputes over molehills and unable to find creative solutions without replicating the problems that got you stuck in the first place.

If you can stop for a moment and analyze or understand your problem before trying to solve it, you will be much more effective. It is nearly always better to discuss the problem in detail with your opponent before coming up with a proposed solution. You can begin by trying to reach agreement on how the problem started, what caused it, whether it is linked to similar or related problems, and the extent of its impact and nature of its effect on you and others.

Research on problem solving indicates that the effectiveness of solutions increases 85 percent once the true problem has been identified. For these reasons, consider spending most of your time identifying and analyzing the problem. Resolution will emerge effortlessly once a well-defined problem has been mutually identified by all interested parties. In analyzing your conflict, try to answer the following questions:

- What exactly is the conflict about? Why is it about that?
- When did the conflict begin? Why then?
- Who else does it impact or involve? Why them?
- What kind of conflict is it? Why that kind?
- What aspects of the conflict have you overlooked? Why those?
- How has your understanding of the conflict changed over time?
- What caused or aggravated the conflict?
- How would you analyze the conflict? What variety of conflict is it?
- Can you break the conflict down into separate parts?
- How would you prioritize these parts?

It may seem counterintuitive for you to solve your problem by *not* coming up with solutions and simply staying with the problem, yet it works. When we consult with organizations that are stuck in conflict, we sometimes ask people to meet in small teams to analyze and prioritize their problems and watch as they laugh cheerfully and work collaboratively while analyzing twenty or thirty major problems.

When we ask them why they are enjoying themselves, they say that they feel relieved to be finally talking about what they all know about but have been unable to discuss. Most people feel relieved just to meet others who have the same problem and are excited because discussing their problems automatically increases the possibility of finding solutions.

We then ask them whether, during the time they were conducting their analysis, they experienced any of the twenty or thirty problems they identified. Rarely does anyone say yes. We then ask why, if their problems are so deep and all-encompassing, did they not experience even one of them during this process, and they begin to see that their problems become less weighty when they face them together.

Your problems will also become easier to solve when you include your opponent in the effort to solve them and when you work in teams, set clear process rules, create identifiable goals, operate by consensus, and talk openly and honestly about the sources and nature of the problem without having to come up with immediate solutions.

Separate Commonalities from Differences

When we work with labor and management teams to resolve grievances or collective bargaining disputes, improve cross-departmental relationships, or develop skills in negotiating, we sometimes ask each group to meet separately to identify their goals for their relationship with the other group. We always find, even with bitter, antagonistic, rancorous groups, that they share most of their goals and basically want the same kind of relationship.

We ask them to again meet separately and this time to identify what they and their opponents are doing that is undermining their ability to achieve these goals. Again, we find they are nearly always in agreement. We then ask them to meet in small, bilateral teams to discuss what they might do instead and how they could make their goals a priority in all their communications and throughout their relationship. Afterwards, they are able to discuss their conflicts and disagreements without feeling angry and overwhelmed.

In conflict, we generally focus on how different we are from our opponents. These differences are important to understand and work through, but it is equally important to recognize how focusing on differences makes it difficult to remember what we have in common. We all share multiple interests as human beings, and if we are unable to bring them to mind in the midst of our conflict, we can at least recognize that we have our *conflicts* in common.

It is paradoxical, yet true, that at the very moment we become poles apart, we also become linked and inseparable. Our conflicts point out to us not only how we are different but how we care about the same things. Simply recognizing that your human wants and desires are similar to those of your opponent will permit a bond to grow between you. As your awareness of this bond grows, it will become easier to talk over your problems and collaborate in negotiating solutions.

This does not mean that you should eliminate or understate your differences, because your conflicts are important sources of learning, improvement, change, and richer and more creative solutions. But if you can discuss your differences and at the same time recognize what you have in common, you will not speak or act as though this connection did not exist between you.

The following questions can help you create a context of commonalities in which to discuss your differences:

- What are three things you have in common with your opponent?
- If you were unable to identify three, what inside *you* made it difficult?

- How much do you actually know about your opponent?
  What is one thing you do not know, but would like to?
  How could you find out?
- What are some things you have assumed about your opponent without trying to find out whether they are true or not? How have these assumptions influenced your behavior?
- What are three values, beliefs, goals, or principles you and your opponent have in common?
- What are three solutions to your conflict that you both might accept?

To highlight what you have in common with your opponent, consider identifying your core values, asking your opponent to do the same, and then sharing your values with each other. Most people share a number of values, so the chances are good that there will be several you have in common, and these can be used as criteria to judge your future behaviors and discourage resorting to behaviors you do not like. This does not mean forgiving what your opponent did, but denying yourself permission to do the same in return.

Indeed, it is possible to define an enemy as anyone you give yourself permission to speak or act toward in ways that do not reflect your core values. For this reason, identifying what you have in common with your opponents can be transformational, not only because you will begin to see them differently, but because doing so will allow you to be more powerful in solving the problems their behaviors created and encourage you to surrender the idea that your conflict can be defined in terms of "either/or," rather than as "both/and."

Separate the Future from the Past

The world has been embroiled in countless bloody conflicts, most of them fueled by an accumulation over generations of pain, anger, humiliation, revenge, and retaliation. The carnage of centuries lives on through succeeding generations. This is the price of failing to distinguish between past and future, a price that is paid years after the events that triggered them have passed into history and their details have been forgotten.

If, in these conflicts, the combatants could have agreed on what they wanted for their children or hoped for their future, if they had been able to let go of what happened in the past and decide to create a different kind of future, they might more easily have found a path to resolution.

In every conflict, the past weighs heavily on the present. This is especially true in conflict-avoidant organizations, those where conflicts are routinely suppressed, denied, settled, and incompletely resolved. In these organizations, conflicts are allowed to fester and multiply, or they are isolated, shunned, and sidelined. More often, they are passed on to others through gossip and rumors and are nursed and hoarded, sometimes for lifetimes.

We once resolved a dispute in a school in which the faculty had rejected and forced out three principals in less than six months. The divisiveness was so intense that even the factions had factions, and their anger and bitterness at one another made the entire educational community angry, frightened, and miserable. No one knew what to do.

We started our intervention by asking the faculty, staff, and administration to introduce themselves and to offer one suggestion for how they could make this the best school in the state. We wrote their ideas down on flip charts and posted them around the room. We then asked whether anyone disagreed with any of these ideas. No one did.

We congratulated them on having reached complete consensus on what needed to be done and then asked the stunned audience, "What would you rather spend your time doing today: proving you were right, or working on these ideas and making this the best school in the state?" The response was unanimous. They all wanted to put the past behind them and focus on their future. We still had to spend time addressing the underlying issues and cleaning up the past so it would not leak into their future, but we ended the day with high morale and enormous enthusiasm about working together to improve their school.

We sometimes ask people who are arguing bitterly if they think they will *ever* convince the other person that they are right. They always say "no." The only healthy, intelligent thing to do then is to give it up! In truth, we will *never* succeed in convincing our opponents that we are right and they are wrong. This is partly because we are only describing what is right for us and do not really care about what is right for them, and partly it is because what we think of as "right" is tied to blaming them for who they are or what they did in the past without considering what we both want for the future.

We can disagree forever about what happened in the past, or about who said and did what to whom, or who did it first, or who was most at fault. None of this will get us anywhere. We each have our own stories to tell based on what we perceive and filter through our own emotions, preconceptions, and needs. We sincerely believe our stories to be true because if they were not, we might see ourselves as wrong, or bad, or at fault. We do everything we can to avoid these outcomes, but ultimately none of it really matters.

Recall a conflict in your organization and how radically people's stories differed from one another. You might have wondered whether you were even working in the same organization! Each person in conflict recalls entirely different facts, draws different conclusions, and identifies different heroes and villains. Everyone sees each other through different lenses and perceives events differently based on their vantage points, needs, and roles at the time and therefore comes away with wildly different memories they each feel passionately about, even years afterwards.

You will be far more successful in resolving your disputes when you stop debating endlessly over who is to blame for the past and instead focus on how to solve your problems in the present or what you both want for the future. The following questions can help you examine some areas in which you may be able to agree about your past, present, and future:

- What are some issues you have been unable to agree on in the past?
- Are your disagreements about the past concerned with who is at fault or to blame for what happened?
- Is it likely that you will ever succeed in resolving these issues or that the other person will ever agree with you?
- If not, what would it take for you to give up your efforts to convince your opponent you are right?
- What would the consequences be for either of you if you could agree on the present and the future?
- What might you have to give up? What might you gain?
- What do you both want for the present?
- What are your goals for the future? Why not focus on this instead?

Focusing on the past or seeking revenge for the pain you have experienced can prevent you from being able to let it go. Holding onto a painful past merely draws it into the present; reduces the likelihood of having a different future; and denies you resolution, closure, and inner peace. Creating a dialogue with your opponent over what you want for the present or the future can give you a better framework for communicating and allow you to share your present realities and explore your hopes and dreams.

Separate Emotion from Negotiation

We are all emotional beings. And as we have discussed, when we suppress our emotions, they do not disappear, but simply submerge and pop up elsewhere, preoccupying our conscious and unconscious attention. These unresolved emotions then distract us and make it difficult to focus our attention on finding logical or strategic solutions to our problems.

At the other extreme, when we vent destructively or dump our emotions onto others, we escalate our conflicts and become unable to identify or stick to our real priorities. We fail to see the forest for the trees and have difficulty remembering what is truly important. As a result, we tend to behave destructively, rapidly reach impasse, and assume it is impossible to solve our problems.

While it is important not to suppress or negotiate your emotions, it is equally important not to negotiate emotionally. Emotions should be acknowledged, not negotiated, and then released so you can solve your problems without being tempted to make emotional decisions that are not to your long-term benefit.

Your primary goals in emotional processing and conflict resolution are to communicate your emotions and hear them recognized by your opponent, not as ends in themselves but as transitions to creative problem solving in which you set your emotions aside, realistically assess what is best for you, and come to an agreement. When you suppress your emotions, you become less able to make reasoned choices. Instead, you will act emotionally at a time when you need to think logically.

If you are unable to express your emotions, you will also find it difficult to work your way free of them. Repressing deep feelings will force you to focus considerable energy on keeping them in check, which will prevent you from paying attention to what is happening around you. In this way, internal blindness leads to external blindness and to your "truths" becoming increasingly distorted.

In conflict, one person is often more emotionally expressive than another, and it is difficult for more than one person to express emotions at a time and still feel heard. In these situations, it is important to encourage some form of emotional release so that acknowledgment, dialogue, or grieving can take place because if it does not, these unexpressed emotions will leak into the negotiation process and generate petty, pointless arguments about things that really do not matter in the long run.

The following questions can help you identify the emotional obstacles in your conflict. We hope they will encourage you to express them constructively and say or do whatever you need to say or do to let go of them so you can negotiate nonemotionally.

- What emotions are you feeling in your conflict?
- What do you need to say or do to let go of them?
- Have you tried communicating your emotions to your opponent? If so, what was his or her response? If not, why not?
- How could you express your emotions more constructively or skillfully and not produce responses in your opponent that you do not like?
- Do you know what your opponent is feeling emotionally? What have you done to find out? What might you do instead?
- What level of permission have you given your opponent to express emotions to you?
- What would it take for you to give your opponent greater permission?
- What could you do to encourage your opponent to express his or her emotions, let them go, and negotiate more logically?
- Have your emotions gotten in the way of your ability to negotiate logically? How?
- Have your opponent's emotions gotten in the way? How? How could you get them out of the way?

Separate Process from Content

Conflicts that concern content—the accuracy of information, data, facts, chronology, precise recollections, and similar matters of substance—are difficult to resolve when you cannot convince the other side of the accuracy of your information. On the other hand, conflicts that concern process—*how* you go about working together—can be defined more flexibly and provide both sides with sufficient common ground to reach an agreement.

In international negotiations, process is enormously important. In the talks that ended the Vietnam War, the parties argued endlessly over the size and shape of the negotiating table, who would be entitled to speak, how many days of discussion there would be, what issues would be on the agenda, and what would be communicated to the press. Both sides understood that if they could reach agreements on these process issues, they would create a starting point for agreements over content.

In organizational disputes as well, reaching agreement over process issues can help pave the way for agreements over content. Many corporate departments, schools, nonprofits, and government agencies have been able to negotiate their differences and improve their communications simply by developing detailed ground rules and reaching process agreements. Process agreements present the following advantages:

- They build areas of trust between people who do not trust each other.
- They create a boundary around the conflict that safely contains it.
- They allow people to settle the rules of debate or dialogue that will operate within procedural boundaries.
- They eliminate small, petty conflicts that would otherwise get in the way of resolving larger ones.
- They encourage a sense of order and predictability about how things will happen.
- They provide a sense of fairness and equity.
- They encourage a feeling of ownership of process.
- They help people identify issues that need to be solved or negotiated and in what order.

- They normalize having a conversation about what is not working in the relationship.
- They encourage a constant monitoring of process issues and continuous improvement in negotiation skills.

In the conflict resolution sessions we lead, the first agreements we reach are generally about ground rules or process. We do this because it is easier to agree on how people will talk to each other than on what they will say, they make everyone responsible for process improvement, and we can arrange the process so as to allow a deeper, more constructive content to emerge.

In addition, small, seemingly unimportant procedural agreements can be used to gradually increase the level of trust and communication between adversaries, pave the way for future dialogue over issues regarding content, and encourage collaborative problem solving.

Here are a number of sample common process or ground rules from which you can select those that could be most helpful. We have listed several ground rules that are optional and will probably not apply to your situation. Before beginning your next discussion, try proposing that you mutually agree on at least some of the following ground rules.

The undersigned parties hereby agree

- To be voluntarily present at each session
- To engage in no retaliations or reprisals for anything that is said or done during the session
- To agree on who may participate in the discussions
- To agree on when and where we will meet
- To keep all our communications during these sessions confidential, except for communications we expressly decide to share [alternatively: To ask that no one's name be used in connection with any statement made during the session]

- To agree on which issues will be discussed and in what order
- To reach all substantive decisions through consensus
- To publicly support all consensus decisions made by the group
- To agree on time lines for each meeting and when to take breaks
- To begin, end, and return from breaks on time
- To allow one person to speak at a time without interruptions
- To focus on issues, situations, and behaviors rather than on personalities
- To sincerely try to listen objectively, openly, and nonjudgmentally
- To break into caucuses or separate meetings at either side's request
- To not keep whatever is said in caucuses confidential to other participants, unless the person making the statement specifically requests it
- To agree on how to handle public announcements and press releases
- To agree on what will happen if no agreements are reached
- To agree on what will happen if confidentiality is breached
- To be present in a spirit of good faith and problem solving
- To be honest and address real problems
- To act with courtesy and not engage in disruptive behavior
- To agree on how to select mediators or arbitrators, if needed
- To maintain a "cease-fire" during these sessions [alternatively: To agree on a list of actions that will be avoided by both sides while these meetings continue]
- To resolve all disputes regarding process, interpretation of these ground rules, or content agreements through mediation before a mutually agreeable mediator

In most cases it should be easy for you to reach consensus with your opponent on a few of these ground rules. If you run into difficulty, first decide whether you really need that ground rule. If you do, try brainstorming alternative language that addresses your opponent's legitimate interests. If this fails, try reaching agreement on an interim ground rule that will at least allow you to discuss the reasons your proposed ground rule is unacceptable, then tailor a new draft to the reasons that are given. See if you can separate the process and content issues in your dispute using the following questions:

- How could the process you are using to communicate be improved?
- How might changing the process affect the content of your communications?
- Do the process conflicts you are having reveal underlying content issues? How? What are they? How might they best be addressed?
- Do the content conflicts you are having reveal process problems? How? What are they? How might they best be addressed?
- Which of the process rules suggested above might be agreeable to you and your opponent?
- What might you do if they are not?

If at any time you become stuck while negotiating the content of your dispute, try shifting your focus and returning to process issues. If you are able to change your process, the content of your dispute might be resolved more easily as well.

Separate Options from Choices

Before agreeing on a solution to your problem, try expanding the range of possible alternatives. Do not assume your options are limited. Play with ideas, and brainstorm all the alternatives you can think of. If you select a solution before considering all the possibilities, you could reduce your chances of finding the best method of resolving your dispute or discovering options that appeal to both sides.

Options are not fixed choices, but creative possibilities. Rather than pointing to a single choice that could lock you into a final position before you are ready, try opening up the possibilities by jointly brainstorming all the options you can. Creativity comes into play when you search together for new ways of solving problems, rather than arguing over whose solution is better.

The most effective way of generating options is to give your imagination full sway. This means not evaluating or rejecting anyone's suggestions until all the ideas have been expressed. It also means encouraging wild, funny, and creative ideas. It means, as you each come up with new ideas, piggybacking on each other's suggestions and improving earlier proposals. Above all, it means going for broke—asking for everything you want. Here are some processes you can use for brainstorming options:

Impromptu Brainstorming

- Group members call out their ideas spontaneously.
- A recorder writes down the ideas as they are suggested.

Round Robin

- Each member expresses his or her ideas in turn.
- Anyone can pass on any round and not suggest an idea.
- The session continues until everyone passes.
- Ideas are recorded as they are suggested.

Secret Ballot

- Everyone writes their ideas on a slip of paper.
- The ideas are collected and organized.
- The ideas are exchanged, so that each person and group has some other person's and group's ideas. These are discussed, prioritized, and presented by someone different from the one who originally made the suggestion.

Subconscious Suggestion

- Each person thinks of words that may seem unrelated but can be used to generate ideas about the problem.

- Everyone forgets about the problem entirely and tries to solve a dramatically different problem.

- Someone picks an object, and everyone describes it in terms that could be applied to the problem.

Each of these methods has its advantages and disadvantages. While impromptu brainstorming is spontaneous, it has the disadvantage that a few vocal individuals in a group can dominate the conversation while others remain silent. Round robin, on the other hand, involves everyone but takes longer to complete. Secret ballots are useful when there is a high degree of distrust but allow people to take cheap shots and not own their critical ideas. Subconscious suggestion is extremely creative but can strike some people as a diversion or too "touchy feely" for practical problem solving.

The object of these methods is to help you identify the alternatives that lie somewhere between the ones you want and the ones your opponent wants. The following questions can help lead you to finding creative options:

- What are the options that are possible for resolving your conflict? (List everything you can think of as quickly as possible, without considering whether you think your ideas are realistic or acceptable to your opponent.)

- Of these, which are your top three possibilities?

- What are three silly, outrageous, or impossible options, and how might they be reframed to apply to your problem?

- How is the problem like an object you see in front of you? What options can you derive from this list?

- What ideas might your opponent suggest for resolving your dispute that you have not considered?

- What do you think would happen if you searched for solutions together?

You will be able to imagine many more solutions if you disengage your thinking from whether they will be successful or acceptable to the other side. There will always be time after brainstorming to analyze your choices and communicate them to your opponent. We suggest you do so after you have considered all the options you can.

Separate Criteria from Selection

One way to resolve a difficult conflict is for you to agree with your opponent on a set of criteria for a successful outcome, the elements that would make up a perfect solution, or what it would take to satisfy both of your interests. If you can discuss and agree on appropriate criteria *before* selecting a solution, you will be better able to judge whether the option will be viable or successful.

Many conflicts are not resolved because people are unable to agree on criteria or standards to use in prioritizing, or selecting between multiple options. Some of the criteria we have found most useful in resolving disputes include:

- Jointly seeking the advice of an expert
- Equality of treatment or outcomes
- Agreed-on ethical standards or shared values
- A ranking and weighting of priorities
- The least costly alternative
- The least time-consuming alternative
- Barter or exchange one thing for another
- What the likely legal outcome would be
- Tradition or precedent
- What it would cost to buy or replace the current approach
- An agreed-on mathematical formula

- Chance (for example, a coin toss)
- Whoever has the greatest emotional commitment or investment in an alternative
- Letting each side take turns picking based on subjective preference

Asking people who are at an impasse to agree on the criteria they will use to decide what outcome is best can quickly unlock a conflict. While Fisher and Ury in *Getting to Yes* refer to "objective" criteria, we believe there are some highly useful, mutually acceptable criteria that are purely subjective or even based on chance.

You can move the decision-making process to a higher level of effectiveness and mutuality by allowing others to identify what criteria they think of as fair *before* deciding who will get what. This will help them feel they are acting with integrity and encourage them to accept the outcome, even if they lose. Using the following questions, try to identify the criteria you might use to select the best solution to your conflict:

- What are all the available criteria for selecting the best option to resolve your dispute?
- What would make any solution seem fair?
- How could you accomplish what you both want?
- How have other people handled the problem?
- What expert opinion might be useful?
- What would happen if you went to court?
- What ethical or values considerations might influence your choices?
- Why do you think a particular suggested criterion will not work? Do your reasons suggest a way of modifying the criterion so it will work?
- What would make you both feel like you won?
- What insights about your conflict have you gained by making this distinction?

If you and your opponent can agree on criteria for selecting a fair solution, you will create a mutually acceptable framework for shaping the resolution process and increase trust between you, even if the end result is not what everyone wants. As you generate options and test them against criteria, you will shift your communications from being about what is wrong to being about what approach you can use to best resolve your conflict and improve your relationship.

Separate Yourself from Others

All conflicts create identity confusions and boundary violations. We are confused by the difference between who we are when we are with someone we like and who we are when we are with our opponent. We are confused by the boundary between what we think and feel and what our opponent thinks and feels, between our anger and our compassion, between what the other person does that touches us and what we absolutely cannot fathom, between our values and our conflict behaviors.

The emotional exchanges that take place during conflict tend to blur the lines that separate us from our opponent. When we are in conflict, we can easily lose sight of who we are, of the distinction between what is rightfully ours and what belongs to our opponent, of what we know is right to do and what our negative emotions are tempting us to do instead.

By arguing only for your own solutions, you may appear to be trying to control others or telling them what they ought to think, feel, or do. When they argue back, you may feel they are trying to do the same to you. It is therefore crucial in resolving your conflict that you recognize what legitimately belongs to you and what actually belongs to them. For example, it is clear that both the conflict and its resolution belong equally to both of you.

Here are some questions and statements that can help you make the separation between you and your opponent. They are all phrased in terms that demonstrate your acceptance of responsibility for your role in the conflict, but they can also be phrased to achieve the same result with your opponent:

- "What is it I did that you are upset about?"
- "I understand that's what you think. Would you like to hear what I think?"
- "Here is what I understand you are asking for: [specific statement]. Is that correct?"
- "What do you think I'm asking for?" "Would you like to know?"
- "Here's where I believe you're right, and here's where I disagree with you." [specific statements for each]
- "Instead of using the word 'you,' would it be possible for you to make the same statement using the word 'I'?"
- "What do you see as the main differences between us?"
- "What do you see as our main similarities?"
- "What role would you like me to play in this conversation?"
- "I can hear that you feel I am being controlling. Would you like to know what I'm really worried about or afraid of?"
- "Thank you for your ideas. I appreciate your concerns and hearing your point of view. Would it be okay if I think about what you said and let you know my response tomorrow?"

It is important that you are clear, both within yourself and with your opponent, about what you want and feel. State directly what your ideas are, and listen in the same spirit. Avoid making assumptions about what your opponent wants or thinks or feels. If this effort fails, it may be necessary to communicate more directly about your confusion regarding the boundaries between you.

Sometimes it may be necessary to actually stop the conversation and say something like, "I'm sorry for interrupting, but I find it very difficult to listen to you when you make negative judgments about me because I find myself becoming defensive and angry. I want to be able to hear what you have to say and would appreciate it if you would focus on the problem or what I did, rather than on who I am. If you can't do that, I suggest we find a neutral person to help us continue this conversation."

We suggest you consider asking yourself or your opponent the following questions to discover what you might need to do or say to separate yourself from others in the conflict:

- Do you feel there has been a boundary violation in your conflict? In what way? How did it happen?
- Have you done anything to encourage or give permission for this kind of boundary violation?
- Have there been similar boundary violations in your past? If so, are they related to what is happening in your conflict now?
- What defines the boundaries, definitions, and distinctions between yourself and others in your conflict?
- What could you do or say to more clearly define the boundaries between yourself and others?
- Is it possible that your opponent feels you have violated his or her boundaries? How could you find out?
- If you have, would you be willing to stop? Would you be willing to apologize?
- What might change in your conflict if you and your opponent were able to clarify this distinction?

These questions reveal that you are willing to take responsibility for your role in the conflict. They demonstrate that you are willing to give up the victim role and separate yourself from your opponent. This means accepting the idea that you are standing alone together and capable of forming positive rather than negative connections with each other. If this is not possible for either of you, it may be necessary to back away, move on, and adopt a more distant relationship.

In summary, orienting yourself to creating open, honest communications; listening actively, empathetically, and responsively to your opponent; and acknowledging intense emotions can help you separate what matters from what gets in the way of resolution and position you to take constructive, committed action to resolve your disputes.

By listening actively, empathetically, and responsively to your opponent, you will not only improve your ability to hear them more clearly and understand what they need to have happen for the conflict to be resolved, you will also be able to separate who they are from what they are doing. This will allow you to cease being hostile and adversarial and become more balanced and authentic, both in your relationship with them and internally within yourself.

As your stance and attitude shift from being a hostile adversary to being a curious listener and creative problem solver, you will also automatically shift from a mode of *being* that is preparatory and poised for impasse to one that is participatory and poised for resolution. Whatever action you ultimately take will then be based on what is really important in your conflict and who you authentically are.

We all form alliances with others through love, acceptance, and affirmation or through pain, rejection, and negativity. When we are in conflict, the fear of separating from others, of being less when the conflict disappears, or of being judged for what we have said or done can become overwhelming and block us from reaching resolution. As we separate what matters from what gets in the way, we clarify our disagreements and become able to take committed, collaborative action to de-escalate or end them.

Many managers and employees feel inauthentic and paralyzed by their conflicts. One employee we spoke to described her feelings when talking to her opponent as "sinking into quicksand of negativity." Unresolved conflicts block us from acting intelligently, strategically, and with genuine commitment. We become incapable of seeing ourselves clearly, understanding our adversaries, or feeling that they understand us. These responses make it more difficult to identify the underlying issues we need to address, notice opportunities for constructive collaborative action, or commit to what we know we need to do.

Yet the truth is that every conflict *already* contains its own resolution. The secret is to locate it, unlock it, and discover the hidden opportunities for resolution that lie hidden within it. We can locate and unlock these opportunities by listening for the profound and vulnerable moments in our conflicts, deciphering their cryptic signals, unveiling their secret structures and processes, and separating what matters from what gets in the way.

These approaches can reveal to us what our conflict is really about, allow us to imagine fresh alternatives, and work with our opponents to resolve them, provided we are able to stop rewarding and learn from their difficult behaviors, as revealed in the next strategy.

Stop Rewarding and Learn from Difficult Behaviors

If you feel guilty, you invent a plot, many
plots. And to counter them, you have to organize
your own plot, many plots. But the more you
invent enemy plots, to exonerate your lack of
understanding, the more you fall in love with them,
and you pattern your own on their model. You
attribute to the others what you're doing yourself,
and since what you're doing yourself is hateful, the
others become hateful. But since the others, as a
rule, would like to do the same hateful thing that
you're doing, they collaborate with you, hinting
that—yes—what you attribute to them is actually
what they have always desired.

—*Umberto Eco*

It may not be enough for you to focus your attention on listening, acknowledging emotions, satisfying interests, and separating what matters from what gets in the way, as discussed in previous strategies. Despite using these earlier strategies, you may find that your attention is increasingly drawn to the *person* whose difficult or unreasonable behavior triggered your anger, deepened your frustration, blocked your achievements, kept you at impasse, and justified your distrust. In your fantasies, you may think that if you could only make that person disappear, your conflicts would be over.

Yet by focusing your attention on the person or their personality, you can lose sight of the problem, forget what you have in common, take your opponent's actions and statements personally, become frightened or angry or defensive, cause your opponent to do the same, and become unable to avoid having unpleasant interactions with someone you increasingly distrust and dislike.

Think of the most difficult person in your life. Yes, *that* one, the one who comes to mind immediately. Consider the possibility that by accepting the challenge of working through your conflicts with that person, you could experience a resolution or transformation, not only in your conflict with your opponent but in your ability to resolve *every* conflict with similar people for the rest of your life. It is our aim in this strategy to assist you in discovering how to do so.

Defining the Problem *Is* the Problem

The way you look at a problem has an immediate impact on the range and variety of options you are even *capable* of imagining in trying to solve it. Some options will simply not appear unless you define the problem correctly.

There are three main ways of defining the problem of your conflicted relationship with your opponent. These consist of identifying the problem as a difficult person, a difficult personality, or as a difficult behavior.

People in the workplace often point their fingers at each other and claim that the other one is difficult or crazy and cite this as the reason they or the organization are not more successful. We heard finger-pointing responses like those that are quoted below from the staff at a large countywide agency that was trying to "reinvent government."

> My manager is the type that doesn't level with people. Giving a straight message is not part of how he does business. Things happen to people and they don't know why because there's no communication from the powers that be.

We have difficulty as a management team working together as effectively as we should. There is too much discomfort among the personalities that are present. The majority of people are open to carrying on a dialogue, but one person has a strong personality. She either makes pronouncements or doesn't say anything. Socially, she's delightful, but when things are pushed or tense, it's very difficult to talk with her. She thinks she's right and is not open to coaching.

These complaints were useful in identifying important problems and pinpointing ineffective behaviors. But they also attribute these problems to specific individuals based on their difficult nature as people or as personalities. Their comments nonetheless reveal that it is not the people or their personalities but the behaviors they are engaging in, and other people's responses to them, that are creating the real problem.

None of these interviewees took responsibility for their part in creating, aggravating, or continuing the problems they complained about. They did not go to the people they were accusing and offer to give them the honest feedback they gave us. Once they labeled the problem as consisting of someone else's person or personality, they were able to avoid having to critique their own behaviors and responses, and because of how they saw the problem, by definition there was nothing they could do to solve it.

In response, we encouraged them to shift the way they were defining the problem and, instead of seeing the issue as one of difficult people or personalities, to see it as one of behaviors that were difficult *for them* because they did not have the skills to handle them successfully. We recommended that they focus instead on the actual statements, behaviors, and actions other people were taking; on alternative skills they might use in response; on giving timely, honest, and empathetic feedback; and on not rewarding behaviors they did not want to continue experiencing.

Finally, we suggested that by taking responsibility for improving their own communications, rather than blaming others, giving up, expecting someone else to solve their problem, or trying to change other people's nature or personalities, they could begin to solve what would otherwise appear to them to be a problem without a solution.

Identifying the Problem as a "Difficult Person"

Many of us refer to the people with whom we are in conflict as "problem people." We label our opponents as "dishonest" or "negative" or describe them as "controlling," "mean," "manipulative," "lying," or "incompetent." When we are angry, we may use even less pleasant words to label and diminish them or humiliate them in front of others as we feel they have humiliated us.

The effect of using these words, however, is to shift our attention away from what the other person *did* to who they *are*. Yet by doing so, we have made it more difficult to resolve the conflict because defining the problem as a *person* means that the only remedy is to fire them, shoot them, or otherwise remove them from our presence. The first of these solutions is usually impossible, the second is illegal and immoral, and the third is unlikely and ineffective in the long run because it succeeds only in transferring the problem somewhere else. In addition, it leaves us feeling powerless and frustrated when confronted by similar behaviors in the future.

Worse, identifying the person as the problem creates a justification for acting against others in inhuman, antagonistic ways and dismissing their concerns and humanity as we feel they have dismissed ours. Ultimately, this gives us permission to, in some way, annihilate them, either by gossip, character assassination, or in the extreme case, even by murder, because by definition, nothing less will solve the problem once we have defined it as the person.

When we define a *group* of people as the problem, we automatically create a justification for genocide. Historically, genocide has always been preceded by a campaign of vilification and stereotyping directed against a group of people, with the purpose of identifying the entire group as "the problem." Any statement that begins with the words "they are" and adds the words "stupid," "lazy," "incompetent," "evil," or "naturally inferior" and consequently "brought it on themselves" automatically creates a justification for genocide.

It is precisely "the person is the problem" as a way of thinking that is responsible for producing malicious, revengeful, inhuman, murderous, and genocidal solutions to our conflicts, all of which are rationalized by labeling the problem as personal, inborn, and unchangeable.

The difficulty with this way of thinking is that, on a personal level, we have all at some time or another been "incompetent," "difficult," or "problem" people who "brought it on ourselves." For this reason, there can never be a limit to our capacity for malice, genocide, and revenge or a barrier to our participation—if not in large-scale malicious behaviors, genocides, and acts of revenge, at least in the small acts of malice and revenge and the minigenocides that take place every day in nearly every workplace.

For example, when conflicts occur between departments, divisions, or specialized functions within an organization, they often become personalized, and an entire group's relationships turn adversarial. Each group then considers the problem only from its own point of view and blames those in the other group for having caused, aggravated, or tolerated it. They label their opponents as incompetent, untrustworthy, or stupid and judge the individual members of the group based on the stereotypes they have created. This prevents them from communicating and collaborating to solve the problem and keeps the organization from working as an integrated whole.

The attitude that the person is the problem, which can be found in some form in nearly every conflict, is a stereotype that is nearly identical in form and consequence to those that support deeper prejudices, such as racism, anti-Semitism, sexism, and homophobia. Stereotyping means turning people into caricatures of themselves by taking a common actual characteristic, exaggerating it out of proportion, ignoring the diverse ways in which it manifests itself, collapsing the individual into the group or category, omitting all the natural complexity of the real human being, and making it cruel.

When we stereotype our opponents, it is usually because we cannot find any convincing justification for the pain or fear we have experienced at their hands. Or we are afraid that they will retaliate for the injustices we have done to them, or we are angry at them, even if only for the pain they have caused us by being on our conscience.

Our logic in stereotyping our opponents is ordinarily quite simple: If we are basically good and they intentionally hurt us, they must be bad. Or: If we want to end the conflict and are unable to, it is because they are being unreasonable. The value of this way of thinking is that it simultaneously lets us off the hook from having to improve our own behavior, gives us permission to act aggressively against them, and allows us to claim the role of victim.

Identifying the Problem as a "Difficult Personality"

When we define the problem not as the other person but their difficult *personality*, we identify what needs to be solved as the product of inherited genes, decades of family and peer conditioning that even long-term psychotherapy may not be able to fundamentally alter, or both. In essence, we will have defined ourselves into a corner with only a set of psychological manipulations and long-term remedies that, even if we are skillful, may not allow us to escape injury at their hands.

Labeling our opponents personalities as the problem or judging their character as defective does not automatically lead to revenge or genocide, but it does give us permission to permanently dismiss them. As a result, we can avoid discussing the problem with them and withdraw or act in a manipulative manner against them. It absolves us of responsibility for whatever we may have done or failed to do that created or aggravated the problem and augments our self-image as the powerless victim of someone who is crazy.

Both these ways of thinking justify our reluctance to exercise empathy or compassion, ask honest questions, acknowledge our opponents emotions, discover their interests, and work together to solve the problem. If we reconstruct this chain of reasoning backwards, we can see that it is primarily a rationalization for throwing up our hands and doing nothing.

The real reason we believe people or their personalities are the problem is that we simply do not know what to do to resolve the conflict and have given up trying. Yet part of the reason for our failure is the way we have defined the problem. As long as the problem is defined as a person or personality, it is axiomatic that there is nothing we can do to resolve it, other than for someone to leave the workplace, and if our opponent is the one who started it, it is only fair that he or she should be forced to leave rather than us.

Yet when we understand the true nature of our conflict and begin to listen openly, honestly, and empathetically to our opponent or when creative solutions are suddenly discovered and a real resolution takes place, we no longer see our opponents as bad people or unreasonable personalities, and they immediately and inexplicably become human to us. Simple logic then compels us to recognize that it was not *them* but our attitude that changed, both toward them and toward the conflict. We are then compelled to conclude that the entire mental construct we created about who they were and what terrible people or difficult personalities they were was fallacious and self-serving from the beginning.

The truth is that we get into conflicts with people whose personalities we define as difficult because their behaviors are difficult for *us* because their actions and statements trigger something in us that we have not resolved or that make us feel powerless in their presence. In other words, we have chosen a way of relating to them that is unskillful and unsuccessful and do not know what else to do or say. In this way, we have become part of the problem and unable to find a way out.

We were recently asked to resolve a highly emotional dispute within the board of directors of a large labor union representing thousands of people in the transportation industry. While the union was fully engaged in bargaining for a new multiyear contract, the directors were busy attacking one another. The secretary of the union had simply had it with the personal attacks directed against her and began to respond in kind with dismissive, smug, challenging, and provocative statements to her opponents on the board.

As these exchanges grew more heated and tempers flared, they moved further away from addressing the real issues, which were increasingly being obscured in a fog of recrimination, defensiveness, and retaliation. The real issues flowed from the dysfunctional way the organization was operating, the failure of the officers to respond to telephone calls from members on hot topics, a perceived lack of respect between members of the board, conflicts over who should lead the union, arguments over styles and strategies for negotiating with the company, and significant differences in union philosophy over how militant or collaborative they should be.

All these issues could have been resolved or, if not, at least openly and honestly addressed through dialogue and informal discussions without being nasty and personal. The conflict had gotten so far out of control that several directors refused to participate in a facilitated informal problem-solving process to find solutions to these problems until after they had officially reprimanded and punished the secretary for allegedly disobeying a resolution of the board. The focus of their attention was on trying to punish her for what they saw as her "hostile personality," rather than on solving the problem. As a result, the bitterness simply increased, and an opportunity for meaningful dialogue was lost.

What they might have done instead was to have openly, honestly, and empathetically addressed the difficult issues in their relationship: first, by identifying the ways they had all contributed to the deterioration of their communication and agreeing to speak more respectfully to each other in the future; second, by targeting specific aspects of the secretary's behaviors that were felt to be disrespectful, letting her know how her behavior was affecting them, suggesting alternative ways of behaving that were more respectful, treating her with equal respect, and indicating what they would do if she continued; and third, refocusing their attention on the high-priority problems both sides recognized needed to be addressed in order to assist the membership.

Identifying the Problem as a "Difficult Behavior"

We believe the alternative to labeling the problem as a "difficult person" or a "difficult personality" is to see it as a "difficult behavior." By shifting the way we describe the problem, we can discover a number of more effective approaches of solving it, and as everyone has changed their behavior countless times, they can easily do so again.

By ceasing to identify the problem as the person or their personality, you allow others to consider what they are doing without feeling they have to defend themselves or counterattack. If what other people are doing does not work for you or the way they are acting or communicating is not successful in convincing you, they can ultimately be brought to recognize that they need to improve their tactics, and that this can be done without having to think of themselves as bad people or flawed personalities.

As a result of this shift, your opponent will feel more respected, empowered, and responsible, both for the conflict and for its resolution. Everyone can understand that they can become more skillful in handling other people's difficult behaviors, and doing so is far more pleasurable, interesting, and effective than feeling attacked or forced to defend yourself.

When you confront difficult behaviors in colleagues or coworkers, it is best to begin by asking yourself three questions. First, have their behaviors been rewarded in any way by you, others, or the culture of the organization in which you are working? The chances are good that they have, perhaps only by offering them the attention they have been craving and been unable to receive through positive behaviors.

Second, are their behaviors a coping mechanism or way of adapting or surviving in a dysfunctional system? What you experience as difficult behaviors may merely be a diversion to draw attention away from the fact that they are working beyond their capacity or skill or are afraid of being fired. Or it may be that it is not the person but the organizational system that is dysfunctional, and they are being blamed for not fitting into a "shaming and blaming" environment that is not meeting their needs.

Third, is it possible for you to become more skillful in your responses and stop indirectly rewarding behaviors you see as a problem? Your negative responses to difficult behaviors may actually be reinforcing or perpetuating them. In organizations, as in families, "misbehaving children" and "squeaky wheels" receive the greatest attention, thereby rewarding them for using difficult behaviors, and drawing attention from more serious problems, or raising issues everyone else has been ignoring.

Why People Engage in Difficult Behaviors

While we often experience the difficult behaviors of our opponents as irrational, it is more often the case that they only *appear* irrational because we have not taken the time or asked the probing questions that could reveal the reasons that are actually motivating them. Rather than labeling or stereotyping our opponents as irrational, if we want to resolve our disputes, we need to find out why they are behaving in ways that appear senseless or irrational to us and what rewards or benefits they may actually be receiving for engaging in behaviors we find bothersome.

Every behavior we find difficult presents us with a "why" question we usually have not found a way of asking. As a result, every honest, empathetic question we ask someone who is engaged in difficult behaviors can lead to a more accurate description of the reasons they chose to use those behaviors. And every accurate description of their behaviors can also lead us to a potential strategy for stopping or discouraging them.

This lesson was made clear to us as we tried to assist a group of employees in reaching consensus on a design for an employee coordinating committee. One person refused to go along with the group's consensus and adamantly refused to accept the design. Her "difficult behavior" created considerable conflict and criticism within the group, but she held firm, seemed to enjoy the conflict, and smiled as she stood her ground.

We discovered by asking her "why" and other open-ended questions that her real issues had nothing to do with the coordinating committee design but were with her own work team, where she had been unsuccessful in raising or solving problems. We realized she was trying to draw attention to these issues in a roundabout way by discussing them in a larger group. We talked about her problems privately and went with her to a team meeting where we addressed the issues that concerned her. Afterwards, she accepted the design, solved most of her problems, and became a leader of the coordinating committee.

There are many reasons people engage in difficult behaviors at work. Sometimes they are upset as a result of personal problems at home, unfair criticisms from managers, lack of respect from peers, actions of which they are ashamed, topics they feel unable to discuss directly, poor self-esteem, repressed anger over past injustices, or feeling that no one likes them, and they decide to reject others before being rejected by them.

One of our clients is the president of his own business and judges every action of his executives and managers in terms of their loyalty to him. If they make their family life or health a priority, he sees it as a personal rejection and evidence of disloyalty. Yet his greatest unresolved issue is his *own* commitment, dedication, and loyalty to his employees! He indirectly guards himself against commitment by creating conflicts with his staff on a regular basis. He would rather distance himself from commitment and use his staff's alleged disloyalty to rationalize his own distancing behavior than confront his issues head-on.

If you are working with people who are engaging in difficult behaviors, first consider: Have you asked them why they are behaving in these ways? If not, why not? If so, is the reason they offered you one that would motivate you to behave in similar ways? If not, is there a deeper, underlying reason they have not mentioned? If so, have you told them honestly and empathetically how their behavior is affecting you and asked them to behave differently? If not, what would it take for you to do so?

Not Rewarding Difficult Behaviors

In any system, whether at home or at work, you can take the initiative in shifting the focus from blaming or scapegoating to problem solving and address others' difficult behaviors by changing the way you respond to them. You can start by not blaming your opponents personally or focusing on their personalities and by not rewarding their negative behaviors but honestly calling attention to the difficulties they create for you. You can then initiate a search for ways they can satisfy their interests that do not create problems for you.

There are substantial payoffs for dysfunctional behaviors in most organizations. These include becoming the center of everyone's attention, being feared or placated, reprioritizing issues to focus on the ones you are complaining about, controlling a group's decisions through negative power and influence, discouraging anyone from criticizing or confronting you, diverting attention from your mistakes, bringing everyone down to your level, and being promoted or transferred as a way of getting rid of the problem.

Take a moment to analyze how you and your organization may be rewarding behaviors you find difficult. Think of a person whose behavior causes problems for you, and answer the following questions:

- What is the specific behavior they are engaged in that you find most disturbing? (Try to describe it in precise words.)
- Why is that disturbing to you?
- Why do you think they are engaging in it?
- Was there anyone in your family of origin who engaged in similar behavior? How did you respond? Did that work?
- How are you responding to the difficult behavior?

- Are the other people benefiting in any way from your responses to their behavior?

- Have your responses been successful so far in stopping the behavior?

- How could you change your responses to stop rewarding them for behaviors you find unacceptable?

- How are others in the organization responding to their behavior?

- Is there anyone in the organization who is handling the behavior skillfully or is not bothered by it? What are they doing differently?

- What organizational benefits are they deriving from their behavior?

- Have you given them honest feedback about the behavior? If so, how did they receive it?

- Has the work group as a whole given them feedback?

- What feedback have you *not* given them about their behavior? Why not?

- What would it take for you to give them fully empathetic and honest feedback?

- What could motivate them to change their behavior? What would motivate you?

- How could you reward them for behaviors you find more acceptable? How could you support them in changing?

There are, of course, many people with "borderline" personalities who are extremely difficult to work with, whom we label as "crazy" because we find it difficult to understand their behavior, reason with them, or respond successfully to them. Yet there is an enormous difference between being "crazy" and what we call being "crazy like a fox." Most people we think of as crazy are actually consciously engaging in behaviors that, in some way, are working for them and producing at least some of the results they want, usually indirectly.

R. D. Laing transformed the treatment of mental illness in families by recognizing that many of the people we call crazy are simply using strategies that helped them survive their dysfunctional family systems. The same can be said of crazy behavior in the workplace. We have seen many employees who have been labeled crazy who were simply—but unskillfully—trying to survive in a hostile, dysfunctional work environment.

Thus, the first step in ending dysfunctional behaviors is to think of them not as people or personalities but as difficult behaviors. The second step is to stop yourself, others, and the organization from rewarding them. As this will not always be possible or within your control, the third step is to develop a strategy for changing their behavior.

Strategies for Changing Difficult Behaviors

By focusing on your opponent's statements, actions, and behaviors; by offering honest, empathetic feedback; by ceasing to reward negative behaviors; and by taking responsibility for inventing collaborative solutions, it is possible for you to move from feeling hopeless to being *strategic* about stopping your opponent's difficult behaviors.

In the countywide agency we described on pages 198–200, we were successful in helping the parties change their difficult behaviors and powerless responses by getting them to recognize and eliminate the unseen rewards they had created or were complicit in supporting that were actively encouraging difficult behaviors and by helping them develop a strategic approach to the problem.

To help you become more strategic about addressing the behaviors you find difficult to handle, consider the following practical steps we took to help this group shift its focus from defining the problem as a "you" to defining it as an "it" and from reacting defensively to responding strategically.

• *Surfacing the conflict:* We began by interviewing people, noting their comments, and typing them up verbatim. We deleted everyone's names and identifying characteristics to preserve confidentiality, summarized the main issues, and distributed the responses to the entire group without censoring or watering them down. In this way, we surfaced the difficult behavioral issues in the group; turned them into a list of problems to be solved; and placed them on the table for discussion, negotiation, and problem solving.

• *Coaching:* We coached the leader of the organization in how best to respond to these difficult behaviors and how to model openness to criticism and encourage and publicly reward honest, empathetic communications.

• *Teamwork:* In a group conflict resolution session, we assigned everyone to random teams and asked them to read through the comments from our interviews and reach consensus on the top five to seven behavioral issues they believed needed to change. We then asked them to brainstorm five possible strategies for ending them or responding to them more effectively.

• *Process awareness:* We asked everyone to identify processes that could minimize "difficult behaviors," and they cited the ability of the group to give feedback and discuss problems in small teams. They realized that they experienced fewer difficult behaviors when everyone felt listened to and acknowledged, goals were clear, leadership was walking their talk, and they were working collaboratively to solve problems that were important and real to them, and agreed to use these techniques in the future.

• *Constructive feedback:* We gave them a checklist of positive and negative behaviors from our interviews and asked them to identify the ones they wanted to do more of, less of, or eliminate for *themselves*. They discussed their checked behaviors with coworkers, starting with the leader of the group, and asked each person to give them honest feedback on the changes they needed to make. They then thanked the person who gave it and indicated what they were willing to do to change. Everyone assessed themselves and received honest feedback about their behaviors from everyone else, which resulted in far more open communication than had existed before, less defensiveness, and a feeling that everyone could improve their behaviors and support each other in the process.

- *Problem solving:* As the group discussed ways individuals could improve their behaviors, the issue of diversity was raised. They agreed to hire more diverse staff and acknowledge people for having diverse skills and personalities. The group then brainstormed strategies to increase respect for diversity, not only at the top but throughout the organization. We complimented them for tackling a difficult problem strategically and discussing sensitive issues without slipping into difficult behaviors.

- *Shared responsibility:* The problem with the "strong personality" of the woman described in the second of the two interview quotes cited on page 199 was addressed by the group, not only in her team, where everyone gave her honest feedback, but in the large group afterward. When she heard identical feedback from all her coworkers, she suddenly became aware that there was a consistent pattern in her behavior, something that was perceived not only by those she saw as her enemies but by her friends as well, that she could no longer deny or minimize. Several people said the fault was not entirely hers because no one in the group had given her nonjudgmental feedback or fully supported her in changing her behavior.

- *Support for change:* At the end of the session, she asked the group for help in changing her behavior. Rather than being criticized by her supervisor or "enemies," which would have made her more defensive, she agreed to work with three people she respected who volunteered to help her. These "on-the-job coaches" agreed to meet with her every day to focus her attention on specific action items and help her adopt more skillful responses. As a result, she was able to quickly modify her most difficult behaviors, reducing tensions considerably in the department.

While everyone started out thinking nothing could be done to change the negative behaviors in the group, particularly at the top, they were able to bring about significant changes as a result of open communication, honest and empathetic feedback, group dialogue, problem solving, and collaborative mutual support. The same results can be achieved in your organization when you shift from blaming people to solving problems.

Difficult Behaviors Begin in the Family

Your opponents' difficult behaviors probably began long before you entered their lives. Most difficult behaviors reflect engrained patterns that are developed in response to unresolved issues or unmet needs from our early childhood and strengthened by repeated use in our schools and families of origin.

Consider, for example, whether there are any hidden patterns in the behaviors *you* find most difficult—whether there is anything that connects all the people whose behaviors have troubled you. Consider whether these difficult behaviors may have originated in your childhood and whether you or the "difficult people" in your life may be acting out emotional patterns that have *nothing to do with each other* but are simply left over from the past, most likely from your, or their, family of origin.

Difficult behaviors usually originate in our inability as children to get our needs met either because we were deprived and did not get enough or because we were smothered and got too much. In either case, we developed compensating behaviors that have remained with us for the rest of our lives. As in tuning a musical instrument, excessive tightness will produce a high, shrill sound while excessive slackness will produce a thick, dull one. Each of us was born with emotional needs and responses that were "tuned" in our families of origin. As we adapted to the difficult behaviors and cultures in our families, we learned compensating behaviors we carry with us into our adult lives and act out at work, generally without understanding why or where they originated.

If our parents, siblings, or peers responded to us in ways we felt were inadequate or excessive, we may have developed compensating patterns of behavior that limit our ability to participate in mutually beneficial adult relationships. If, for example, we sought affection as a child and did not receive enough of it, we may experience distrust and as adults be unable to commit to a team or develop close relationships with colleagues. Or we may be plagued with a constant fear of rejection and become rejecting ourselves or distant and overly defensive to feedback. Or we may respond in an opposite way and become clingy and dependent or excessively vulnerable to signs of rejections or sometimes to similar responses of clinging and defensiveness in others.

We have often found that people in conflict engage in behaviors their opponents find difficult to handle because they are reminiscent of a parent or sibling with whom they have not yet fully resolved their differences. Sometimes they are people who developed patterns of compensating behavior that are exactly the opposite of each other, or they engage in behaviors the other person had to struggle to overcome, or they simply remind them of the difficulties they had as children in getting their needs met.

Thus, we can think of our conflicts and responses to our opponents as mirrors pointing backward to our own childhood issues. Conflict can be defined as a relationship with someone whose behaviors we find difficult, and these behaviors nearly always point backwards to issues we have not fully resolved in our own lives. When we fully resolve these issues, our opponents' behaviors cease to bother or entrap us, and we become more skillful at handling what we now regard as their idiosyncrasies.

In one organization in which we consulted, two women managers had been asked to create a fast-forming team to develop a new product for a premier customer. Corporate management was about to pull the plug on the project because they were locked in conflict and could not collaborate. At one point, we privately asked April, the senior engineer, whether Sharon, the team leader, reminded her of anyone in her family. She said that as a child she felt she had never been good enough to meet her parents' standards. They were distant and judgmental, and she felt she would never gain their approval because they could not acknowledge who she was. Not surprisingly, she had a similar complaint about Sharon. April felt that everything she did was criticized by Sharon, and her work was devalued through personal distance, cool objectivity, and formal review. Rather than disliking Sharon, she desperately wanted her praise, support, and recognition for being creative.

Sharon, on the other hand, had an alcoholic father who filled her life with uncertainty, lack of respect for emotional boundaries, and instability. She complained that April was unreliable, never cleared plans with the team, always came up with unexpected reactions, and was too needy. Rather than rejecting April, Sharon wanted her to work with the team and become more predictable. We asked them to share their stories with each other, which broke their impasse and allowed them to begin problem solving.

Later, at a team retreat, we asked everyone to tell a story from their childhood that had shaped their team expectations. Their stories revealed the core issues between them, as it had between Sharon and April, and they were able to see more clearly the emotional buttons they were pushing in each other.

The team members gave each other honest feedback and agreed to do so again if they started slipping back into their old behaviors. They were each able to say what the others could do to avoid pushing their buttons and, in a written agreement, developed a set of strategies for communicating and working together. With support from each other, the teams led by Sharon and April became a powerful product development group and in a later morale survey were found to be among the most satisfied employees in the company.

Not every conflict will end like this. In most cases, difficult behaviors are too deeply engrained, practiced, and integrated with identity and self-doubt to be given up so easily. In addition, considerations of privacy and the conflict-avoidant, emotionally averse cultures in many organizations generally discourage managers and employees from asking questions about emotional patterns or early family life in a public setting. In this case, it took outside consultants, caucusing, teamwork, and considerable effort to produce the conditions in which this conversation could result in resolution.

It's Your Button

We all have emotional buttons that get pushed from time to time by someone's difficult behaviors. Some of these buttons are obvious, and the people who seek our attention will quickly learn where they are located. Others, however, are hidden, convoluted, disguised, and less open to view. These we need to own and reveal or explain to those who push them.

For example, we were consulting in an organization where an internal candidate who was favored for promotion to a marketing analyst position behaved insensitively to an interviewer and pushed his buttons during the hiring process. At the interview, when he informed her of some of the pressures she might encounter on the job, she responded, "You don't need a marketing analyst, you need a psychoanalyst." And when he told her about difficulties in meeting the needs of their customers, she responded, "You should just give them Prozac."

As it turned out, this member of the interview team was taking Prozac and deep in psychoanalysis. He was furious with her and rejected her out of hand. Other team members thought her comments had been flip but still felt she was the best candidate and did not want to reject her. Their very different reactions created a serious conflict on the team.

When the other team members showed empathy for his upset reaction and did not defend her behavior, he was able to join them in agreeing to give her honest feedback and reinterview her for the position. When he told her how deeply he had been hurt by her comments, she cried, apologized sincerely for her insensitive remarks, and was given the job.

When we are able to identify the specific behaviors that push our buttons and speak honestly and vulnerably about them, we can often defuse them and become less emotionally reactive when someone pushes them. We also increase our balance, health, mental focus, integrity, and internal strength when we find the courage to talk openly and vulnerably about what upsets us and suggest alternative behaviors that will be more successful with us.

Most often, what pushes our buttons are behaviors *we* were not allowed to get away with, or were punished for engaging in, or would secretly like to engage in ourselves, or that reflect back some part of ourselves we do not like, or that we should have objected to earlier but did not, or that elicit emotions we have walled up deep inside and, as a result, lack the skills to handle.

Remember that even though someone pushes your button, it is still *your* button, and you always have a choice in how you respond. Being able to choose your response strategically from among multiple alternatives will reduce your feeling that the other person is able to control you, make you feel more skillful, and increase your sense of power in the relationship.

Techniques for Working with Difficult Behaviors

If you always have a choice about how you respond to difficult behaviors, every encounter with a difficult behavior can be thought of as a test of your character and skill. You can respond to the behavior by blaming the person who engages in it and washing your hands of responsibility for solving the problem or by seeing it as a challenge and using it to increase your capacity for awareness, empathy, and honesty and your ability to respond skillfully. When you choose the second approach, you will discover opportunities for personal growth and character development that are not available when you choose the first.

As we have indicated, there are three fundamental ways of responding more skillfully to people who engage in behaviors you find difficult. First, you can take responsibility for your own attitudes and behaviors, including those that trigger difficult behaviors in others. Second, you can listen to what they are saying and observe what they are doing empathetically, in an effort to understand what may be taking place beneath the surface of their behavior. Third, you can communicate honestly to them that what they are doing is difficult for you to handle and suggest an alternative. These steps will help you learn how to improve your character, skills, communications, and relationships.

When you focus your attention on self-improvement, you become less vulnerable to other peoples' behaviors and encourage them to alter the way they are acting merely by changing the way you respond to what they do. For example, if they yell at you, you can *lower* your voice in response, instead of raising it. If you cannot inspire change in them, you will at least feel better about your own participation by following these steps and honestly addressing the real issues.

If these steps do not produce the desired results, you can still benefit from the exchange by learning something new about yourself or them or by discovering how you can live with the problem without losing touch with who you are and your long-term goals. In any event, you will feel better about yourself for trying.

Learning skillful techniques for handling difficult behaviors is a lifelong process. We recommend that you consider the following checklist of techniques and attitudes we have found useful in communicating and responding to people who are engaged in difficult behaviors:

- Accept other people and their ideas and feelings about the issues that divide you as legitimate from their perspective, without imposing any preconceptions or agendas of your own. Next, focus on their behavior and the deeper reasons why it bothers you.
- Do not try to unilaterally determine either the process or the content of your communication about your conflict. Do not start by indicating how it should be resolved or how other people should change their behavior. Begin by entering into dialogue with them over the issues as "its."
- Be willing to collaborate in defining what is wrong with your communication and relationship. Take responsibility for your participation and contribution to what is not working between you.
- Express curiosity about the reasons for the other people's behaviors and the sources of the conflict between you. Do not assume you already know the answers.

- Search for a deeper, more empathetic understanding of the other person. Focus on the behaviors you are least able to understand. Ask yourself what would make you behave that way.
- Be willing to observe and release hostile feelings and judgments. Openly acknowledge your own lack of skill in responding to behaviors you do not like.
- Work collaboratively to find solutions. Start by thinking of something you can do to improve the situation.
- Express your desire to understand what lies beneath the surface of the conflict and discover the real issues and problems. Tell the truth about what is happening and express a desire to improve your relationship.
- Take responsibility for your false expectations. Ask questions to uncover their interests, expectations, and desires.
- Rigorously respect personal boundaries and differences, including your own. If you or they cannot, it may be necessary to temporarily distance yourself from them to regain your balance.
- Accept paradoxes, enigmas, riddles, and contradictions in others' behaviors as well as in your own.
- Strive for perfect integrity in your behavior.
- Model the degree of openness to introspection, feedback, and evaluation that you would like to see from the other person.
- Keep an open mind and an open heart. Give the other person the benefit of the doubt, without necessarily agreeing that what they are doing is right.
- Be unconditionally respectful, courteous, acknowledging, and hospitable, regardless of the other person's allegations or behaviors.
- Hold on to your sense of humor, irony, and play. Most conflicts are not as important as they seem.
- Reach for completion and closure with the other person and for yourself. Make your agreements, understandings, decisions,

and responsibilities concrete. Follow up to make sure they are working and, if not, correct them.

Each of these techniques and attitudes has a common core, which is to center yourself in who you are, act responsibly toward others regardless of how difficult they behave, and cultivate your capacity for empathy and compassion. As you become more aware of your participation in the dance of conflict, you can be more open, honest, and vulnerable; give others more powerful feedback about their behaviors; and be able to coach or support them in becoming more effective and authentic in how they interact with you.

As you pursue this strategy, we believe you will discover that you can transform even the most difficult behaviors and use them to identify the issues that can change your life. These techniques can encourage you to focus less attention on your opponent and more on increasing your own skills and capacities by practicing attention, awareness, empathy, and commitment. These changes take time, but the time will be well spent, particularly if you consider all the time you have already wasted being upset about your opponent's difficult behaviors and feeling powerless in responding to them.

Changing Difficult Behaviors in Organizational Cultures

As we noted in the first strategy, culture powerfully shapes and influences how we think about and handle our conflicts. Yet many organizations have developed cultures that foster and reward the difficult behaviors that aggravate conflicts. Even if you improve your skills in responding to difficult behaviors, manage how your buttons get pushed, and heal unresolved wounds from the past, if your organizational culture does not enthusiastically support open, honest, and empathetic communications and collaborative forms of problem solving, you will continue struggling for balance.

Every organizational culture includes a set of norms for acceptable and unacceptable behaviors, unspoken expectations regarding relationships and interactions, and implicit rules for how to work effectively together. Most often, these rules are invisible to people inside the culture, yet they shape everyone's thoughts, feelings, and relationships.

Generally, when we want others to change, we give them advice or try to encourage or manipulate them into doing something that fits our expectations and needs but not necessarily their own. We are like the monkey in the African story who places the fish safely up in a tree so that it will not drown.

If you want to end the difficult behaviors in your organization and increase opportunities for skill development, resolve chronic conflicts, and improve collaboration, you will need to reshape its culture so as to welcome and support these efforts and do so in ways that recognize the legitimacy of other people's interests.

One definition of organizational culture is that it is what everyone knows and no one talks about. But you cannot change a culture if you do not talk about it. Indeed, every culture defends itself against change, creates obstacles to new ways of thinking, and resists any alteration in its core values. This is what gives cultures their tremendous staying power. To change an organizational culture, it is therefore necessary to reveal and discuss its features and the ways it defends itself against change.

There are countless defenses against organizational change employed by managerial cultures. Among these are the following, several of which were first catalogued by Henry Mintzberg:

- Rewards for competition, individualism, and selfishness
- Conditioned passivity and reactiveness
- Isolation, fear of being fired, and social fragmentation
- Separation into distinct professional, departmental, and hierarchical subcultures
- Reliance on formal rules, policies, and external forms of discipline

- Conflict suppression and avoidance, with rewards for accommodation and aggression
- Stories of victimization and demonization
- Tolerance of covert behaviors, dysfunctional conduct, and unresolved conflict
- Lack of support for candor, whistle-blowing, or anything that might reduce profitability

A powerful tool for creating dramatic cultural change is simply to talk about the shared values, ethics, norms, and standards by which people in the organization want to live and secure everyone's agreement to honor and promote them. By clarifying values, ethics, norms, and standards and committing to them, you can redefine what is expected, what is important, and how your behaviors will be perceived and responded to by others.

If you are able to work with coworkers in your organization to define a set of shared values, ethics, norms, and standards, it will be much easier to differentiate the difficult behaviors that undermine these values from those that support them. You can then work together to create an environment that discourages difficult behaviors across the board and supports people in finding constructive alternatives that still allow them to get their needs met.

Nearly every organization has at least one member who frequently engages in destructive or difficult behaviors, most often in private, but sometimes also in meetings and group discussions. Despite the damage these behaviors cause, nearly everyone in these organizations fails to recognize that they have the ability to act in unison to publicly identify, minimize, and transform these behaviors.

As independent mediators and consultants, we have the advantage of being outsiders in every organizational culture and, as a result, are allowed to do and say things that insiders would be discouraged from, or punished for doing or saying. This allows us to work with insiders and help them design and implement group processes that differ from—and even contradict—key elements of the organization's culture.

Yet cultural insiders can have a significant impact on cultures that tolerate or reward difficult behaviors if they approach them in the right way and do not adopt responses that reinforce or legitimize those behaviors. It is possible, for example, for anyone in an organization to speak up when difficult behaviors take place during a meeting and ask whether everyone in the group is comfortable with what is happening and, if not, whether they want to handle it differently.

It is always possible for anyone to say to someone who is engaging in difficult behaviors, "I'm sorry, but this conversation is not working for me. Could we discuss this issue without yelling at each other?" Or at the end of a meeting, to ask with complete impartiality whether it would be possible to go around the room and ask each person to make one suggestion as to how the next meeting might be more useful and effective.

It is equally possible to stop someone as (or after) they have engaged in behavior you find difficult, ask their permission to give them honest feedback, and then describe—using "I" statements—how their behavior has affected you. You can then ask them what you can do to support them in behaving differently. It is possible to ask your fellow team members to write down what is working and what is not in each team member's communications and behaviors and schedule a meeting where everyone gives each other honest feedback.

A more hard-hitting approach but one that we have found effective in intractable cases is to either have a process observer or audiotape or videotape a typical meeting or interaction, then ask each person how they would describe their behavior and request honest feedback from the others.

We often find that people who are engaging in difficult behavior feel isolated, harassed, and alone. By drawing them in, acknowledging their needs and interests, refusing to accept their behaviors, and suggesting constructive alternatives, you can sometimes shift their attitude and style without rewarding the problem behaviors.

Classroom teachers know that "problem children" are often willing to give up their antagonistic attitudes toward other members of the class when they are included or assigned a role or job that is valued by others. As the poet Edwin Markham wrote,

> They drew a circle to shut me out,
> Heretic, rebel, a thing to flout.
> But Love and I had the wit to win,
> We drew a circle that took them in.

For example, several years ago we worked with a team of teachers from a school in Chicago that was having tremendous difficulty with one of its team members. Fred, the only man on a team with four women, refused to take part in team meetings. He sat on the side grading papers while the others tried unsuccessfully to draw him in. He routinely expressed his contempt for the team process, which he called "touchy-feely" and regarded as an interference with his right to teach in whatever way he wanted.

Toward the end of one team meeting, Fred announced that he was leaving early because he had been called to the principal's office to meet with a complaining parent. The other team members stopped him as he got up and said that because they were a team, if there was a complaint it should be directed to the team as a whole, and they would all go with him.

They adjourned the meeting and went together to the principal's office, where they spoke to the parent about Fred's outstanding teaching abilities and helped him see how he might be more effective in reaching a child who was engaging in difficult behaviors. After that, Fred became an active, enthusiastic team member and an ardent supporter of the team process. They found a way of drawing a circle that took him in.

Giving Feedback and Evaluation

As we have indicated, one way of discouraging or preventing the difficult behaviors that aggravate interpersonal and organizational conflicts is for people who routinely work together to give each other frequent, open, honest, empathetic, and timely feedback about what is working in their relationships and communications and what is not.

Relationships are living, constantly changing, and highly sensitive to external environmental influences. Yet they also seek stability and try to defend themselves against harmful changes. As a result, like all living things, they require continuous honest feedback in order to grow, evolve, adapt—and simply stay alive. When feedback dies, relationships start to wither and fall apart, resulting in less caring and more conflict.

Feedback is simply an honest, empathetic, nonjudgmental, subjective response to another person's communications or behaviors. It is most effective when it is

- Opened with a self-assessment by the person giving it
- Begun following a request for permission
- Delivered as an "I" statement
- Reciprocally exchanged
- Given by one's peers
- Offered constructively
- Specific and detailed
- Balanced and fair
- Communicated in real time
- Presented without anger or judgment
- Supportive of learning, growth, and change
- Accepted with sincere thanks from the person receiving it
- Taken seriously by being used to promote improvement

Evaluation is a more objective, less personal response that is oriented to assessing the effectiveness of an action, strategy, or project. It is useful in teams and conflict resolution to assess what worked and what did not, to indicate possible ways of correcting course, and to reach closure. Unlike feedback, evaluation focuses on events and deeds rather than on feelings or behaviors.

When applied to people, personalities, or behaviors, evaluation usually implies judging, criticizing, grading, or exercising power or control over another person, usually to their detriment. Yet when applied to actions, strategies, or projects, it is an excellent way of identifying why one approach was successful and another was not and correcting in midstream.

Feedback and evaluation are best done reciprocally, collaboratively, and in tandem so that no one feels they are in a one-down position, immune from learning, or not encouraged to participate in assessing what is working and what is not and working together to improve it.

It is always best to start an evaluation process by giving yourself honest, risky feedback, then inviting your opponent or members of your team or group to follow suit. In this way, you can model the level of honesty and nondefensiveness you expect from them and have your feedback be received more openly when it is the their turn. Afterwards, sincerely thank them for their comments and offer feedback to them. Once you have completed the process, turn it in a circle by evaluating what worked and what did not during the feedback process and identify ways of improving it.

Responding to Difficult Behaviors in Meetings

Anyone who works in an organization has spent considerable time in meetings. With any collaborative group process, such as team building, strategic planning, and organizational change, people end up meeting frequently with their peers and coworkers. The number, variety, and pace of organizational meetings have increased steadily over the years, while our skill and effectiveness in conducting them has lagged behind.

Difficult behaviors tend to blossom in meetings, where they leave people feeling frustrated and powerless. You have no doubt been in meetings at which you felt trapped or held hostage by behaviors that were difficult or painful. While nearly everyone feels there is little they can do during such meetings, other than remain silent and wait for them to end, our experience has been different.

For example, we consulted several years ago with an organization that was undergoing a massive change process in which meetings seemed designed to increase frustration and distrust. The group's vice president, Cathy, was a "nice person" with few organizational skills. She meant well and was technically proficient but seemed unable to create a clear agenda, delegate tasks, or answer important questions.

On the other hand, Ted, the organization's comptroller, loved to dominate meetings and used them to attack, criticize, cajole, and blame others for their failures. Everyone dreaded attending meetings with Ted and spent their time ducking his barbs and holding back their anger.

We were told by a group of employees that Ted's behavior had to stop or "the organization will implode." At the next meeting, we asked each person to write down on a sheet of paper one suggestion for making the next meeting more effective. At the end of the meeting, we read out their comments to the group. Most of the suggestions were for Ted to stop his dominating behavior.

Ted was shocked and immediately agreed to do so if the rest of the group would take more responsibility for making their meetings efficient. In the discussion that followed, we broke the group down into small brainstorming teams and used a round robin process to brainstorm creative ideas for improving their meetings. As a result, Ted became merely one participant among many and was unable to dominate the discussion.

After the teams reported their ideas and reached consensus on needed changes, we asked for volunteers to draft a set of procedures and ground rules for their next meeting, facilitate it themselves, and spend five minutes at the end discussing how it went in order to improve the next session.

The meeting was a great success, and as a result, they agreed that they would rotate facilitators and recorders for every meeting, reach consensus on ground rules for respectful communications and behaviors, discuss issues more frequently in small teams, use a round robin process for brainstorming, and evaluate each meeting at the end. Finally, they had a structure for their meetings and were able to control their comptroller.

There are many ways you can respond to difficult behaviors in the meetings you attend. Most of these methods do not require advance agreement by the participants and can be implemented unilaterally. In doing so, it is important to distinguish between people who simply disagree with the direction a meeting is taking or with a policy or decision being made by the group and those who are intentionally engaging in difficult behaviors or being disruptive.

It is important to actively encourage criticism and disagreement and allow them to be heard and discussed. Constructive conflicts make meetings interesting and useful, and efforts need to be made to satisfy the legitimate interests of anyone interested enough to disagree. It is especially important not to be frightened simply because someone feels passionately about a subject or issue. While passion is sometimes experienced by others as anger, an obstacle to open dialogue, a judgment of the other side's integrity, or a block to consensus, it actually represents deep caring and can easily be expressed and responded to without triggering negative side effects.

If you are facing problems with people who are exhibiting consistently difficult behaviors, consider bringing one or more of the following ideas to your next meeting and asking those present to select the ones they want to follow or discuss further. This will raise the issue of difficult behaviors openly and identify ways of limiting or managing them.

- Before the meeting, discuss with people who regularly engage in difficult behavior what they could do to make the meeting more successful.

- Inform them that one of the topics on the agenda will be a discussion of what happened at the last meeting. Ask them to say what they think should be done differently in the future so that meetings can be more satisfying to them and others.

- Interview them and model active, empathetic, and responsive listening. Be explicit about what you want to accomplish. Listen as you would like them to listen to you.

- Meet with other group members before the meeting. Ask them to include this person and acknowledge or validate their contributions. Ask them to calmly yet honestly confront difficult behaviors or keep to the agenda and refuse to engage in diversionary arguments.

- Negotiate ground rules for future meetings.

- Create listening teams—in which everyone pairs with others with an opposing or different point of view and each presents their partner's perspectives to the group—to build understanding, empathy, and acceptance of diverse positions.

- Create a "fishbowl" discussion of issues where pairs of opponents discuss the issues for ten minutes while other group members observe the process and give them feedback. Call time-outs and invite observers to offer feedback on the process.

- Draw out your opponent's motives and respond directly to these, rather than to their statements or behavior or even the content of their issues.

- Offer an honest personal, vulnerable response to their actions. For example, say, "I feel powerless to accomplish anything when you get so angry or talk so much during our meetings."

- Give them a special task or role in the meeting that is valued by the group, such as facilitating, recording, observing the process, or time keeping.

- Ask each person to summarize the other side's arguments. Ask the other side if the summary was accurate and to correct it if it fell short.

- Suggest a role reversal. Ask those who have been silent to do all the talking for five minutes and those who were talking to remain silent, then debrief. Or ask critics to argue in support and supporters to criticize, then debrief.

- Create a moment of silence so everyone can think about what just happened in the meeting, then ask people to share their thoughts.

- Find some basis for agreeing with the person who is engaging in difficult behavior. Ask, "If everything else were acceptable, would that still be an issue for you?" and "If so, why?" Then discuss that.

- Support or agree with the interests that are being expressed and limit your disagreement to process or content.

- Reframe other people's statements to show how they might communicate them more constructively. Ask, "Is this what you are saying?"

- Acknowledge their feelings and ask whether others share them. If not, move on.

- Allow only clarifying questions at first, and schedule debate or discussion afterward.

- Post issues neutrally on a flip chart without anyone's names, or refer to them as "proposal A and proposal B" to defuse ownership and "political" reasons for opposition.

- Post opposing points of view so that everyone knows they have been heard and the point does not need to be repeated. When it is repeated, place a conspicuous check mark next to it.

- Request a straw vote on their proposal or point of view to see if there is any support for continuing the discussion.

- Post the significant contributions people made during the meeting to create a sense of group ownership. If this does not work, consider using names to record the number of contributions, disruptions, or times each person spoke.

- At the end of the meeting, ask everyone to make one suggestion for how the next meeting might be improved.
- Agree on ground rules for the next meeting and sanctions if they are repeatedly violated.
- Ask a professional to facilitate the meeting.
- Bring in a mediator to resolve issues separately with those who are engaging in difficult behaviors.

Before moving too quickly to silence difficult behaviors, consider whether you may not have engaged in some yourself and whether the real reason for other people's difficult behaviors might not be an absence of listening, a suggestion for improvement that has not been heard, or a procedural flaw in the meeting itself. Walk in the other person's shoes for a while in your imagination and consider how you would feel before putting a stop to what may actually be a healthy response to an unhealthy or dysfunctional situation.

Difficult Behavior as Resistance to Change

Personal and organizational changes are constant occurrences in our lives, and many of us struggle to adapt to changes for which we are unprepared. As we search for the sources of difficult behavior, we can see that many are simply disguised forms of resistance to change and result from a failure of leadership or an unwillingness to involve people from the beginning in defining both the process and content of needed changes.

For example, we watched a cynical vice president at a telephone company overwhelm a creative, innovative, enthusiastic department director with demands for meaningless paperwork as a way of resisting her effort to restructure the organization into self-managing teams. We witnessed an entire staff in a public school sabotage a school reform effort because their ideas, suggestions, and contributions had not been solicited or respected. We saw the department chief of a large government agency undermine the efforts of his social work staff to provide more responsive customer service by refusing to meet with a planning delegation and demonstrating his complete disinterest in what they had to say by opening his mail as they tried to present their plans to him.

Rapid, constant, disruptive change is now a fact of organizational life. The difficult behaviors that emerge during a change process often take the form of resistance and a fear that change will lead not to improvement but loss. The result is conflict because every change involves loss, insecurity, and fear, and these often translate into anger and resisting behaviors.

Nonetheless, it is possible to organize the change process in such a way as to reduce resistance and the difficult behaviors that reveal it. For example, we all know that change takes place more smoothly when

- Everyone is involved in planning it.
- People know where it is headed and what it will actually do.
- There is effective leadership in carrying it out.
- Goals and outcomes are clearly and collaboratively identified.
- Small changes are tested first.
- False expectations are exposed and discouraged.
- People who resist the change are won over or moved to neutrality by having their objections answered and their interests met.
- Conflicts are addressed openly and resolved fully.
- Feedback, evaluation, and self-correction are built into the process.

The difficult behavior you experience from coworkers may actually be an expression of their fear that change will result in unacceptable loss, anxiety that they may not have the skills to succeed under the new system, or worry that something valuable may get thrown out by mistake. Or it may simply be a lack of opportunity to grieve over the loss of old relationships and ways of working that are about to be dismantled.

If you can welcome people who are engaging in difficult behaviors for these reasons and affirm or even celebrate their gift of different perspectives, if you can view their resistance as an opportunity to improve the substance as well as the process of change, and if you can encourage their criticism and see their dissent as a contribution to your understanding and improvement, you will be able to see your opponents as allies and jointly do battle against what made you opponents in the first place.

Imagining a World Without Difficult Behaviors

Every difficult behavior represents a lesson we can learn, a challenge we can rise to, a skill we can develop. By simply suppressing those who engage in difficult behaviors, we may actually be eliminating a unique opportunity to learn from them. This idea lies at the heart of the following story related by Anthony De Mello, S.J.:

> There was once a rabbi who was revered by the people as a man of God. Not a day went by when a crowd of people wasn't standing at his door seeking advice or healing or the holy man's blessing. . . . There was, however, in the audience a disagreeable fellow who never missed a chance to contradict the master. He would observe the rabbi's weaknesses and make fun of his defects to the dismay of the disciples, who began to look on him as the devil incarnate. Well, one day the "devil" took ill and died. Everyone heaved a sigh of relief. Outwardly, they looked appropriately solemn, but in their hearts they were glad. . . . So the people were surprised to see the master plunged in genuine grief at the funeral. When asked by a disciple later if he was mourning over the eternal fate of the dead man, he said, "No, no. Why should I mourn over our friend, who is now in heaven? It was for myself I was grieving. That man was the only friend I had. Here I am surrounded by people who revere me. He was

the only one who challenged me. I fear that with him gone, I shall stop growing." And, as he said those words, the master burst into tears.

Carlos Castaneda, author of the Don Juan chronicles, has written about the value of having a difficult person or "petty tyrant" in one's life because only through a petty tyrant can one learn patience, endurance, and perseverance. What would we be without the difficult behaviors of others? Who would we become without enemies, troublemakers, boat rockers, and gadflies? What one person finds difficult, another will find useful or indicative of integrity or determination. Literature, drama, and popular culture would be uniformly bland, boring, and useless without the tension of difficult behaviors. History would cease, and social progress would certainly come to an end.

In some Native American cultures there were individuals who were highly regarded for doing everything opposite to the way it was supposed to be done. If everyone danced clockwise, they would dance counterclockwise. If everyone cried, they would laugh. They did so in order to preserve the harmony and balance of the universe, which is not one-sided but consists of a unity of opposites. Just as there cannot be an up without a down, there cannot be easy behaviors without difficult ones. Difficulty can therefore be thought of not simply as what other people do but the *attitude* we bring to what they do.

Charles Swindoll has written powerfully about the importance attitude has in determining how we live our lives:

> Words can never adequately convey the incredible impact of our attitude toward life. The longer I live the more convinced I become that life is 10 percent what happens to us and 90 percent how we respond to it.
>
> I believe the single most significant decision I can make on a day-to-day basis is my choice of attitude. It is more important than my past, my education, my bankroll, my successes or failures, fame

or pain, what other people think of me or say about me, my circumstances, or my position. Attitude keeps me going or cripples my progress. It alone fuels my fire or assaults my hope. When my attitudes are right, there's no barrier too high, no valley too deep, no dream too extreme, no challenge too great for me.

You can always choose not to have difficult people in your life and go elsewhere. But if you choose to go elsewhere, make sure you do not give up too soon, let yourself off the hook, and lose an opportunity for growth, resolution, and transformation. If you do not take time to understand the behaviors that are difficult for you and how you have contributed to them, wherever you go you will find yourself in the presence of someone who acts exactly like the one you resisted and left behind and feel unprepared to respond effectively.

Our final recommendation regarding this strategy is that instead of focusing on eliminating other people's difficult behaviors or leaving, you focus on trying to learn from them. It is important to recognize that every difficult behavior is difficult *for you* for reasons only you can learn to appreciate. You can use their behaviors to investigate your own discomfort, improve your skills, monitor your own behaviors, and improve your relationships by confronting and working through your difficulties, rather than blaming them on others. You can stretch your honesty, empathy, and compassion by learning more about what makes you and others engage in these behaviors. You can search harder for creative, collaborative solutions and create circles that draw in those who have felt excluded.

Solve Problems Creatively, Plan Strategically, and Negotiate Collaboratively

The formulation of a problem is often more
essential than its solution, which may be merely
a matter of mathematical or experimental skill.
To raise new questions, new possibilities, or to
regard old questions from a new angle, requires
creative imagination and marks REAL advances.
                —*Albert Einstein and Leopold Infeld*

A first set of strategies for resolving conflict consists of opening it up, encouraging it to unfold, and seeing what lies hidden inside. This includes understanding the culture and context in which the conflict occurred; listening actively, empathetically, and responsively to your opponent; acknowledging and integrating intense emotions; searching beneath the surface for hidden meanings; separating what matters from what gets in the way; and not rewarding but learning from difficult behaviors.

A second set of strategies consists of shutting the conflict down, encouraging it to end, and finding practical solutions for the problems you uncover. This includes finding creative solutions to the problems that you reveal, strategically planning how you will avoid them in the future, and collaboratively negotiating your ongoing disagreements. Doing so means generating options and criteria, reaching consensus, planning, and committing to action as part of a process that will end in resolution, completion, and closure—or, if not, in an agreement to disagree.

After you have listened actively, empathetically, and responsively to your opponent and been listened to in return; after you have acknowledged and processed your emotions, searched beneath the surface to uncover hidden issues, and separated people from problems, positions from interests, and the future from the past; and after you have learned from your opponent's difficult behaviors, you will have gone a considerable distance in defining the problem and can begin the search for creative solutions.

Problem solving is a watershed point in every conflict, where the entire process shifts from expansion to contraction, emotion to logic, and large-scale exploration to practical implementation. It is the place where analysis turns practical, the sacred becomes pro-fane, and the deeper meaning of your conflict gets translated into a practical question of who is going to do what and by when.

If you are stuck in a conflict and have not yet felt listened to, or acknowledged, or that its deeper meanings have been understood, all your problem-solving efforts will be premature and often inef-fective. This is partly due to a natural tendency in the beginning to see what *you* want as the only possible solution. As a result, your problem-solving ideas will nearly always be influenced by your emo-tional responses to your opponents and rarely take into account what they want and why, the nature of their emotional needs, what is hidden beneath the surface, or what is logically possible and ra-tionally beneficial for both of you.

For example, in our mediation practice, it is not uncommon to hear litigants demand a million dollars in settlement. But that sum tells us more about the pain they have suffered than what a judge or jury would be likely to award in damages if they went to court. It is *intended* to inflict pain on the person whose wrongful actions caused their distress and indirectly communicate how much harm their ac-tions caused.

If our goals are to resolve our dispute without forcing our oppo-nent to surrender, engage in constructive dialogue over our com-mon problems, and reach consensus on a set of practical solutions that will result in ending them, we need to surrender our search for emotional compensation for the wrongs that were done to us. What caused the conflict is now over, past, and done with. The only re-maining question is whether we are willing to let it go, solve the problems that led to it, and move on with our lives, or whether we would rather the conflict continue to cause us pain and be allowed to undermine our future.

To end your conflict, you will need to shift gears and start calculating logically and practically. You will need to decide what you actually need and can realistically get and move from focusing on the problem to focusing on the solution. This means ending the period of emotional processing and moving on to creative problem solving, strategic planning, and collaborative negotiation. It means releasing yourself from rage, recrimination, and revenge and substituting redress, restitution, and reconciliation.

Conceptual Preparation for Creative Problem Solving

There are three important conceptual or attitudinal shifts in preparing to engage in the problem-solving process. To begin with, it is important to encourage a positive attitude toward problem solving by opening possibilities for resolution through imagination and creativity, putting aside the assumption that yours is the only solution, letting go of the need to punish your opponent, and realizing that the conflict does not have to end in a win-lose outcome.

Second, as you release yourself from the rigidity of assuming that the only possible solution is the one you suggest, you will see that the problem-solving process works best when it is collaborative, open, honest, and inclusive of everyone involved in the problem. Problem solving need not be a lonely process. By inviting others to join you in solving the problem, you enrich the solution pool with ideas no single player could possibly envision.

Third, it is important to openly address the issue of process: in other words, *how* you will go about solving the problem. If you approach it with a learning orientation that is open, transformational, and thrives on the paradoxes, enigmas, riddles, and contradictions that constitute the core of most problems, you will be far more successful in revealing fresh options. This shift in thinking is perhaps the most powerful of all. The philosopher Ludwig Wittgenstein described this opportunity and the shift required to achieve it:

Getting hold of the difficulty "down deep" is what is hard. Because, if it is grasped near the surface, it simply remains the difficulty it was. It has to be pulled out by the roots; and that involves our beginning to think about these things in a new way. The change is as decisive as, for example, that from the alchemical to the chemical way of thinking. The new way of thinking is what is so hard to establish. Once the new way has been established, the old problems vanish; indeed, they become hard to recapture.

Each of these conceptual or attitudinal shifts can help you design a more effective, creative problem-solving process. Yet each can also be an end in itself and, as Wittgenstein described, an opening to transformation in the way you see yourself, your opponent, your organization, and your conflict. These possibilities are revealed in the more detailed analysis of each shift that appears below. As you begin the practical work of problem solving, consider what you might do to shift the attitude you bring to your task.

Shift One: Adopt a Positive Attitude Toward Problem Solving

We witnessed a dramatic transformation in the attitude of a college president who was widely respected for her strong leadership skills but, due to severe budget cuts, became embroiled in a number of bitter conflicts with faculty and staff. After being subjected to several angry, vitriolic public attacks, she became torn between responding in kind and simply giving up and leaving.

In the midst of this crisis, an accrediting association conducted an audit and determined that if the parties to this conflict could not create a shared governance program and work together more collaboratively, its educational credentials would be in jeopardy.

The president took this warning as an opportunity to shift her attitude from one of defensiveness and counterattack to support for shared governance and creative problem solving. She began by indicating that she wanted to work with the representatives of all factions to develop a shared governance structure for the campus. She convened a work group that included all the warring parties, agreed to meet with them over several months to design a planning and governance structure, and promised to forward their recommendations to the board of trustees and support their adoption.

Once the work group began meeting, she did not slip back into hostile or hierarchical attitudes but participated fully in the sessions, calmly and openly debated issues, humbly offered suggestions, and actively encouraged her opponents to participate and make recommendations. As the process evolved and solutions began to emerge, previously hostile participants began to shift their attitudes from suspicion and resistance to optimism and support.

By reorienting her attitude, the president was able to send a positive message regarding her intentions and become a model for others. As a result, a collegewide planning council was created to plan programs, govern the college, and encourage collaboration and problem solving among all constituency groups.

If you can approach problem solving with a positive attitude; if you can experience your conflict as an opportunity, adventure, or challenge; if you can avoid taking your problems too personally or seriously, you will be far more successful in solving them. Perhaps the greatest obstacle to doing so is the persistence of negative emotions and adversarial behaviors directed at your opponent.

One of the purposes of the six strategies presented previously is to assist you in getting to a place where it is possible to solve your problems without being sidetracked by negative emotions. A key function of emotional communication is to allow you to complete and let go of your negative feelings, allowing you to have a conversation with your opponent that is *only* about the problem and not about emotions or difficult behaviors.

Your attitude is a critical element in determining how successful you will be in solving your problem, particularly when you consider solutions that fall short of total victory. There are a number of personal attitudes you can cultivate to help you become a better, more creative, and successful problem solver. As you review this list of possible attitudes, consider which ones you would like to apply or practice more often.

- Acceptance of the existence and full complexity of the problem
- Calmness in the face of paradox or contradiction
- Empathy with the person you see as the source of the problem
- Complete openness to all possible solutions
- Optimism about the chances for success
- Balance in approaching the problem
- Curiosity about where it originated
- Awareness of your own role in creating or sustaining it
- Courage about addressing difficult or dangerous issues
- Relaxation that allows intuition and subconscious ideas to arise
- Playfulness to encourage creative thinking
- Surrender to the possibility of resolution

What is your attitude when you confront difficult problems? Are you curious, relaxed, and playful? Or are you defensive, stubborn, and argumentative? At each moment you have a choice about how to respond to your problems, and the attitude you reveal will play a significant role in ending the problem. As you search for solutions, try to express the attitude you would like to experience coming from your opponent. The difficulties you encounter will then seem less like obstacles or problems and more like hurdles, adventures, and challenges.

Shift Two: Approach Problem Solving as a Collaborative Process

We observed a vivid example of collaboration and creative problem solving in an organization making the transition from hierarchical, command-and-control management to democratic, self-managing work teams. One of the key teams was failing, responsibilities were falling through the cracks, morale was extremely low, and there was no effective team leader. Team members were blaming each other and escalating their conflicts, and the whole process had come to impasse.

The head of the organization wanted immediate action. Forgetting the lessons he had learned during the team training about empowering others, he called the team manager into his office and read him the riot act, including a veiled threat that if *he* did not solve the problem, his job was in jeopardy. This conversation took place at such a pitch that people down the hall could hear every angry word.

The team manager used the same inappropriate hierarchical managerial style when he met with the team, barking out a series of orders about how to implement his solution to the problem. As a result, everyone felt even more frustrated, disempowered, and upset, and their performance became even worse.

After the teams complained bitterly about what happened, we met with the manager and executive, conveyed the team's feedback, and gave them some coaching. We suggested that they personally go to the team, acknowledge and apologize for their mistakes, and work with the team to collaboratively assess the problems, determine what went wrong, and try to fix them.

The executive and manager took our advice, apologized to the team for trying to impose their solutions, and conducted a collaborative analysis of the problems they were having. They worked together to understand the problem and finally reached consensus on a solution everyone was able to accept and implement. A win-win outcome was produced through active involvement and participation in the problem-solving process and the creation of a united approach, which already solved part of the problem.

When you are ordered by your boss to solve a problem you did not participate in defining or handed a solution you did not help in creating, you will most likely react with resentment, apathy, cynicism, resistance, or rebellion. But when you participate actively in defining the problem, search collaboratively for solutions, and agree on a unified approach to implementation, you are more likely to respond with enthusiasm and eliminate a significant source of impasse.

In hierarchical organizational cultures, there is an unspoken understanding that the role of a manager is to solve problems and that any manager who cannot do so is probably incompetent. But the true role of the manager is *not* to solve problems but to increase the ability of employees to solve them collaboratively with a minimum of managerial advice.

Hierarchical organizational cultures tend to encourage isolated, individual, competitive problem solving; yet, as Warren Bennis and Patricia Ward Biederman astutely observed in *Organizing Genius: The Secrets of Creative Collaboration*, the problems we are now being asked to solve are increasingly complex and actually *require* collaborative solutions:

> In a society as complex and technologically sophisticated as ours, the most urgent projects require the coordinated contributions of many talented people. Whether the task is building a global business or discovering the mysteries of the human brain, one person can't hope to accomplish it, however gifted or energetic he or she may be. [T]here are simply too many problems to be identified and solved, too many connections to be made. . . . [I]n a global society, in which timely information is the most important commodity, collaboration is not simply desirable, it is inevitable. In all but the rarest cases, one is too small a number to produce greatness.

Shift Three: Solve the Problem of How to Solve Problems

After you decide to address your problems creatively and collaboratively, the next step is to focus your attention on the way you are going about trying to solve them. This is because, as Albert Einstein famously remarked, "Our problems cannot be solved with the same level of thinking that created them."

There are many approaches you can take to solving your problems, but most people approach them with the attitude that they are adversaries or enemies that need to be defeated or controlled, rather than seeing them as opportunities for learning and improvement or exciting journeys and adventures. You will face problems all your life, but only rarely will you actually stop to consider how you might improve the way you go about trying to solve them.

For example, consider the following comment from a report by Michael Maccoby in *Harvard Business Review* on the success of Japanese management techniques, which makes it clear that we can approach our problems more creatively if we see them as opportunities for improvement:

> When I visited the Toyota assembly plant at Nagoya [Japan] I was told that there were an average of 47 ideas per worker per year of which 80 percent were adopted. I couldn't believe it; this meant almost an idea from each worker every week. The Toyota manager said, "I think you in the West have a different view of ideas. What you call complaints, we call ideas. You try to get people to stop complaining. We see each complaint as an opportunity for improvement."

Creating a shift in attitude toward problems, and redefining complaints as opportunities for improvement, is more than a minor change in terminology. It can, if implemented, leverage an enormous transformation in the way you think about your problems. It can do so by redefining problems as mutual responsibilities and as sources of learning, growth, self-actualization, pride, and creativity. It can do so by interpreting complaining as merely pointing to something that is not working for someone. It can do so by recognizing that complaints are simply negative expressions of dissatisfaction that can easily be turned in a positive, constructive direction, merely by asking, "What would you suggest we do to solve that problem?"

The traditional approach to problem solving is very different. It begins with a *control-oriented* methodology that leaves our opponent out of the process, uses power to control process and outcomes, and sees problems as enemies to be eliminated or defeated. This widely used conventional approach produces results that are often disastrous, sometimes creating more problems than existed before starting.

An alternative strategy is to begin with a *learning-oriented* methodology that fully includes your opponent; uses interests to share control over process and outcomes; and sees problems as allies, partners, teachers, and opportunities for exploring, improving, and learning from your problems. The following chart describes these fundamentally different problem-solving styles. Take a closer look at the consequences of each, and choose the one you think will produce the most satisfying long-term results.

Orientation to Problem Solving

	Control Orientation	Learning Orientation
Goals	• To assert sufficient control to ensure that problems as you define them are solved in ways you see fit	• To maximize my opportunity to create alternatives and test whether they work or not
Assumptions	• Other people can't be influenced • Problems can't be solved unless they are solved "my way"	• Other people can be influenced • I can be influenced • Constraints can be altered
Strategies	• Unilaterally impose your solutions and act as though you are not doing so • Do not request feedback about your own ideas • Shoot down others and don't share reasons why • Reflect privately on results	• Identify shared responsibility for problem definitions and for solutions • Encourage others to react to your plans, and do the same for others • Experiment off-line with alternatives • Discuss results publicly
Consequences	• Low team commitment and responsibility • Public "group think" • Private politicking and subterfuge • Polarized group dynamics • High risk to raise difficult problems	• Increased team participation • Higher team commitment and responsibility • Increased willingness to raise problems • More resources to tackle them • More creativity and better solutions

Source: Adapted from Diana Smith's "Working Paper"

The most effective problem-solving process is not one in which you seek to control outcomes or rush to solutions but one in which you seek to learn from what went wrong: step back, analyze the problem, and investigate it for a while to uncover its secret sources. After you have reached a full and complete understanding of the issues involved, you will more easily discover solutions.

It is extremely difficult for most of us to overcome our natural desire to control and immediately rush to solve our problems, yet we discover much more by living with them, learning from them, and only afterwards trying to solve them. Moreover, our problems are often complex and express underlying paradoxes, contradictions, and polarities that cannot be collapsed or resolved by simple means. They should not be treated as "things" to be changed or conquered but as natural phenomena that can be explored, learned from, and accepted for what they are.

Paradoxical Problem Solving

In our book *Thank God It's Monday!* we identified paradoxical problem solving as one of fourteen values needed to make workplaces more humane, user friendly, and effective. In that book, we cited an example we want to repeat here because it succinctly expresses what we mean by the usefulness of paradoxical problem solving:

> One of our most unusual assignments was to facilitate an intensive three-day planning process for a world-renowned science museum that wanted to create a national teacher-education center. It was unusual because they did not want a linear, final plan as an outcome. Rather, they asked that the process capture and preserve the paradoxes, dissimilarities, conflicts, and wide variety of contradictory ideas that would be generated by a diverse collection of staff, science teachers, and international representatives of the science, political, and education communities whom they wanted to invite to attend the session and critique their ideas.

To solve the problem of how to design a teacher-training center and organize its programs, they wanted to hold on to all their open questions, to list the main paradoxes and dissimilarities, and to keep all the richness and complexity of their uncertainty. The "charette" planning process we facilitated involved producing several prototypes which they would live with, discuss, and review. They used these models as sources for a final design workshop from which they created an ultimate plan. This plan was also left open so the center could evolve organically at its own pace, shifting between the four models that were generated during the charette. The paradox of moving in four directions at once created a more powerful program than coming to a single path through a linear process.

Paradoxes, riddles, contradictions, enigmas, and polarities are an integral part of nature and essential to creative human thinking. It is impossible, for example, to "resolve" the conflict between up and down, light and dark, plus and minus, hot and cold, or inner and outer without at the same time integrating and abolishing both. The same can also be said of life and death, pleasure and pain, good and evil, right and wrong, truth and falsehood, or conflict and resolution. It is impossible to eliminate one without simultaneously integrating or eliminating the other. This idea was insightfully described by Italian novelist Umberto Eco:

> In those halcyon days I believed that the source of enigma was stupidity. Then . . . I decided that the most terrible enigmas are those that mask themselves as madness. But now I have come to believe that the whole world is an enigma, a harmless enigma that is made terrible by our own mad attempt to interpret it as though it had [a single] underlying truth.

Our greatest teacher in learning how to live with paradoxes, riddles, contradictions, enigmas, and polarities is everyday life. We need only accept the challenge of living our lives fully and at the same time be conscious of the certainty that they could end at any moment. The paradoxical problem we all face is discovering how to accept death as a natural part of life while not surrendering to it and learning how to live fully in the moment with the certain knowledge that it could end at any time.

Similarly, by accepting your problems, learning from them, wrestling with them, and at the same time not immediately solving them, you will be able to discover the deeper paradoxes they express. As you become aware of these paradoxes and do not try to reduce them to a single solution, you will become more open to learning and allow the interplay of diverse contradictory realities to inform your problem solving. Doing so will enrich your life immeasurably, helping you solve your deepest problems.

Obstacles to Creative Problem Solving

After you have solved the problem of approaching your problems with a closed mind and shifted your attitude toward problem solving; after you have rejected a control orientation and adopted a learning orientation; and after you have seen your problems as rich, complex, and paradoxical, there remain a number of additional obstacles to successful problem solving. Here are a few of the most common obstacles, many of them based on work by Bolman and Deal in *Reframing Organizations:*

- You are not sure what the problem is. Your definition of the problem may be vague or competing, and many problems may be intertwined.
- You are not sure what is really happening. Information may be incomplete, ambiguous, or unreliable, or people may disagree as to how to interpret the information that is available.
- You are not sure what you want. You may have multiple goals that are unclear or conflicting or both. Different people may want different things but do not openly discuss them, creating political, value-based, and emotional conflicts.

- You do not have the resources you need. Shortages of time, attention, money, and support may make difficult situations even more chaotic.

- You are not sure who is supposed to do what. Roles may be unclear, there may be disagreement about who is responsible for what, or roles may keep shifting as problems come and go.

- You are not sure how to get what you want. Even if you agree on what you want, you may be unsure or in conflict over how to get it.

- You are not sure how to communicate what you want to others so they understand it. You may hesitate to communicate what you want for fear of offending others.

- You do not know what is possible. You may not have explored all the options or disagree about which alternative to focus on first.

- You are not sure how to determine if you have succeeded. You may be unsure what criteria to use to evaluate success. If you know the criteria, you may be unsure how to measure them.

- You are not sure what you did that was responsible for your success. Once you succeed, you may be unsure whether your efforts were responsible and, if so, which ones.

Each of these obstacles can be successfully overcome, and many can be quickly removed. For example, you can ask your opponent to identify the problems they think are most important and brainstorm solutions together before arriving at a decision. You can observe the problem over a period of time and see how it shifts. You can identify the key elements in the organizational culture that most need to be changed. You can broaden your definition of the problem or analyze what worked, what did not, and why.

For example, we observed an organizational disaster that took place because the key players lacked a shared understanding of the issues and selected the wrong problem to solve. The CEO of a small, successful consulting firm was angered by the failure of his

leadership team to generate adequate sales and produce enough revenue to keep the company in business.

In his view, the problem was that the members of the leadership
team were just not doing their work and were not committed to
finding clients or selling business. As a result, his solution was to yell
at them and tell them they had to bring in more business or they
would no longer be part of the leadership team.

The leadership team, on the other hand, defined the problem as
the CEO's hostile, blaming, micromanaging behavior. By focusing
on whether they were trying hard enough or he was being supportive enough, they both took a simplistic view and chose the wrong
problem to solve. They tried to control each other and the problem,
rather than learning from it, because they were not sure how to get
what they wanted or how to work together more effectively.

We suggested they stop midsolution, back up, and meet to better define the problem. They divided into small teams and used a
brainstorming process to answer the following questions: Where
have we been successful and where have we not in our efforts to generate revenue and sell business? What do we need to do to be more
successful? How can we target and coordinate our efforts to make our
work more successful? What role can each of us play in this process?
What are we each willing to contribute to increasing our business?

As they answered these questions, their entire attitude changed,
and there was a burst of commitment and creativity in developing
strategies to solve the problem. They agreed on a new set of programs, incentives, and sales initiatives, and each member of the
leadership team identified a number of personal contributions they
could make to improve business.

The team also created strategies for working more cooperatively
and supporting one another. They delineated a time line, targeted potential clients and results, and everyone affirmed their commitment
to produce more revenue. The CEO agreed to stop yelling, blaming,
and micromanaging. The solutions were owned by everyone, and
they were able to market the company in a more positive way so that
by the end of the year, everyone's sales and bonuses had increased.

Five Steps in Creative Problem Solving

How can you implement all these ideas and approaches and adopt a learning orientation to solve your problems? How exactly do you come up with creative ideas? In the middle of a conflict, how do you invent options and create alternatives that can satisfy both sides' interests and open up possibilities of resolution and transformation?

One definition of conflict is simply being stuck in a problem and unable to figure out how to solve it or trying out various solutions, none of which has yet succeeded in solving it. To continue moving in the direction of problem solving or, at the very least, better understand why your problem is so difficult to solve, we find it useful to break the process down into a series of discrete steps and undertake each step separately.

Problem solving is fundamentally a five-step process. The first step is to become aware of the problem and accept it as something that needs to be solved. The second step is to collaboratively define and clarify the elements and nature of the problem so you can better understand how to approach it strategically. The third step is to jointly analyze, categorize, and prioritize the elements of the problem. The fourth step is to generate options, assess alternative criteria, and jointly invent solutions that satisfy everyone's interests. The fifth step is to take specific, concrete, committed action to solve the problem; evaluate your results; and give each other feedback so you can learn from what you did and continue to become better problem solvers. Here is an analysis of each of the five steps, along with a series of helpful substeps:

Step One: Admit You Have a Problem and Decide to Solve It

- Instead of saying your opponent is "the one who has the problem," recognize that any time you are in a relationship and the other person has a problem, you have a problem, too.
- Clarify what is delaying or preventing you from solving the problem and what the continuation or cessation of the problem would mean to you.

- Specify all the short- and long-term costs to you, your opponent, your coworkers, and your organization of *not* solving the problem.

- Choose to commit whatever time and energy may be necessary to solve the problem.

- Ask your opponent whether he or she agrees that you both have a problem and is willing to discuss and work through it.

Step Two: Collaboratively Define and Clarify the Problem

- Before meeting with your opponent, gather as much information as you can about the elements and nature of the problem.

- Try to define the problem with as much precision as you can, separating it from the people and personalities who were involved in creating it. Write down a concise statement of the problem, and continue revising it until you are satisfied.

- Meet with your opponent and ask how he or she would define the problem. Then state clearly and concisely, incorporating elements from your opponent's definition, how you would define the problem based on what you have learned about it.

- Jointly identify the barriers or difficulties that need to be overcome and the questions you need to answer in order to solve it.

- Jointly decide what information you could gather that will help you identify the best possible solution, who will be responsible for gathering it, and when you will next meet to let each other know what you discovered.

- After completing these steps, redefine the problem.

Step Three: Jointly Analyze, Categorize, and Prioritize the Problem

- Meet with your opponent or with a team of people to analyze, categorize, and prioritize the elements that make up the problem.

- Separate and define the emotional elements that have distorted your perception of the problem. Discuss them separately, then return to analysis.

- Break the problem down into smaller, bite-sized pieces, separate them from one another, and consider each piece separately.

- Compare the problem with other problems, noticing their similarities and differences, and ask how those problems were solved.

- Identify the perfect state in which the problem no longer exists, and work backward from the future to the present.

- Examine the ways the problem has been affected by the context and relationships that surround it. Consider the history of the problem and its evolution over time.

- Clarify factual inconsistencies, hidden assumptions, false expectations, implicit value orientations, cultural myths, unexamined stereotypes, and clichéd ways of thinking about the problem.

- Search for the structural, systemic, contextual, and environmental sources of the problem.

Step Four: Invent Solutions That Satisfy Everyone's Interests

- Decide whether the information you have gathered is sufficient to solve the problem. If not, return to earlier steps.

- Jointly generate options through brainstorming.

- Incorporate objections, disagreements, and concerns into the solution.

- Develop appropriate criteria for determining whether you have been successful in solving it.

- Predict the probable costs, consequences, and impact for each proposed solution.

- Consult with experts, critics, coaches, anyone who will be impacted by the solution, and complete strangers for feedback on proposed alternatives.

- Search for solutions that include and are able to satisfy everyone's interests.
- Test your hypotheses or conclusions through a pilot project or test run, agree on the questions it should answer, and fine-tune the solution based on results.

Step Five: Jointly Act, Evaluate Results, Acknowledge Efforts, and Celebrate Successes

- Jointly create a strategy or set of goals, an action plan, and a timeline for solving the problem, and identify targets, mileposts, and due dates.
- Engage in committed action together to solve the problem.
- Give each other feedback on what you are each doing that is working and what is not. Agree to stop doing what is not working for anyone.
- Periodically evaluate interim results.
- Ask critics or opponents of the solution to participate in the feedback and evaluation process.
- Make midcourse corrections wherever needed.
- Summarize what you learned from the problem and the process of solving it. Communicate what you learned to others.
- Identify ways of improving the problem-solving process in the future.
- Define your next problem and start all over again.

Conflict Resolution, Problem Solving, and Strategic Planning

When we are stuck in a problem or conflict, it is easy to see it as exclusively personal and divorced from its organizational sources. Yet our problems cannot be understood or solved separate from the organizational environments in which they occur. These environments directly affect the problem-solving process, making it easier or more difficult to navigate.

Moreover, many of the problems and conflicts we face in the workplace are not personal, or isolated incidents, but chronic, predictable, and either created or aggravated by the organization itself. What we experience as a personal conflict or problem may actually be an organizational one that is merely disguised as a personality dispute or as interpersonal conflict.

This is because organizational conflicts take place only between individual people while the structures, systems, cultures, processes, and relationships that actually created them remain largely invisible. These conflicts become apparent only when we cease being emotional, analyze carefully what took place from an organizational point of view, and realize that what we experienced is not unique but is happening repeatedly and to other people as well.

In our experience, there are five widespread, chronic sources of workplace and organizational conflict: a lack of clear and courageous leadership; a lack of agreement over values, vision, mission, and goals; a lack of clarity regarding roles and responsibilities; a lack of support for collaboration and participation in decision making over issues that are important in people's lives; and a lack of equality and fairness in the distribution of resources and pay.

To resolve these complex, systemic sources of workplace conflict and eliminate many of the chronic disputes that have been generated by dysfunctional organizational structures, systems, cultures, processes, and relationships, it is necessary to utilize a higher order of problem solving, one that is capable of generating not merely personal and tactical solutions but organizational and strategic ones as well.

The principal technique we use to address these issues consists of what we call "democratic strategic planning." When strategic planning is conducted hierarchically and bureaucratically, it becomes restricted to the top of the organization and turns into an empty process that recreates the systemic problems it is trying to solve. Managers merely go through the motions, agree on a set of beautiful yet empty slogans, then "shine it on," and continue doing what they were doing before they began. Employees feel excluded from the decision-making process, blame management for glitches and mistakes in the strategic plan, rationalize being apathetic and cynical, and either blindly obey orders, reluctantly go along, or quietly sabotage the implementation of the plan.

When participation is restricted, leadership is lacking, roles and responsibilities are unclear, and values, vision, and mission are narrowly defined, planning turns hierarchical and bureaucratic, causing it to focus on tactical short-term problems that can be solved relatively easily. These plans usually describe a future that sounds nice but is too simplistic, or pathetic, or uninspiring or that uses grandiose words to restate the status quo.

When this happens, strategic planning begins to be seen as unnecessary and a waste of time, and employees either decide it is worthless, or that it is better to simply figure things out along the way, or that events are moving too fast to engage in any kind of planning, or that there is too much conflict in the organization for anyone to be able to plan strategically. As a result, the main problems remain unsolved and conflicts increase.

Democratic strategic planning, on the other hand, encourages people at all levels in the organization to participate in redefining their futures—especially those whose participation is essential for any long-range plan to work. A simple democratic strategic-planning model starts by empowering cross-organizational, cross-functional teams to define and drive the planning process. Everyone in the organization then uses a collaborative, consensus-based, inclusive process to identify and answer several foundational questions, among which we often include the following:

- *Values:* What ethical principles and shared values do we want to live by? What do we want to stand for?
- *Vision:* Where do we want to go? What do we want to finally achieve? Why?

- *Mission:* Who are we? What are our main strengths and weaknesses? What do we do best?
- *Barriers:* What stands or might stand in the way of getting where we want to go?
- *Strategies:* How can we successfully overcome these barriers in a way that is consistent with our principles and values and who we are? How do we get to where we finally want to go?
- *Goals or objectives:* What do we need to achieve in the next year to get where we want to go? How do we break our strategies down into achievable subparts?
- *Action plans:* Who is going to do what to achieve each one of our goals? By when? What resources do we need to be successful?

It is useful to keep in mind that there are a number of fallacious ideas and ways of thinking that seem to automatically flow from the strategic planning process. For example, Harvard management theorist Henry Mintzberg has identified a number of fallacies, which we have subsequently modified in order to better describe the difficulties we have seen individuals and organizations encounter in trying to solve their problems or resolve their conflicts through strategic planning. These include the fallacies of

- *Prediction:* thinking you can know what is going to happen
- *Reductionism:* thinking complex phenomena can be reduced to simple, bite-sized bits
- *Separation between planning and doing:* thinking planning can take place in the absence of action
- *Formalization:* thinking formal processes can alter informal realities
- *Personalization:* thinking personally about systemic problems
- *Closure:* thinking it can ever be over

To these, we can add two others, the first of which philosopher Alfred North Whitehead called "the fallacy of misplaced concreteness," meaning that we may think that a problem is solid or exact when it is actually fluid and imprecise. The second is what we call "the fallacy of immutability," meaning that most of the problems we face in the workplace are in motion and changing from moment to moment. This requires us to make our efforts at problem solving as agile and capable of evolving as the problem we are attempting to solve.

What matters most in democratic strategic planning is not merely finding a solution to our problem but engaging in constructive dialogues with our colleagues over important workplace questions and continually working to improve our problem-solving processes, skills, and relationships.

Simply by democratically addressing strategic issues and collaboratively planning responses encourages everyone to reflect on their work experiences; become more responsible for their actions; own the results of their work processes; collaborate in responding to problems; reach consensus over critical issues; consciously plan their futures; and engage in united, coordinated, committed action.

In the process, they will experience the pleasure of honest and open dialogue, passionate commitment, teamwork, camaraderie, self-fulfillment, and enjoyable interactions, communications, and relationships, all of which will help solve their problems and resolve their conflicts, and are therefore at least as important as coming up with useful strategies and solutions.

Conflict Resolution and Consensus Decision Making

Throughout these problem-solving, strategic-planning, and conflict resolution processes, decisions need to be made by participants regarding the attitudes, approaches, and methods they will use; the solutions they will implement; and how they will implement them. Yet these decisions are made before the problem has been solved and therefore in ways that are likely to include or replicate it. As a result, they will consciously or unconsciously upset people, undermine their relationship, or trigger a fresh round of conflict. To avoid this outcome, it is important to solve the problem of *how* you are going to decide to solve the problem.

There are six fundamentally distinct decision-making processes from which individuals, teams, and organizations can choose in trying to solve their problems. Rather than picking one as a template for all situations, it is better to become fluent in all six and choose the right one for each variety of decision. These six fundamental methods of decision making, followed by an illustrative phrase that expresses each, are as follows:

1. *Notification:* "The following decision has been made and will be implemented by Friday."

2. *Consultation:* "I would like your thoughts on this issue before I make a decision."

3. *Delegation:* "You decide, and let me know what you decided."

4. *Voting:* "The majority will decide."

5. *Consensus:* "I am willing to accept the wisdom of the group, can live with the decision, and feel it addresses my most important needs and interests."

6. *Unanimity:* "We need to be in 100 percent agreement in order to implement this solution."

In considering which decision-making process you will use to solve your problem, notice that as you progress from notification to unanimity, the time required to make a decision increases, as does the degree of unity and ownership that follows when you implement the decision. The choice of which process to use will depend on the kind of problem you want to solve.

For example, rapid, unilateral decision making often works well when the issues are clear, the stakes are minimal, and the time for deciding is short. Yet individuals and organizations that routinely make unilateral decisions and rarely if ever use consensus or unanimity experience higher levels of conflict and distrust than those that periodically take time to make sure everyone is on board and in consensus or unanimous regarding the decision.

It is most important for you to be clear about which method you are intending to use and why so as to avoid triggering future conflicts because some people assumed, for example, that the process would be one of delegation while others assumed it would be one of consultation. When the parameters and limits of the decision-making process have not been made clear, participants may, for example, work hard to come up with a delegated decision that is subsequently rejected, leaving them feeling disrespected, disempowered, and distrustful.

Voting is widely considered to be the ideal form of decision making in a democracy, but significant problems arise whenever a large minority loses an important vote. Voting is a "rights-based," "winner take all" process that can cause polarization and bad feelings to undermine relationships. Because voting permits full participation, it is preferable to notification for many purposes, yet can also be highly competitive, contentious, and unnecessarily adversarial. In these circumstances, voting is less preferable than consensus, which is based on interests, does not result in anyone winning or losing, invites participants to modify their ideas to meet everyone's needs, includes the useful ideas of dissenters and resisters, and encourages participants to own the results.

Nevertheless, it is clearly inappropriate, for example, to use consensus to decide what someone else is going to eat for lunch or say in the course of a meeting. It is equally inappropriate to use notification to decide what employees will do in teams or to vote on whether the majority in a group will treat their minority colleagues respectfully.

Each problem needs to be considered separately in order to select an optimal decision-making process. What is most important is that everyone involved in implementing the decision accept the *way* it was reached. This suggests that it is best to use consensus or unanimity to decide which decision-making process should be used for any given purpose.

Consensus is the preferred method for making team decisions because it is naturally collaborative, includes everyone, involves them in brainstorming and selecting options, promotes understanding and ownership, respects and learns from dissent, and prevents sabotage after the decision is made. It is highly democratic because it allows everyone to have an equal voice regardless of their position in the organizational hierarchy, encourages differences of opinion to surface and be incorporated in the solution, and increases unity and a sense that the group is moving in a common direction. Here are some typical statements that indicate that consensus has been reached:

- "I can say an unqualified 'yes' to the decision."
- "I find the decision acceptable."
- "I am willing to support the decision because I trust the wisdom of the group."
- "I can live with the decision, although I'm not enthusiastic about it."
- "I do not fully agree with the decision and need to register my disagreement. However, I do not choose to block consensus."

You will know that consensus has been reached when every participant feels the process was fair, there was sufficient opportunity to influence the outcome, and they are willing to live with what was decided by the rest of the group and support it as though it were their first choice. A lack of consensus, on the other hand, can be recognized in statements like

- "I feel there is no clear unity in the group."
- "We need to do more work before I can reach consensus."
- "I feel I haven't been heard."
- "I do not agree with the decision and feel the need to stand in the way of its being accepted."
- "I strongly (or repeatedly) disagree."

There is a common misunderstanding that consensus requires everyone to "be a team player" and surrender their opposition so as to satisfy the group. In our view, consensus requires the opposite. Consensus can become a cover for coercion when it is used to suppress the open and honest expression of differences or to compel formal agreement and only appear to solve problems collaboratively. Consensus, in our mind, means refusing to compromise over principles, going deeper into what is preventing agreement, and holding out for better solutions.

In seeking consensus, it is important not only that you be clear about the process and encourage others to express dissenting opinions, but also that you avoid rushing decisions or asking people to vote before it is absolutely necessary. It is equally important that you actively encourage everyone's participation, prevent anyone from dominating the process, and agree to avoid acting unilaterally until it has become completely clear that consensus cannot be reached.

While consensus is the best form of decision making for problem solving in connection with conflict resolution, there will always be people, times, and places when it will fail. If, after providing ample time for dialogue and making a clear and committed effort, it becomes obvious that consensus cannot be reached, here are a number of steps you can take:

- Use brainstorming to expand options.
- Separate out the issues over which there is no consensus to return to later.
- Bring in a subject matter expert to advise the group.
- Break issues down into separate pieces and try to reach consensus on each piece separately.
- Look at objections to see if solutions can be created to them while moving ahead with the proposal.
- Create a small team of representatives from each side to brainstorm, prioritize, and recommend solutions.
- Take the decision to a larger group for suggestions or additional problem solving.

- Reach consensus on shared values, commonalities, principles, interests, or criteria; then develop procedures or guidelines for further problem solving that flow from them.
- Use the same process with vision, mission, goals, barriers, strategies, or action plans.
- Look for hidden issues or agendas, and address them privately or publicly.
- Refer the issue to a completely uninvolved group to develop compromise proposals.
- Take a break and allow time for reflection.
- Bring in a mediator or facilitator to help bring about consensus or resolve the underlying dispute.
- Ask proponents to meet separately and return with three to five suggestions for compromise.
- Divide into factions and create a dialogue.
- Table the decision, or decide not to decide.
- Take a straw vote.
- Vote based on majority rule.
- Prepare majority and minority reports and submit them to a higher level.
- Allow the minority group to continue trying to convince the majority to change its mind.
- Allow the group's primary decision maker to decide.

Collaboratively Negotiate Your Differences

Negotiation skills are a critical component in problem solving and conflict resolution. To solve any problem, it is first necessary to negotiate a common definition of what needs to be solved, a process for solving it, and a solution that will be implemented. If after using all the techniques outlined above you are still unable to arrive at a mutually acceptable solution to your problem, it will be necessary for you to negotiate and either discover a better solution, reach a compromise, or agree to disagree in ways that will not be disrespectful or interfere with your ongoing communications and ability to work together.

In any conflict, it is possible to negotiate in two fundamentally opposite ways: either aggressively, based on positions, in search of win-lose outcomes; or collaboratively, based on interests, in search of win-win options. Most people who are stuck in conflict or in the grip of intense negative emotions tend to negotiate aggressively, asserting and debating their positions, and trying to win or cause their opponent to lose.

Collaborative negotiation, on the other hand, is a process in which both sides negotiate to satisfy both sides' interests, reject the use of negative and destructive tactics, and seek win-win outcomes. Sometimes collaborative negotiation results in a mutually acceptable lose-lose compromise in which each side receives only part of what it wants or needs, and sometimes it results in a temporary cease-fire that leaves the fundamental dispute unresolved. More often, however, it is a key element in resolving conflicts, encouraging positive and constructive communications, and building successful relationships.

It is common for people to view conflicts as negative and collaboration as positive; yet, in highly successful organizational cultures, conflict and collaboration are inextricably linked. Collaboration without conflict results in formality, conformity, and politeness that feels inauthentic and lacks creativity and substance. It is less important to successful organizations that people be polite than it is for them to openly express their differences, communicate honestly and empathetically, and work together to find solutions that creatively combine their diversity, unity, and interdependence.

Collaborative, interest-based negotiation techniques encourage people *not* to suppress their differences, which results in their effective disenfranchisement, but instead to speak up and become organizational citizens. The collaborative approach to conflict acknowledges that everyone needs to discuss, probe, challenge, engage, debate, and participate in making decisions regarding issues that are important to them and to do so in ways that leave them stronger, more successful, and more united.

This cannot be done without openly and honestly discussing the issues that divide them, without negotiating their disagreements in the context of a larger set of agreements and shared values, and without searching collaboratively for solutions that satisfy both sides' interests.

Negotiation is therefore as important a strategy and skill to learn in resolving conflicts as listening, responding to emotions, separating what matters from what gets in the way, learning from difficult behaviors, and creative problem solving. To do so, it is important for you to consider, as with problem solving, not only *what* needs to be negotiated but *how* you will negotiate it, the subconscious assumptions you are bringing to the negotiation process, and the relationships you are subtly creating through the ways you interact with your opponent throughout the negotiation process.

Aggressive Versus Collaborative Negotiating Styles

Everyone negotiates everything all the time. Most often, we negotiate to secure *quantities* such as money, time, or space. Yet, while we are doing so, we are also indirectly negotiating *qualities*, which are invisible and rarely discussed openly. Thus, for example, while we are negotiating the amount of office space we will receive, we are actually negotiating our status within the workplace, and while we are negotiating for our salaries, we are also indirectly negotiating recognition and respect for our work.

Usually, qualities are far more important to us than quantities, and it is not uncommon for people to pay a high price in trust for a small victory in dollars. In conflict resolution, it is important to openly negotiate both. If you care about the people on the other side of your conflict or are in an important ongoing relationship with them, you cannot afford to negotiate only for quantities.

Indeed, simply assuming that you are merely negotiating quantities is already an implied statement that qualities do not matter to you and that you prefer your future relationships and communications to be formal, cold, and distrusting. To obtain the qualities of relationship and communication you want, you need to negotiate them as well, and you will do so as much by your style as by the substance of what you negotiate.

In negotiating quantities and qualities, there are two fundamentally differing negotiating styles from which you can choose. Aggressive negotiators generally move *against* their opponents in a competitive struggle for power and unilateral victories. They believe it is acceptable to reduce or destroy trust by being inflexible, intimidating, demoralizing, withholding, or threatening. They often browbeat their opponents, conceal facts and motivations, refuse to listen or compromise, attribute blame, define problems as caused solely by their opponent, and manipulate the process to get what they want. The aggressive approach to negotiation is generally an outgrowth of the control orientation to problem solving discussed earlier.

Collaborative negotiators, on the other hand, generally adopt a learning orientation to problem solving and move *toward* their opponents in a mutual effort at improvement and win-win outcomes. They listen respectfully, establish common ground, emphasize shared values, discuss issues openly and honestly, and take responsibility for creating problems as well as for implementing solutions. They unconditionally act in a uniformly trustworthy, fair, objective, and reasonable way. They refuse to manipulate the process and consistently work for what *both* sides want or need. The collaborative approach is an outgrowth of the learning orientation to problem solving.

Aggressive negotiators generally make exaggerated demands and offer few concessions. If concessions have to be made, they do so grudgingly and make small ones. They create "false issues" to gain advantage elsewhere. Collaborative negotiators, on the other hand, work to establish credibility and good faith by making significant concessions, sometimes unilaterally. They are clear about their priority issues, seek the highest joint outcome so that both sides can feel they won, and minimize the importance of false issues.

Because the aggressive approach generates greater distrust and misunderstanding between the parties, agreements often take longer to reach and consume greater resources. There are more failures and a stronger likelihood of retaliation, even when the aggressive approach "wins." In the context of ongoing relationships, an aggressive style usually results in smaller gains over the long run than a collaborative one and reduces trust.

For these reasons, whenever you are in an ongoing relationship, as everyone is in the workplace; whenever you are likely to negotiate repeatedly over persistent problems; and whenever you are seeking to negotiate in such a way as to maximize your own personal satisfaction, it is nearly always better to adopt the collaborative approach.

Preparing for Collaborative Negotiation

One reason the collaborative style is more successful in resolving conflicts than the aggressive style is that the elements and techniques involved in the collaborative approach dovetail nicely with those used in other interest-based and collaborative work processes.

In preparing to engage in a collaborative negotiation, it will be useful for you to identify and understand the principal elements in the process, both for yourself and your opponent. Several of the elements listed below are derived from Roger Fisher and William Ury's classic text on negotiation, *Getting to Yes*, which we highly recommend. After each element are several questions to help you prepare for collaborative negotiation.

- *Goals*: What are your goals for your relationship and for the negotiation? What do you want? What does the other side want?
- *Issues*: What issues does each side want to see addressed? In what order? Which are real priorities and which are not?
- *Interests*: Why do you want the things you want? Why is the other side asking for what it wants?
- *BATNA*: What is each side's "best alternative to a negotiated agreement"? What is the best that could happen if no agreement is reached?

- *WATNA*: What is each side's "worst alternative to a negotiated agreement"? What is the worst that could happen if no agreement is reached?

- *Options*: What creative solutions can you identify that could satisfy both of your interests?

- *Relationships*: What will the impact of these proposed solutions be on your ongoing relationship?

- *Criteria*: Are there criteria or standards that could help you agree on what is fair?

- *Reality testing*: Are the ideas proposed realistic? Will they work for both sides?

- *Satisfaction*: What do both of you need in terms of content, process, and relationship to feel satisfied with the outcome?

- *Commitment*: What are both sides willing to commit to do to make the proposed solution work?

- *Improvement*: What can you do to improve trust and make the next round of negotiations more successful?

The best way to prepare for collaborative negotiation is to spend a great deal of time listening to your opponent and trying to understand his or her interests. As Abraham Lincoln famously remarked, "When I'm getting ready to reason with a man, I spend one third of the time thinking about myself—what I'm going to say—and two thirds thinking about him and what he is going to say."

The Collaborative Negotiation Process

Participating in collaborative negotiations is not a matter of simply preparing or having the right intent, although manifesting a collaborative intention can be extremely important. It is also a matter of using the right process. Just as the process used in a typical adversarial negotiation enhances the probability of stalemate or impasse, there are a number of processes that can be introduced at each stage in the collaborative negotiation process to encourage a successful outcome.

The processes listed below can help you move your negotiation in a more collaborative direction and improve outcomes to the satisfaction of both sides. Many of these steps are best taken before the negotiation even begins, others are best taken during the process, and still others are best implemented after it is formally completed.

Before Negotiation Begins

Agree on Ground Rules for the Negotiation Process. Establish a timetable, and agree on a set of ground rules for the negotiation process. Include confidentiality and other ways of improving trust, together with fail-safe devices, reset buttons, and escape hatches in the event that collaboration fails. Ground rules can also include a preamble or joint statement of the reasons each side decided to use a collaborative bargaining process, which affirms their intention to reach a full resolution.

Form a Joint Process Improvement Team. Form a joint team for process improvement that operates by consensus and sets agendas, suggests and reminds people of ground rules, stops the process when it is not working, and makes certain the negotiation is running smoothly. By agreeing on an agenda, you can help keep your focus on issues that are of primary concern to everyone. The experience of coming to consensus on process improvement proposals can give both sides a sense that their goals are achievable, particularly if collaborative negotiation is a new experience.

Agree on Common Goals for Your Relationship. Meet together for a few minutes to agree on four or five goals you each have for your relationship in the future. Alternatively, develop lists of goals separately, then come together and share your lists, marking the ones you have in common or on which you can easily agree. Next, separately identify the problems or barriers that stand in the way of achieving your joint goals. Share your results again, and mark the ones you have in common or on which you can easily agree. Next, jointly brainstorm strategies for overcoming the barriers and achieving your common goals. Reach consensus on all the strategies you can, and postpone the goals, barriers, and strategies you were unable to agree on for later discussion.

Identify Issues and Interests. If groups are in negotiation, call a joint meeting, ask people to sit alternately around a circle rather than on opposite sides of a table, and use a facilitator, joint process observers, a flip chart, and someone to record ideas. Start a round-robin process in which each person identifies an issue or problem for negotiation, says what is important about the problem, and offers one reason why it is important. Continue around the circle until no one has any more issues or problems. Next, group the issues into a single, manageable list. Together, or in small joint teams, analyze, categorize, and prioritize the issues under each topic, and identify any common principles or values you share with respect to how they should be resolved. Follow typical problem-solving procedures, and brainstorm recommendations for each problem, then list these before starting actual negotiations. Have the list typed up for everyone to revise, use, and improve as ideas change. Afterwards, let the process observers report on what they saw, and agree on ways of improving future negotiations.

Develop Shared Vision or Values. As an alternative to the first two steps, meet together to create a vision of where you would like to go or what you would like to create together. Next, analyze the barriers or hurdles that stand in the way of getting there, and agree to take small steps to overcome them. Or agree on a set of shared values for your behaviors with each other. List the actual behaviors either of you are engaging in that either support or undermine those values, agree to encourage the supporting behaviors and discourage the undermining ones, and give each other feedback so you know when you are doing either.

Discuss Past Negotiation Experiences. Meet informally to discuss in detail what happened during the last round of negotiations. If you are involved in group negotiation experiences, ask participants to switch sides and dramatize through role-playing their worst and best negotiation experiences. Then, after the role-play or discussion, brainstorm ideas on how you can improve the process the next time around, or make recommendations for specific improvements. Alternatively, ask each side to separately identify the behaviors *their* side engaged in during the last round of negotiation that they think did not work for the other side, share them, request feedback from the other side, and agree not to repeat them.

Develop BATNAs, WATNAs, Options, and Positions.   Meet separately to identify your own best and worst alternatives to a negotiated agreement for each of your own interests and those of the other side. Next, brainstorm alternative ways of achieving those interests, and develop initial, fallback, and bottom-line positions. Share these lists confidentially with each other, or discuss them openly in the group.

Meet Informally.   Build trusting relationships through socializing, storytelling, informal gatherings, and personal sharing. Consider holding a retreat or having a potluck dinner, barbecue, seminar, sports event, family party, or other social event to give everyone an opportunity to get to know each other on a personal level.

Receive Joint Training in Collaborative Negotiation.   Meet together and agree to participate in a joint training session on techniques for collaborative negotiation, effective communication, relationship building, or conflict resolution. Use courses, workshops, and outside consultants to raise issues and improve your skills. Training can add an element of openness to the negotiation process and allow both sides to share a learning experience and adopt the same language and techniques.

Use an Outside Facilitator or Mediator.   Jointly hire an outside facilitator or mediator to assist you and the other side throughout the negotiating process. An experienced outsider can bring a fresh perspective, give both sides honest feedback and personal coaching, and help resolve disputes before, as, and after they occur.

Seek Advice from Allied Third Parties. Form a joint advisory committee or board consisting of representatives from concerned outside groups or third parties who may be affected by the success or failure of your negotiations. Report to them periodically on your successes and failures, and seek their advice or intervention when you get stuck.

Hold a Facilitated Public Forum. Consider holding an open public forum, facilitated by a third party, where representatives of all interested groups can openly discuss the issues being discussed in the negotiation. This public venting process can be useful in putting an end to rumors, gossip, and past history. It can be an opportunity for people to be heard and develop fresh ideas before moving on to problem solving or after an impasse has been reached. After the group has analyzed the issues, ask them to suggest alternatives or recommendations, and take time to consider their contributions.

Jointly Research Alternative Methods of Negotiating. Research might include jointly reading collaborative bargaining classics such as *Getting to Yes* by Fisher and Ury or *Getting Past No* by Ury or jointly researching alternative negotiation literature, experiments, and methods. Both sides might agree to contact or visit individuals and organizations that have used collaborative negotiation techniques and interview participants or consultants to learn their ideas about what worked, what did not, and how to improve the process.

Choose Negotiating Team Members Jointly. Select people to negotiate who have good interpersonal skills and who are respected and seen as credible in the eyes of people on the other side. You might consider allowing the other side to veto anyone they do not trust or even to select one or more members of your own bargaining team.

Keep Lines of Communication Open.　Allow sufficient time to communicate fully with each other, and plan to meet on a regular basis, with added sessions when needed. Make sure both formal and informal lines of communication are left open, and ask to meet with the other side in an informal setting away from the table if you get stuck or run into problems.

During the Negotiation Process

Meet in Comfortable, Informal Surroundings.　Meet, if possible, off site, and avoid an "our side against your side," across-the-table setting. Sit in an alternating pattern rather than on opposite sides of the table if you can. Use a round-robin speaking order. Dress informally. Bring food and beverages. Welcome the other side, and allow time for informal personal conversation. Help both sides feel they are part of the same team.

Use Experts.　Designate someone who has subject matter expertise, a strong interest in a particular area of the negotiation, or an ability to solve problems. Ask this person to meet with both sides beforehand and agree on information protocols and procedures and, if possible, on joint recommendations.

Create a Single Version of the Facts.　Both sides can spend time working together to develop agreement on a single set of facts, especially when chronology, essential facts, and economic information are critical to reaching an agreement. This will prevent senseless disagreements over questions that have only one right answer and ease tension over potentially hot issues.

Eliminate Surprises.　Ask the other side to reveal their bargaining agenda in advance, and agree that both sides will avoid surprise demands at the last minute. Joint agenda or process-improvement suggestions can be used to limit and prioritize topics for discussion. Each side should be clear about the maximums they are willing to concede and the minimums they are willing to accept. Keep in mind in doing so that there will necessarily be trade-offs and compromises and that either or both sides may have to alter their expectations in the interest of improving their relationship.

Allow Your Opponent to Save Face. Search for opportunities to support your opponent in looking like a committed participant in the process, appearing to negotiate effectively, and not losing face with their employers or supporters. Often the need to save face is a driving force in motivating negotiators to dig in their heels or agree on unclear language, and claiming victory can make the other side feel they suffered a defeat.

Record Everything. Pick a mutually acceptable recorder to note the issues, discussions, recommendations, ideas, actions taken, and issues for future discussion. Minutes of meetings should be available to both sides. At the end of every session, ask each person to give a brief plus-and-minus evaluation of the process used during the session and suggest what could be done to improve the next session. Make sure these ideas are included in the minutes and that changes are implemented at future meetings.

Negotiate in a Spirit of Problem Solving. Agree that anything that is a problem for one side is a problem for both. Refocus your attention on the future, recognizing that you are not only in the same boat but likely to remain there and that it ultimately does not matter which end of the boat is leaking because you will all end up going down together. Therefore, do not adopt strategies that run the risk of jeopardizing long-term relationships. Make a good-faith effort to resolve all issues through a collaborative process, and approach your problems with the idea that it is "us versus it" rather than "us versus them" or "me versus you."

When You Get Stuck, Change the Process. If the process is not working, change it. You can even just stop cold and start over again. If you get stuck, appoint a facilitator, recorder, timekeeper, or process observer, or bring in an outside mediator or facilitator to advise you on how to make the process work. Encourage process interventions and improvements and regular discussion of process problems, and elicit ideas for continued improvement.

When You Get Stuck, Open Up the Negotiations. If you get stuck, allow other concerned individuals to observe the negotiations and provide you with feedback. You can allow customers, coworkers, colleagues, community members, or partners to express their sentiments, and ask observers to make suggestions about how they think you might resolve difficult issues or break impasses. Then meet and consider new strategies. Alternatively, you can videotape your session, play it back, ask people to comment on what they see, make changes, and erase the tape or keep it confidential.

When You Get Stuck, Jointly Generate Options. Jointly brainstorm options or alternatives based on the interests each side has expressed. Choose the best alternative, then fine-tune or improve it by incorporating the other side's ideas. You can also identify the barriers to achieving each objective and create specific, concrete solutions to overcome these barriers. Consider asking each side, "What would it take for you to give that up?" Then look for options that satisfy those interests. Alternatively, ask each side to meet separately and identify what they would want or need in exchange for agreeing to what the other side is requesting, then meet and discuss ways of expanding the scope of the negotiation process to include these requests.

When You Get Stuck, Work to Resolve the Impasse. Specifically identify and name the issues that still require resolution. Reach consensus on terminology or the reasons for overcoming impasse. Have each side state the reasons the other side's proposal is unacceptable and suggest specific ways it might be improved. Delegate small, bilateral subteams to discuss a problem, prioritize options, and report back on their top choices or consensus recommendations.

Extend the Negotiations.   Create year-round negotiations, and build small negotiations into everyday life. Do not wait for an agreement to end, problems to develop, or conflicts to occur before sitting down together to agree on how you will act to resolve issues with each other in the future.

After Negotiation Ends

Improve the Process.   At the end of the process, ask each person to summarize his or her experience, and thank the other side for whatever they did that helped the group negotiate more collaboratively. Ask each person to indicate what worked for them and what did not in the negotiations and to say one thing that could be done to improve the process the next time around.

Publicize Your Accomplishments.   Generate support among nonparticipants for the collaborative process. Focus on what you achieved, but do not hide what you did not. Periodically remind yourself and others how much worse it could have been if you had used an adversarial approach.

Support the Other Side in the Eyes of Its Constituency.   Acknowledge the legitimacy and cooperation of the other side, not only to the participants personally, but to their constituencies as well. In group conflicts, beware of praising the other side's negotiators too highly. Recognize that some people are afraid of collaboration and need to feel their particular self-interests have been satisfied adversarially. Negotiators always need to strike a balance between cooperating and pressing aggressively for the satisfaction of their needs. Because they are expected to be strong advocates for opposite sides, professional negotiators cannot become too closely aligned with each other. When a settlement proposal is presented, both sides should take steps to alleviate the concerns of constituents who feel they may be sacrificing something because agreement was not reached through an adversarial process.

Remember the Problems. Make sure both sides recall the problems and issues that were encountered during the negotiation, topics that were postponed or not fully resolved, and glitches in administering the agreement afterwards. Keep everyone informed, and try to solve the problems, if possible, before returning to the negotiation process. Encourage people who were not happy with the process to air their feelings, and hear them out. Take their comments not as criticisms but as suggestions about what did not work for them and what might be done better in the future.

Honor Your Agreements. Be committed to fully honoring the agreements you reach. Nothing undermines collaborative negotiation more than the failure to live up to what you agreed to. In groups, create a joint evaluation team to follow up and make sure that all the agreements are being honored, and fine-tune any that may require adjustment.

Continue Solving Problems. Keep a list of unresolved issues or problems to which you will return to in the future, and continue your search for solutions. Also, keep a record of objections or complaints that were expressed about the process or the agreement. If necessary, stop and reopen negotiations to discuss these issues. In groups, establish a joint team to identify problem areas that cropped up following negotiations. Put a process in place for defining how these issues will be handled, making sure that channels are available for resolving these issues outside negotiations and that everyone is aware of their existence. The primary purpose of collaborative negotiation is not only to reach agreements but to create mechanisms for solving future problems without negotiations, improve relationships, and institutionalize the ability to satisfy both sides' long- and short-term interests.

Continue Negotiating. Do not allow unresolved issues to pile up. Negotiate solutions to problems before, during, and as soon as possible after they occur. Identify ongoing issues and create a permanent way of searching for solutions in those areas. Schedule regular problem-solving meetings to deal with ongoing issues before they have a chance to get blown out of proportion. Meet regularly, even if there are no items on the agenda, in order to continue trust building, communication, and problem solving.

Continue Communicating About the Success of Collaboration. New people who enter the process or join the organization should receive an orientation to the collaborative-negotiation process and be trained in its methods. While collaborative negotiation is based on common sense and a team approach to problem solving, it should not be taken for granted or assumed that everyone will understand it. Make efforts to rotate leadership and include different people in the process to broaden the range of support. Offer year-round opportunities for negotiators to continue improving their skills.

Evaluate Your Personal Participation. Honestly assess what you did and did not do during the negotiations. Consider what you actually accomplished, at what cost, and what you still need to accomplish. Communicate your self-assessment to others.

Celebrate Your Successes. Take time out to jointly celebrate what you have accomplished. Hold a party or open house. Congratulate yourself and the other side generously on what you have jointly done.

Committed Action

Having hopefully brainstormed, planned, or negotiated creative solutions to your problems, you now face a choice: you can either act on your agreements in a committed way or pass the responsibility for making them work onto someone else. If you are committed to deepening your understanding, improving your relationships, learning from your problems, resolving your conflicts, and transforming yourself, your opponent, or your organization, you will succeed only by committing to work through them until they are resolved.

Thus, the last step in creative problem solving, strategic planning, and collaborative negotiation is implementation, and successful implementation requires commitment from both sides. Your ability to solve problems, implement strategic plans, and negotiate agreements all ultimately depend on your willingness, before, during, and after using the processes we have outlined, to engage in clear and committed action.

Committed action is different from going through the motions, taking a stab, or giving it a try. It means taking risks, making a stand, and acting before the real outcome can be known. It is not only the final step in the problem-solving process but the ultimate, pragmatic meaning of integrity, values, ethics, collaboration, and leadership. Without it, even the best solutions become worthless, and the most effective processes and techniques dissolve into dust.

Committed action simply and finally means that you are willing to solve your problems, plan for the future, and negotiate with your opponent in a collaborative manner. It means you are prepared to stand by your agreements, allow the past to remain in the past, and act in the present in such a way as to bring about a qualitatively different future.

Until problem solving translates into commitment and commitment into action, you can easily delude yourself into thinking you are resolving your conflict when you are actually only playing it safe. But in your willingness to risk change, it will immediately become apparent how far you have traveled and how far you still have to go.

Commitment is an indication of how close you feel to the problem. The more removed you feel, the less committed you will be to solving it. If you are not concerned about it, you will not be willing to act in a committed way to make it right. Commitment therefore measures the degree of your authenticity and integrity. It signifies ownership, not simply of outcomes but of processes, relationships, ethics, and values.

Every action is a choice, and your choices belong to you, including the choice of not choosing. Committed action means taking responsibility for your choices and the effects they have on others. Initially, it does not matter whether your choices are conscious or unconscious, well-intended or hostile, accidental or on purpose, petty or grand. What matters is that you take responsibility for them and do not try to diminish or deny their consequences.

Committed action therefore both requires and reinforces integrity. It models for your opponents how to be responsible and true to what they believe in. It encourages closure by allowing you to feel complete about what you have done and will help you discover who you and they actually are.

The Transformational Power of Problem Solving

Our greatest challenge is not to solve the problems we are fighting over but to solve the problem of how we think about and approach them. Sometimes if we define something as a problem, it becomes one, whereas if we do not define it as a problem, it disappears and ceases to demand our attention. Sometimes we present ourselves and others with problems so that we will have something important to work on because problems are more interesting and challenging than solutions, and life without problems can seem pretty dull. Sometimes we think we are solving one problem when what we are actually subconsciously working on is a far deeper problem, such as who we are or want to become. And sometimes the real problem is the one who is trying to solve it.

Thus, it sometimes happens that we do not actually solve our problems so much as we learn from, transcend, and outgrow them. We usually think of our problems as external; yet, for every external problem we face, there is an even more interesting and perplexing internal one that we may or may not be facing. In this way, every external solution or transformation we can find is likely to correspond to an internal one that is subtly demanding our attention.

As a result, we can begin to see that all our problems and conflicts reflect internal calls for growth, learning, and transformation that we have mistakenly assumed originated from outside. When we see our problems as capable of being solved internally, we gain a critical new perspective on them, which in many cases is the same as solving them. As Carl Jung brilliantly wrote:

> The greatest and most important problems of life are all in a certain sense insoluble. They must be so because they express the necessary polarity inherent in every self-regulating system. They can never be solved, but only outgrown. . . . What on a lower level, had led to the wildest conflicts and to panicky outbursts of emotion, viewed from the higher level of personality, now seemed like a storm in the valley seen from a high mountain-top. This does not rob the thunderstorm of its reality, but instead of being in it, one is now above it.

Thus, our problems and problem-solving methods form an inseparable element in our own growth, learning, evolution, and transformation. As we learn to solve each type of problem, we make room for another, higher, more advanced type of problem to take its place. Thus, as Buckminster Fuller reminds us: "Once you solve your problems, what you get is a higher order of problem."

If you have tried all these techniques and none of them have worked; if you have followed all the steps we have outlined and still been unable to reach your opponent, solve your problem, resolve your conflict, or negotiate your differences, it is now time to explore more deeply the sources of your opponent's resistance, consider asking a mediator to help resolve your dispute, and redesign your organizational structures, systems, and cultures in order to encourage conflict prevention and resolution.

Explore Resistance, Mediate, and Design Systems for Prevention and Resolution

> Discourage litigation. Persuade your neighbors
> to compromise whenever you can. Point out to
> them how the nominal winner is often a real
> loser—in fees, expenses and waste of time. As a
> peacemaker the lawyer has a superior opportunity
> of being a good man. There will still be business
> enough.
>
> —*Abraham Lincoln*

Some conflicts may prove to be beyond your skill or ability to handle, even if you have tried all the techniques and suggestions we have outlined in preceding strategies. You may simply be too close to the problem to respond creatively, or the issues may be too complex for you to resolve on your own, or the emotions or positions may have become too entrenched, or the organizational culture may be discouraging resolution, or your opponent may be too committed to keeping the conflict going for psychological reasons you are unable to approach, assuage, or abolish. What do you do then?

If you are still unable to resolve your conflict, it may now be time for you to reassess your options, explore the hidden sources of resistance to resolution, consider using a mediator to help end the dispute, and turn your attention to ways of redesigning your organizations' structures, systems, and culture so as to prevent and resolve disputes before they escalate.

Success and Failure in Conflict Resolution

Before proceeding, it is important for you not to feel you have failed, even though you are at impasse and have so far been unable to reach a resolution. In the first place, statements about success and failure are often deceptive and inaccurate. Second, success and failure in conflict resolution depend sensitively on what both you and your opponent did or said and were capable of doing or saying in response; on the level of awareness, self-confidence, and integrity on both sides; on each person's readiness to learn and change; and on the actual nature and meaning of your conflict.

Moreover, sometimes what seems to be a success turns out to be a failure, and vice versa. For example, you may succeed in coercing your opponent to accept your proposal and undermine your long-term relationship, or you may settle a superficial issue and provoke a deeper conflict that is much worse. Or you may fail to resolve a conflict and later discover a better solution, rebuild trust, or learn an important lesson as a result.

In addition, the likely outcome of your success is that you will repeat what you did successfully and as a result be less likely to grow, learn, or change. Yet the likely outcome of your failure is that you will critique what you did, experiment, take risks, and be more creative, and as a result be more likely to grow, learn, and change. So which is the success and which the failure?

If your goal is to learn from your conflicts, labeling your efforts as successes or failures may not be helpful. The real questions are: Did you improve your skills? Did you make any discoveries? Were you seduced by your desire for success? Were you willing to experiment and take risks without fear of failure? By answering these questions, you may realize that failure often consists of trying too hard to succeed, while success consists of being willing to accept the possibility of failure.

Winston Churchill, in the midst of war, famously defined success as "proceeding from failure to failure with undiminished enthusiasm." A similar definition can be applied to conflict resolution, which always begins at impasse and remains there until, sometimes for no discernable reason, an opening appears and resolution becomes possible.

The implications of reversing our attitude toward success and failure are far-reaching. They suggest that we adopt a learning orientation with respect not only to problem solving but also to exploring the deeper reasons for resistance to resolution, to understanding the nature of mediation, and to redesigning our organizational structures, systems, and cultures. In so doing, we discourage conflict suppression and avoidance and encourage its prevention and resolution. Doing so *automatically* makes us more successful simply by allowing us to develop better skills in listening, emotional intelligence, honest dialogue, collaborative negotiation, and creative problem solving.

As you take these next steps and consider how you can explore the sources and reasons for resistance, keep in mind that the reasons for resistance run deep and often point to truths we have been unable to hear or refuse to learn, that your opponent undoubtedly sees you as the source of resistance and has similar lessons to learn, and that if you allow yourself to risk failure, you will succeed whatever happens.

Some Reasons for Resistance

There are many reasons we get stuck in conflict and end up in impasse. In fact, we are *always* at impasse in all our conflicts until the moment when we arrive at a solution that works for both sides. Impasse simply means that whatever we have been doing has not worked, and we need to try something different.

Everyone who resists resolution always does so for a reason. Instead of thinking of their refusal as unreasonableness, craziness, or difficult behavior, start with the assumption that *all* resistance reflects an unmet need. Sometimes it is simply an indirect request to be listened to more respectfully, to indicate that their deeper needs have not been met. As a result, it is important to find out what unmet needs may be causing the stalemate and search together for solutions that can move the process forward.

For example, we were asked to assist in resolving a dispute in which an employee, Sam, had applied for a position as team leader, a job for which he felt qualified because he had spent six months as team coordinator on a successful project. His manager, Betty, disagreed and favored a more traditionally qualified candidate because Sam had not had any leadership training.

When Betty told Sam the job was not his, she felt bad but covered it over by being abrupt, insulting, and insensitive. She surprised him because he thought she liked his work and that the job was his. He tried to convince her he was qualified, but she did not want to take time to listen and brushed him off.

As a result, Sam went to the organizational ombudsman in charge of conflict resolution to request a hearing and to human resources to file an internal grievance. He complained bitterly to his colleagues and "bad-mouthed" Betty, who became angry and retaliated when she heard about his insulting comments, telling him that if it were up to her he would never get the job. Various proposals for settlement were offered, but Sam was resistant to all of them.

In mediation, we asked Betty to listen actively, empathetically, and responsively to Sam as he presented his case. She did so in a genuine and honest way, and Sam felt respected, acknowledged, and heard for the first time. As a result, Betty was able to apologize for not having listened earlier, failing to acknowledge the excellent work he had done, and making vengeful, retaliatory comments. She admitted that he was highly qualified for the job but merely lacked the required leadership training.

In response, Sam was able to apologize for his efforts to undermine Betty and agreed to withdraw his grievance. Together they agreed that Sam would be included in the next leadership training program to earn the credentials he needed for the position, that the team would be consulted first on future hires, and that Betty would request feedback from the team and coaching from human resources on how to improve her communication skills.

The promotion proposal that Sam finally agreed to was identical to the one offered earlier by the ombudsman. Sam had resisted resolution, not because the proposal was inadequate but because Betty had not listened to him, apologized, acknowledged his skills, and offered it herself.

The reasons for resistance are often subtle and unstated. Sometimes it results from a perception that the process being used to resolve the dispute is unfair or one-sided. One person may not have agreed to use the process, or feel it is being used unfairly, or is not committed to following through. There may not be adequate ground rules to keep the conversation on track, or the ground rules may have been disregarded and previous violations been ignored or condoned.

Sometimes the process is too structured and formal—or, conversely, too unstructured and informal—to allow for a real exchange of views and the real content of the dispute to emerge. Sometimes people feel they have not been listened to deeply or sincerely enough, or the other person has not been honest or empathetic enough, or the other person has tried to manipulate the process.

Sometimes resistance is caused by unresolved issues in the relationship, or one person has adopted an adversarial style or control orientation that is creating a perception of disrespect or prejudgment. Sometimes one person is trying to fix blame, or humiliate the other, or has false expectations of the other that have not been addressed. Sometimes there is a need for an apology or acknowledgment that has not been spoken.

For example, we were invited to a large urban high school that was being torn apart by conflict. The parents had accused the administration of institutional racism, citing remarks made by teachers in their classrooms and data on achievement by students based on their race and national origins. The administration was willing to mediate, but the parents and teachers refused to meet. There was great distrust: by the parents who felt they had been treated unfairly in the past, by the teachers who felt they had been personally attacked by the parents, and by the administration who felt blamed by everyone.

The resistance began to break up when a newly appointed district administrator asked to address the parent group and apologized for the mistakes that had been made in the past. He acknowledged that institutional racism had existed in the school and in the district as a whole and agreed to make it his priority to end it. He indicated his commitment to work with them over the next year to eliminate disparate treatment at the school and make sure that all students were treated equally.

At the same time, he reached out to the teachers and administrators by arguing that institutional racism was not anyone's personal fault and by offering resources and support to improve student achievement. His sincere apology, acknowledgment of the problem, willingness to speak directly to both groups, and commitment to deliver needed resources reduced the resistance and allowed everyone to join forces and create an improved environment for students.

Techniques for Reducing Resistance and Overcoming Impasse

Sometimes listening, apologies, and acknowledgments, while helpful, will not be sufficient to resolve your conflict. If you continue feeling stuck in resistance and unable to move beyond impasse, here are some methods we sometimes use in mediation or other forms of third-party intervention, each of which could help you discover or create a breakthrough. As you read through them, consider how you might adapt, reconfigure, and apply them in your conflict.

• Break the issue down into smaller parts, isolating the most difficult issues and reserving them for last. If you are stuck trying to resolve a large issue, break it down into tiny pieces and try to solve each one separately. Identify the easiest, most manageable parts that might be solved easily, then move on to more complex issues. For example, we once resolved a dispute involving over $500,000 by first reaching sixteen points of agreement on how the parties would talk to each other on the telephone, after which the rest was easy.

• Ask the other side why your alternative is unacceptable, then look for narrow solutions that are tailored to the reasons they offer. If someone rejects your proposed solution because they do not believe it will work, suggest trying it for a month to see. For example, we resolved a sexual harassment dispute by asking the harassee why she refused a generous offer of settlement. It turned out that she did not really want the money as much as she wanted the company to train her, allowing her to move into a higher-level job she really liked. The company agreed, and both sides were satisfied.

- Go on to other issues that might be easier to resolve, or take a break and ask the other person to think about the alternatives you presented. When people take a time out and step away from their conflict, they become more reasonable and realistic about what they need. For example, we often suggest in mediation that both sides think about the problem overnight and come back the next day with three proposals for resolution that they think would be acceptable to the other side. We also find that people become more reasonable after bathroom breaks, in what we call "restroom revelation."

- Review the other side's priorities and any interests you have in common. Go over your priorities together and create a merged list. Identify your interests and see whether they match. For example, we worked with two teachers in conflict who agreed that their top priority was the children. Their shared interests in school safety and improving the language arts curriculum allowed them to create a partnership and overcome their differences.

- Explore hidden agendas, and elicit a willingness to compromise. Sometimes hidden agendas prevent someone from reaching an agreement. If you surface and explore these agendas, you can find a compromise—or see that the one you have advanced is impossible. For example, we worked with a manager whose hidden agenda was to appear managerial to his boss and enhance his chances of promotion by solving problems quickly. An employee with whom he was in conflict understood his agenda and was able to negotiate a solution that made the manager look good to his boss.

- Split the difference. Simply dividing a sum in half and splitting the difference is an easy way of settling a dispute without necessarily resolving it. For example, we once mediated a conflict in which the parties agreed to settle $400,000 worth of claims, and the entire mediation almost fell apart over $35. We suggested they split the difference, and each side agreed to pay $17.50.

• Try to reach agreement on your original expectations. Going back to original conversations and expectations before the dispute began can help you realize that you need to stand by your original agreements. For example, we mediated a dispute between two business partners who had worked together for several years. They were in a heated conflict over how to resolve an unfair division of labor and were considering dissolution. When they recalled their original agreement, which was to share the work equally, they identified all their tasks, broke them into two equal groups, and flipped a coin to decide who would take which ones.

• Look for possible trade-offs or exchanges of services. You may find solutions to your conflicts by discovering collateral needs that can be satisfied, bartered, or traded against each other to resolve the dispute. For example, we mediated a dispute between a model and a photographer over fees for a set of prints. She thought his photographs were unflattering and refused to pay for them. He claimed she had not looked very good when he took the shots and had refused to take his advice when he suggested how she might look better. She wanted a flattering set of prints, and he wanted to be paid and do his job without interference. They traded, accepted each other's conditions, and reached an agreement that he would take the photos while she would accept his suggestions and pay him for his work, including film costs from the earlier shoot.

• Recognize and acknowledge other people's feelings and points of view, and encourage them to acknowledge yours. A common reason for impasse is inadequate recognition or acknowledgment of others' feelings. It is extremely difficult to over-acknowledge someone in a way that is sincere. If your opponent says, "You don't think I'm a very good [whatever]," start by praising whatever he or she does well and offering honest feedback. If you are unable to think of anything positive to say, your emotions have obscured your vision. For example, we resolved a dispute between a male manager and a female employee who told her coworkers that the manager was incompetent and had assigned her tasks she thought were beneath her. The manager complained that she was always resisting his ideas and had a "bad attitude." We asked them to describe three things they respected or liked about each other and to acknowledge each other for something they had done well. It turned out that the entire dispute was based on each person thinking the other one did not like them and acting defensively as a result. As they praised and acknowledged each other, the conflict began to disappear.

• Say you are stuck and ask for ideas. Sometimes telling other people you need help will encourage them to step forward with creative ideas or let go of their resistance to seeing your point of view. For example, we were asked to resolve a dispute in a school in which most of the teachers had requested that the principal be removed. We convened a faculty meeting in which the principal admitted she was stuck and asked for their help. In small groups, the faculty came up with a list of the things she was doing that were causing problems, a list of the things they were doing that were not helping her change, and a list of creative ideas for how they both could improve and work together in the future.

• Ask the other person to indicate what would change or happen if a solution were reached. One reason for impasse is a perception that what will happen when you reach agreement will be unpleasant. For example, we mediated a dispute in which an employee was taking a long time to sign a settlement agreement, insisting that commas be changed into semicolons, then back into commas again. We asked him what he thought would happen if he actually signed the agreement. He dodged the question three times. We asked him if he was ducking the question, and he finally said he was afraid that he would never find a better job than the one he had. We assisted him in accepting the inevitable by strategizing about how he could find a better, more satisfying job, which allowed him to complete the past, let go, and move on with his life.

• Stop the process and consider whether it is helping you get where you want to go. If your process is not working or is preventing open, honest, and empathetic communication, stop it and try to improve the way you are communicating. For example, we mediated a dispute in a federal agency where the director encountered employee resistance to a number of changes she was trying to implement. She ran staff meetings with an iron hand and rarely asked employees what they thought. She did not even give them an opportunity to speak before telling them what they were going to do. We stopped their next meeting midstream and asked her publicly if she wanted to hear what employees thought about her plan. She was forced to say she did, and we changed the process by breaking the large group into small teams of four or five employees, asking them to identify three to five useful elements in her plan and three to five ways it could be improved. Their constructive ideas shocked her, and she realized that her employees were well-meaning and knew how to make her plan work better than she did.

• Compliment others on reaching earlier points of agreement, and encourage them to reach a complete agreement so as to put the dispute behind them and move on with their lives. Every conflict resolution process creates a momentum toward resolution that is increased by periodically recognizing the gains you have made and acknowledging your successes. For example, we met with a team in an information systems department that was blocked from meeting its commitments to clients as a result of an impasse over a strategy for developing software. We convened the team and asked each person to identify one point on which they were in agreement regarding the strategy and one issue on which they still needed to agree. It turned out that they actually agreed on twelve points and only really disagreed over two. We worked with them to identify the problems that were keeping them from reaching agreement over the two, and they were able to come to a complete agreement in three hours.

• Remind the other side what will happen if they do not settle—what each of you stands to lose. Say what you stand to lose if you are unable to resolve the dispute, then ask the other side what they stand to lose, or what it will cost them to continue the conflict. For example, we mediated a dispute between a manager and an em-

ployee where we asked them what they each stood to lose by not resolving their dispute. They both answered that they could lose their
jobs and chances for promotion. We asked them if this was what
they wanted, and they said it was not. Once they saw what was at
stake, they were able to reprioritize, put their less important ani-
mosities aside, and negotiate a working relationship that would
make them both look good.

• Ask for a minute of silence so both sides can think about their
differences and what to do about them. In conflict, it is easy to get
caught up in emotional dynamics and lose the forest for the trees. Silence allows you to stop a process that is not working, reassess your
position, center yourself, and return to what is really important. For
example, we mediated a dispute between an ex-husband and wife
who were business partners in which the husband made a generous
offer to purchase the business from his wife. We asked her how she
wanted to respond, and she said, "I don't know." We asked what she
thought she needed in order to respond, and she said, "I don't know
that either." We asked for a minute of silence to let her think about
it, and before a minute had passed, she said, "I'm afraid that if I say
yes, our relationship will be over." We now understood the real
source of her resistance and supported her in letting go of their old
relationship. She told her ex-husband that what she really wanted
was a friendship. As a result, they were able to negotiate a nonbusi-
ness friendship that would not be emotionally or financially confusing, and she accepted his offer of settlement.

• Ask more questions—not only about the problem but about
feelings, priorities, creative solutions, flexibility, hidden agendas,
compromises, and unresolved issues—then return to agenda setting
and problem solving. If you are completely stuck, double back to
the beginning and ask questions as though you were just starting to
resolve the dispute. For example, we mediated a conflict over a negative performance evaluation in which both sides had hired attorneys. The original reasons for the impasse had been forgotten in a
flurry of legal issues and aggressive advocacy. We asked the parties
to meet together privately without their lawyers and were able to

ask questions that cleared the air, returned them to the original issues, allowed them to agree on changes in the performance evaluation, and got their relationship back on track.

• Generate options by asking the other person to brainstorm ideas with you, without considering their practicality or acceptability. Ask the other person if he or she has any suggestions for how to resolve the dispute, then add your own. Do not critique or evaluate ideas until you have both expressed all the ideas you can. Use a flip chart if the conflict is especially hot. For example, we mediated a dispute between family members who were operating a business in which two brothers were competing to see who would run the operation. We brainstormed options and discovered that neither of them really wanted to run it, they just did not want the other one to look more successful. They agreed that their general manager was far more capable, qualified, and motivated than either of them and that he would get the job instead.

• Ask an expert or third party to identify which alternative is more appropriate or fair and why. Going to an expert or someone who has a reputation for fairness to request advice can often resolve an impasse, as can jointly researching options and discussing the merits of each proposal. For example, in a collective-bargaining dispute we helped settle concerning the salaries of a large group of employees, both sides agreed to consult an expert who was able to put a value on their pensions and benefits and compare their total package with what employees were receiving in similar organizations.

• Ask your opponent if he or she is willing to mediate the dispute or, if not, take the dispute to arbitration, rather than litigating it. If all else fails, bring in a third party to mediate or arbitrate. For example, a mediator can often create the permission and hopefully have the skills needed to resolve the dispute. Often a mediator will succeed merely because he or she is a third party who is outside the conflict and perceived as unbiased or impartial. If mediation is unsuccessful or unacceptable to either side, consider using final and binding arbitration, which is much quicker and less expensive than litigation.

The Organizational Costs of Unresolved Conflict

Most organizations suffer from chronic unresolved conflicts, many of which are triggered by, among other factors, hierarchical structures, autocratic decision making, bureaucratic policies and procedures, dysfunctional processes, overly competitive relationships, ineffective leadership, unclear roles and responsibilities, adversarial attitudes, false expectations, distorted communications, value and goal differences, unresolved responsibility issues, conflict-avoidant cultures, resistance to change, and competition over scarce resources.

A survey conducted several years ago by the American Management Association, responded to by 116 chief executive officers, 76 vice presidents, and 66 middle managers, revealed that these managers spent at least 24 *percent* of their time resolving conflicts. They felt that conflict resolution had become more important over the past ten years and was equal to or more important than strategic planning, communication, motivation, and decision making.

In many organizations, 24 percent is a low-end figure, particularly when minor low-intensity disputes are included. If we add up all the time managers spend listening to complaints, countering rumors, delivering corrective feedback, disciplining employees for conflict-related behaviors, monitoring compliance, and searching for solutions, managerial time dedicated to resolving conflicts easily increases to 50 percent or higher. If we multiply this figure times the number of managers and the average manager's salary, we begin to understand the true organizational cost of unresolved conflict.

On the other hand, when chronic conflicts are resolved, organizations generally experience, among other results, improved productivity; increased morale; reduced waste; innovative solutions; revitalization; better alignment with vision, mission, and values; more targeted strategic planning; expanded participation; more effective communications; increased synergy and teamwork; streamlined processes; enhanced organizational learning; and increased trust.

If this were not enough, many organizations have discovered that by expanding their existing conflict resolution programs, they can substantially reduce litigation expenses and realize significant cost savings. Here are some examples of such savings, cited by Karl Slaikeu and Ralph Hasson, in *Controlling the Costs of Conflict*:

- In the first year of comparison, Brown and Root reported an 80 percent reduction in outside litigation expenses by introducing a systemic approach to collaboration and conflict resolution regarding employment issues.

- Motorola Corporation reported a reduction in outside litigation expenses of up to 75 percent per year over six years by using a systemic approach to conflict management in its legal department and including a mediation clause in contracts with suppliers.

- National Cash Register Corporation reported a reduction in outside litigation expenses of 50 percent and a drop in its number of pending lawsuits from 263 to 28 between 1984 and 1993 following the systemic use of alternative dispute resolution.

- The U.S. Air Force reported that by taking a collaborative approach to conflict management in a construction project, it completed the project 144 days ahead of schedule and $12 million under budget.

- The U.S. Defense Mapping Agency reported that systemic conflict management reduced the cost of resolving a particular set of employment disputes by forty-two hundred hours.

- The U.S. Air Force estimated a savings of 50 percent per claim in one hundred equal employment opportunity complaints using mediation.

If we add to these figures the savings that would be achieved by reducing gossip and rumors, stress-related sick leave, conflict-induced absences and tardiness, reassignment and retraining costs triggered by people quitting over unresolved conflicts, human resources and executive salaries devoted to employee discipline and discharge, and similar expenses related to unresolved conflicts, the figures become astronomical. Thus, in one study of sixteen hundred employees, it was found that

- Twenty-two percent of employees said they had actually decreased their work efforts as a result of conflict.
- Over 50 percent reported that they lost work time because they worried about whether the instigator of the conflict would do it again.
- Twelve percent reported that they changed jobs in order to get away from the instigator.

Thus, while it takes time and money to resolve conflicts, it takes far more time and money *not* to resolve them. Indeed, the time and money spent on not resolving conflicts is clearly far in excess of the cost of implementing the most elaborate and expensive conflict resolution system imaginable.

But there is a still greater cost of unresolved conflict. As organizations face increasing demands for change, conflicts accumulate along the fault lines that lie hidden in their cultures, structures, and systems. These conflicts point directly to what is not working in the organization, while resolutions often reveal new processes, principles, ideas, or relationships that are waiting to be born.

In this way, conflict can be understood simply as the sound made by the cracks in an organizational system, as the first indication of the birth of a new paradigm, as a warning light that is signaling an imminent breakdown, or as a path to organizational improvement and evolution to a higher order of conflict. The opportunity cost of leaving these conflicts unresolved can be measured indirectly in the failure of the organization to adapt, evolve, and change.

Yet most of these chronic conflicts are missed because the organization sees them as purely personal or a result of "personality clashes." Nonetheless, as these individual conflicts accumulate, a point arrives when what appeared as unique and personal is suddenly revealed as common, widespread, and omnipresent throughout the organization—in other words, as the by-products of a dysfunctional organizational structure, system, or culture. Still, these larger issues often get hidden, ignored, or avoided, even when hundreds or thousands of people are experiencing the identical conflict.

Chronic conflicts are a clear sign that an organizational system is unable to reform or repair itself and has erected lines of denial, defense, counterattack, and compensatory rationalization to protect itself against any resolution that might require a fundamental change.

As these defenses aggregate, they produce growing insecurity, fear that the whole structure will collapse, and heightened resistance, even to minor modifications that might trigger an avalanche. As fear of a systemic meltdown increases, even those in favor of change may retreat and seek to preserve or roll back the status quo or deflect the change by focusing on less important issues.

Designing Systems for Prevention, Resolution, and Learning

One reason for these defensive responses is that few organizations possess adequate systems for resolving conflicts, and most do not use the systems they have until after unacceptable losses have occurred. When this happens, the conflict is often pigeonholed as someone else's problem, or beyond the reach of organizational policy, or the expertise of people within the organization to resolve, or the solution does not reach deeply enough into underlying attitudes and relationships, permitting it to come back later to create new problems.

What is needed, therefore, are complex, collaborative, self-correcting conflict resolution systems that are designed to process all disputes within the organization and to build a rich array of diverse alternatives that will lead to prevention and resolution and support organizational learning.

Based on ideas first propounded by William Ury, Stephen Goldberg, and Jeanne Brett, "conflict resolution systems design" encourages organizations to view their conflicts not as isolated incidents but as parts of a system that can be addressed in more than one way, to emphasize integrated systems rather than discrete procedures, and to respond not just to single disputes but to the *stream* of disputes that flows continually within them.

This approach encourages early informal problem solving, mediation, evaluation and monitoring, and de-escalation throughout the life of the conflict. It allows several people to work on the problem from multiple, diverse perspectives, employs alternate methodologies in search for synergistic results, and encourages organizational learning and personal self-correction.

As described earlier, conflicts can be resolved by means of power, rights, or interests. Conflict resolution systems design prioritizes interest-based alternatives such as informal problem solving, mediation, and collaborative negotiation while using rights- and power-based systems as backups and arranging them from lower to higher cost.

Interest-based resolution systems are far more complex than power- or rights-based systems because they offer multiple opportunities for personal, team, and organizational dialogue and learning. Their goal is not victory over others but improving relationships, processes, trust, and communication. Designing interest-based conflict resolution systems includes the following:

- Analyzing the source of conflict, including its connection to systems, structures, culture, communications, strategies, change, values, morale, styles, and staffing, by conducting a "conflict audit" to assess chronic sources of conflict within the organization
- Identifying the core cultural ideas, traditional approaches, and informal mechanisms already in place for resolving conflict and supplementing them with enriched alternatives that emphasize prevention and focus on interests rather than rights or power-based solutions

- Expanding the number and kind of resolution alternatives available internally and externally and arranging these procedures from low to high cost
- Including a full range of options from process changes to binding arbitration, with low-cost rights and power backups, and "loopbacks" to informal problem solving and negotiation
- Encouraging consultation, facilitation, dialogue, coaching, mentoring, feedback, and evaluation and altering behavioral patterns that discourage widespread use of resolution procedures
- Providing training, motivation, skills, support, and resources to make these procedures work, continuing to improve understanding of how these principles succeed and fail, and improving their design

The object of the systems design process is to create conflict resolution mechanisms that match specific organizational needs, resolve individual conflicts, and stimulate personal and organizational growth, insight, change, and learning so that conflicts can be prevented and not repeated.

The most commonly used procedures in the system design arsenal include informal problem solving; peer counseling, coaching, mentoring, and feedback; team building; supportive confrontation; public dialogue and open forums; peer and professional mediation; ombudsman offices; internal appeals boards; organizational review boards; binding and nonbinding arbitration; and similar processes. Here are seven different illustrations, drawn from our experience, of how different organizations have used the process to design unique outcomes.

1. A Fortune 100 corporation decided after a string of costly jury verdicts to develop a comprehensive systems approach to conflict resolution. Human resources staff designed an employee problem-resolution procedure that led conflicting employees through a multistep process. Both sides in any conflict are assigned an "exec-

utive advisor" from outside their business unit to informally advocate for and coach them and meet confidentially to mediate the dispute. If this fails, the dispute proceeds to a "consensus review board" with power to bind the company. If these processes fail, the issue moves to binding arbitration.

2. A technology corporation confronted with angry clients and chronic conflicts between staff members and business partners conducted a conflict audit that revealed disgruntled information systems users, skeptical senior managers, and low morale among staff and vendors who did not believe they could implement the new systems. A staff retreat analyzed these results and reached consensus on a conflict resolution plan that began with an open dialogue session for user groups. The dialogue sessions resulted in several creative ideas for implementing more effective customer service, a better delivery system, and a more powerful technology architecture. Staff from each organization were trained to act as peer mediators and resolve employee and vendor disputes, which led to an overall increase in morale and motivation.

3. A conflict audit at a large manufacturing company revealed multiple disputes between line workers at one of its plants. Angry outbursts, competition among team members, and threats of physical attack were disrupting operations. Human resources staff identified, analyzed, categorized, and prioritized the sources of conflict and noticed how it was reinforced by the organization's culture. A small, integrated team was selected to identify conflict predictors, preventive measures, safety nets, outlets for constructive expression of differences, procedures for resolution, and methods for making them effective. This allowed them to dramatically reduce the risks and costs of conflict, mediate disputes before legal costs accumulated, provide a fair forum for resolution outside the courts, and create a learning environment regarding conflict.

4. Similar results were obtained at a large utility company where a court-based consent decree forced the creation of a conflict resolution system to handle employee complaints, particularly allegations of discrimination based on race. A human resources team

designed a comprehensive conflict resolution system that relied heavily on informal problem solving and mediation by human resources staff. Line managers were trained in its use, resulting in a reduction of hostilities and litigation and improvement in racial relations.

5. A large corporation reorganized its staff into self-managing teams. As managers became team leaders and a largely bookkeeping and accounting staff began managing themselves, they became more service-oriented and adept at strategic planning. As these changes unfolded, conflicts arose within, between, and among the teams based on false expectations, inconsistencies in implementing team values, lack of equity between team members in pulling their weight, old managerial behaviors, and role confusions. Using systems design principles, the teams created new governance structures, communications systems, organizational roles and responsibilities, peer mediation training, and an orientation program for new managers and staff. They developed innovative strategies to address the systemic sources of their conflicts and conducted an open, honest dialogue regarding inconsistencies in the team process, which resulted in dramatic improvements in morale and productivity.

6. A regulation negotiation process was initiated between city staff and neighborhood organizations to help diverse community constituencies reach consensus and avoid a destructive battle over the design of zoning regulations and public policies that directly impacted their lives. This several-month-long process brought civil servants and city planners together with merchants, residents, community organizations, and homeowners, who had fought bitterly with each other for years. In the course of a few meetings, they produced a vision for the future of their neighborhood and informal problem-solving processes for resolving future disputes and reached consensus on a proposed ordinance that was recommended to the city council and adopted unanimously.

7. Similar results were achieved by a citywide homeless task force that brought hostile, opposing parties to complete consensus on a comprehensive set of recommendations for public action.

Those who disagreed most strongly about an issue were assigned to the same small team and asked to work together to research the issue and return to the large group either with consensus or a set of prioritized recommendations. Large-group facilitation and sidebar mediations were used to reduce personalization and refocus on problem solving.

We have used similar processes to assist conflict-ridden schools, colleges, and university departments; nonprofit organizations; partnerships; and community, political, and public interest groups to resolve their conflicts using conflict resolution systems design and to develop processes, techniques, and skills that are at *least* as complex as the problems they are addressing.

In all these diverse organizations and environments, conflict resolution systems design has proved to be a powerful method—not just for preventing, mediating, and resolving conflicts—but also for learning from them and using them to improve collaboration, democracy, morale, and the capacity for successful self-management.

In each of the organizational initiatives described above, our goal was to create interest-based systems that would build the capacity of the organization to respond preventively and proactively to future disputes. The adoption of these initiatives reflected a willingness on the part of leaders and employees inside these organizations to risk trying something new and a strong commitment to put energy and resources into prevention and mediation, rather than into conflict avoidance, grievances, litigation, and cleanup.

What Is Mediation?

Probably the key element in all the conflict resolution efforts we have described—and the most important ingredient in designing interest-based organizational systems—is mediation. If the methods we have so far described in this book have not been successful in resolving your dispute, your next step may be to find an unbiased third-party mediator who can assist you and your opponent in communicating your ideas and feelings to each other, discussing the issues, and finding collaborative solutions to your conflict.

So what is mediation? Mediation has its roots in ancient conflict resolution practices that are common to all preindustrial cultures. Yet it is also a highly modern, intricate, sophisticated set of techniques for depolarizing and depersonalizing conflict. Many of these techniques have already been mentioned in this book, but their effectiveness can be enormously enhanced in the hands of a skilled practitioner.

In essence, mediation is an informal problem-solving conversation that is facilitated by an experienced third party. It is a voluntary consensus-based method of resolving disputes that uses facilitated communication, emotional processing, problem solving, collaborative negotiation, brainstorming, expertise, impasse resolution, and heart-to-heart communications to bring conflicting parties into constructive, creative dialogue with each other.

Mediation differs from litigation and arbitration in that the mediator is not a judge or arbitrator who decides the issues for the parties. It is a process that invites the participants to be creative, collaborative, and responsible for solutions. It is future-oriented and less concerned with deciding who is right or wrong than with solving problems so they do not occur again.

Mediators are not so much neutral as they are "omnipartial" and on both people's sides at the same time. Mediators often work in co-mediation teams that combine diverse backgrounds, cultural experiences, areas of professional expertise, and personal styles. Mediation sessions are generally informal and confidential or "off the record" so as to encourage direct dialogue.

Mediation has proved highly successful in resolving a wide range of conflicts, including interpersonal, workplace, discrimination, public policy, environmental, and organizational disputes as well as divorce, family, neighborhood, and community disputes. It is often able to reach solutions quickly, saving time, costs, and attorney fees and preserving privacy.

Mediation can also help parties learn more effective communication skills and assist them in avoiding a great deal of bitterness and hostility resulting from the way they are communicating and negotiating. On average, experienced mediators resolve 85 to 95 percent of their disputes, although a great deal depends on the insight, competency, training, and experience of the mediator, the timing of the intervention, and the willingness of the parties to participate in the process.

Agreements are often reached in just a single session, and in the workplace it is common for sessions to last from one to three hours. The process is informal and may or may not include attorneys or union representatives. Agreements reached in mediation rarely experience enforcement problems, primarily because they are reached voluntarily based on consensus.

There are many ways of encouraging your opponent to come to mediation. But even if you are certain your opponent will not accept mediation, we recommend that you ask a mediator to try anyway because mediators often convince people to mediate their disputes after they have refused to do so when asked by their opponents.

You can contact a mediator by calling a local or national mediation organization, such as the Association for Conflict Resolution in Washington, D.C., or a personal friend, union or management representative, therapist, lawyer, church, or community agency, or you can contact us at the Center for Dispute Resolution in Santa Monica, and we will help you try to locate someone in your area. Make sure the mediator has been thoroughly trained, is well thought of in the community, and is acceptable to your opponent.

Why Mediation Works

We have conducted thousands of mediations over the past twenty-five years, certified hundreds of people to become mediators, and conducted workshops for tens of thousands of people in mediation and conflict resolution techniques. In the process, we have developed a sense of the value of mediation and an understanding of how and why it works.

Mediation works on many different levels. It is able to stop people from fighting, de-escalate their aggressive behaviors, initiate deep listening and dialogue, acknowledge and affirm negative emotions, facilitate informal problem solving and collaborative negotiation, settle the issues in dispute, resolve the underlying issues that gave rise to the dispute, promote forgiveness, and encourage complete reconciliation.

As mediation works through each of these successive levels in conflict, the skills and experience required to overcome obstacles and move to the next level increase exponentially. At each new level, mediation requires greater willingness and commitment on the part of the participants to resolve their dispute and greater subtlety and artistry on the part of the mediator. But subtlety and artistry at what? What is it exactly that makes mediation so successful?

Mediation is successful for many reasons: because it invites adversaries to become human and real with one another; allows dialogue to take place in the language of metaphor; acknowledges the emotional needs of the parties; and allows both sides to tell their inner, subjective truths, along with their outer, objective points of view.

Mediation is successful because it brings people together through empathy, curiosity, and listening, rather than dividing them in anticipation of revenge or unilateral victory. It draws on their compassion, affection, and love for one another, rather than on their hatred, distrust, or dispassionate neutrality. It invites each side to listen to the deeper meaning of what the other person is saying and *not* saying and encourages them to participate in small collaborations without triggering their distrust and defensiveness.

Mediation is successful because it helps opponents reestablish their lost connections and emphasizes the wholeness of human experience, as opposed to demonizing and rendering it unintelligible. It allows them to surrender, let go, and move on with their lives. It lays open the secret sources of their motivation because it recognizes every human interest as valid and important.

Mediation is successful because it empowers everyone equally and thereby democratizes their conflict, looks to the future rather than the past, and offers constructive feedback as opposed to hostile judgments. It helps people create solutions for themselves and choose to accept them, rather than having them imposed from the outside. It acknowledges that no one enjoys being the object of another person's wrath or being trapped inside their own and releases people from their own rage and fear and that of others.

Mediation is successful because it creates an expectation of resolution, encourages hope, gradually reestablishes trust, and allows people to imagine what it would be like to live in and be at peace. It invites people to move beyond their rigid positions and try to understand each other's underlying interests. It promotes authenticity and unconditional respect, minimizes difficult behaviors, discourages aggressiveness, reduces stress, and encourages mutual compromise.

Mediation is successful because it makes the positive motivation of each person the center and object of the process and because it respects people and accepts them as they are while simultaneously encouraging them to improve. It does not judge their actions or intentions but helps them do what they know is right. It encourages empathy, hospitality, honesty, friendship, partnership, and respect while acknowledging disagreement, anger, disappointment, rejection, denial, aggression, and revenge. It supports each side in getting what it wants and needs and allows everyone to win.

Mediation is successful because it unites reason and intuition, love and self-interest, freedom and order, law and justice. It works because it is unique in every case, yet fundamentally the same in every culture around the world. It provides everyone with the unique opportunity to see their enemy as a reflection of themselves and to see themselves as no greater than the least among them nor worse than the best. It is successful because the possibility of resolution is already inside each of us, trying to emerge.

Reaching Closure

Even if you have not been successful in overcoming your impasse and resolving your conflict, you still need to seek completion and closure. There is a fundamental difference, however, between merely stopping a conflict and completing it, or reaching closure. While stopping a conflict essentially means temporarily stopping the fighting, completion means settling the issues, and closure means resolving the underlying issues and ending it with little or nothing left over.

To reach closure after a conflict has settled or resolved, most people need to feel they have been listened to respectfully and been allowed to release their emotions. They want to feel that they have been able to say everything that is really bothering them and communicate whatever they needed to express to get the conflict off their chest and let it be over.

The paradox is that to fully say everything you are thinking and feeling, let go of the conflict, not hold anything back, and come to closure, there are three essential steps you will need to complete. First, you will need to be willing to acknowledge your own role in the conflict. Second, you will need to be willing to recognize your opponent as a human being. And third, you will need to forgive your opponent and yourself.

You can start to move your conflict toward closure by telling your opponent there are certain things you need to talk about for the conflict to be over for you. Or you can ask your opponent if there is anything he or she needs to say for it to be over. It is important in doing so not to re-escalate the conflict. Therefore, instead of saying, "This is what you did to me," which will only return you to accusations and defenses and initiate a cycle of recrimination, say, "This is what I learned from this conflict about what I need to do to protect myself from behaviors that are difficult for me to handle." This is a statement that reflects a genuine resolution and movement toward closure because it acknowledges your role in creating or continuing the conflict.

The second step is somewhat easier and consists of recognizing your opponent as a real person who is not totally evil but entitled to a basic level of respect and acknowledgment. If you find yourself unable to think of anything positive to say about your opponent, you are probably not yet emotionally ready for closure. Indeed, this is a good test to determine how far you have come in ending your conflict.

It should always be possible for you to say something positive about your opponent, even if it is simply to thank him or her for being willing to meet and talk with you about the problem. You can say, for example, "I know it took a great deal of courage to come here today and face a difficult conversation with me, and I want to thank you for doing that." Or, you can acknowledge your opponent for teaching you some important lessons about how to handle similar disputes in the future, or you can talk about how you are working to improve your skills in conflict resolution.

You can also acknowledge your opponent in areas where you would most like to encourage growth or learning. You can, for example, praise your opponent for facing problems squarely, listening to you empathetically, communicating honestly, being willing to compromise, sticking with the process even when it was difficult, being open and forthcoming about the issues, offering you useful feedback or food for thought, being principled or assertive, reaching a number of agreements, or being willing to commit to a course of action that is likely to end the conflict.

Regarding the third step and forgiveness, it is important first to identify what you need to do or say in order to let go of the conflict completely and find a constructive way of doing so. In preparation, ask yourself: If I end the conflict and do not reach closure, what issues or feelings will be left unresolved? What will happen as a result? What price will I pay? What do I need to do or say to my opponent to reach closure? What positive things could I say about my role in the conflict resolution process? What have I learned about conflict or myself through my efforts to resolve it?

Forgiveness is something you do only for yourself. Fundamentally, it means releasing yourself from the burden of your own false expectations, or as writer Anne Lamont put it, "giving up all hope of having a better past." It means separating the person from the problem and being hard on the problem while being soft on the person. It does *not* mean forgiving and forgetting but remembering what happened and how you felt, then imagining what the other person must have experienced and how it might have felt.

Although it sounds counterintuitive, it is important in reaching forgiveness to identify all the reasons for *not* forgiving your opponent and all the expectations you had that he or she did not meet. Afterwards, you can either choose to release yourself from each of the reasons and expectations you cited or honestly assess what it will cost you, both personally and organizationally, to hold on to them in the future.

Finally, it is useful to design and execute a ritual or ceremony of release as a way of signaling through action that the conflict is really over for both of you. Minirituals and ceremonies can be extremely useful in expressing and consolidating closure, even if they consist only of shaking hands or agreeing to let bygones be bygones. Try to think of some creative ways you might ceremonialize the end of your conflict and a return to collegiality.

As an illustration, we mediated a conflict in which two coworkers had personally insulted each other repeatedly over a period of five years in staff meetings and private conversations. To ceremonialize the end of their conflict, they agreed to jointly request that they be placed on the agenda for the next staff meeting, to tell everyone how they had resolved their conflict, and to each say what they had learned from each other and from the mediation process.

At the staff meeting, they each spoke with an open heart about what they had learned from their experience and hugged each other at the end as a way of showing everyone that the dispute was over for them. During the meeting, you could have heard a pin drop, and afterwards, several staff members came forward and said they also had conflicts they wanted to resolve, and a series of mediation and problem-solving sessions were scheduled as a result.

We encourage you to search for similar creative ways of completing your conflict that have heart and soul in them. We support you in your determination to reach completion or closure and ask you to give the resolution process at least as much energy, insight, courage, perseverance, and commitment as you have given to your conflict.

Our Conclusion

Together we have explored eight strategies that we hope have helped you move your conflict from impasse to settlement, resolution, or transformation. Perhaps you have completely resolved your conflict or moved it to a place where it is easier to handle, or perhaps it remains unresolved. In any case, we hope you have learned that conflict can be a rich source of learning, growth, and improvement in both your personal and your organizational life.

Whenever you encounter conflicts, as we have indicated, you have two basic choices: you can either tighten up, pull back, and prepare to do battle, or you can relax, move toward your opponent, and prepare to participate in a process leading to resolution. Our last question to you is: Instead of tightening up and preparing for battle, would not it be more satisfying to relax and prepare for resolution? Is not the person you become when you are in battle less happy, fulfilled, and connected than the one you become when you are successfully communicating and resolving your conflicts? Which one would you rather be?

As individuals, organizations, cultures, societies, and nations, our challenge is to learn from our conflicts how to resist engaging in warfare, whether it be the small-scale petty wars that occupy much of our time at work, the large-scale international conflicts that destroy lives, or the modern, civilized forms of warfare, such as litigation.

Workplace conflicts, international wars, and litigation are all nourished by antagonistic responses to criticism and differences of opinion, by refusing to accept the gift of dissent, and by being unable to recognize that conflicts can be experienced as journeys and opportunities for learning and improvement.

As individuals, organizations, cultures, societies, and nations, we need to realize that innovation and collaboration flourish *precisely* in the midst of conflict and reject the win-lose limitations supported by conflict-averse, adversarial cultures. If we can learn to experience our conflicts as journeys rather than as wars, as challenges rather than as burdens, and as enormous opportunities for growth and change, we may actually begin to anticipate with pleasure the next chance we have to turn our conflicts into exercises in communication, problem solving, creativity, collaboration, and relationship building.

As we learn to approach our conflicts more constructively, we also reveal new levels of conflict to analyze and work on and make deeper levels of resolution possible. The opportunities for learning and growth that emerge when we improve our conflict resolution skills have the potential to significantly transform our work lives and organizations.

We believe the opportunities to learn from conflict are infinite. We encourage you to keep your openness and capacity for learning alive as your conflicts swell, dissolve, soar, stall, and suddenly vanish in a puff of smoke. We encourage you to find resting places, lookouts, safe harbors, and guides to help you along your way. As you do so, we encourage you to reflect on your experiences and search out the knowledge you need to grow.

You can only locate the opportunities in your conflicts by relaxing and moving toward and through them. To do so, you have to be willing to consider your own limitations, weaknesses, mistakes, and sources of impasse. Yet noticing these obstacles *automatically* creates the possibility of learning to transcend them. And who could be better at highlighting these possibilities than someone whose difficult behaviors encourage you to think the conflict is about them and not about you? Thus, we are all indebted to our opponents for teaching us to become better human beings.

We hope we have encouraged and supported you on this path of self-discovery, learning, and transformation. In closing, we are reminded that at the turn of the century, William James wrote:

> Most people live, whether physically, intellectually or morally, in a very restricted circle of their potential being. They make use of a very small portion of their possible consciousness, and of their soul's resources in general, much like a man who, out of his whole bodily organism, should get into a habit of using and moving only his little finger. Great emergencies and crises show us how much greater our vital resources are than we have supposed.

We hope the same will be true for you in your conflicts, and for this reason, we wish you *great* conflicts, with endless opportunities for self-discovery, resolution, and transformation. Good luck!

About the Authors

KENNETH CLOKE, J.D., L.L.M., PH.D., has been the director of the Center for Dispute Resolution in Santa Monica for twenty-five years and is a mediator, arbitrator, consultant, and trainer. He specializes in resolving complex multiparty conflicts, including organizational conflicts, workplace and labor-management disputes, discrimination complaints, sexual harassment claims, and environmental and public policy disputes. He is an internationally acclaimed speaker on conflict resolution.

He is the author of *Mediating Dangerously: The Frontiers of Conflict Resolution* and *Mediation, Revenge, and the Magic of Forgiveness*. He is coauthor with Joan Goldsmith of *Resolving Personal and Organizational Conflict: Stories of Transformation and Forgiveness; Thank God It's Monday! 14 Values We Need to Humanize the Way We Work; The Art of Waking People Up: Cultivating Awareness and Authenticity at Work;* and *The End of Management and the Rise of Organizational Democracy*, which was selected as the best book on leadership in Germany for 2002 by the German *Financial Times* and has been translated into several languages.

JOAN GOLDSMITH, M.A., Doctor of Humane Letters, has been an organizational consultant and educator for twenty-five years, specializing in leadership development, organizational change, executive coaching, conflict resolution, and team building. She has contributed to organizational change in Fortune 100 companies, government agencies, and nonprofit organizations in the United States, Europe, Asia, Africa, and Latin America.

She has specialized in resolving sexual harassment claims, gender-based conflicts, and public policy disputes. She is the creator of several innovative programs for women, including "Women Leaders: Creating Ourselves at the Crossroads." She is a mediator, facilitator, and trainer in conflict resolution in public, private, and nonprofit organizations. In addition to the books coauthored with Kenneth Cloke, she is coauthor with Warren Bennis of *Learning to Lead: A Workbook on Becoming a Leader*.

Index